Open Society

Re: IMF Conditions p.269.

GEORGE SOROS

OPEN SOCIETY

[
Reforming
Global Capitalism
]

LITTLE, BROWN AND COMPANY

A *Little, Brown* Book

First published in the United States of America by PublicAffairs ™,

a member of the Perseus Books Group

First published in Great Britain by Little, Brown and Company in 2000

Copyright © 2000 by George Soros

The moral right of the author has been asserted.

A CIP catalogue record for this book
is available from the British Library.

ISBN 0 316 85598 7

Book design by Jenny Dossin
Printed and bound in Great Britain
by Clays Ltd, St Ives plc

Little, Brown and Company (UK)
Brettenham House
Lancaster Place
London WC2E 7EN

Contents

Acknowledgments   *vii*

Introduction   *ix*

Part I: Conceptual Framework

1. Thinking and Reality   3
2. A Critique of Economics   38
3. Reflexivity in Financial Markets   58
4. Reflexivity in History   91
5. Open Society as an Ideal   116
6. The Problem of Social Values   138

Part II: The Present Moment in History

7. The Global Capitalist System   167
8. The Financial Crisis of 1997–1999   208
9. Who Lost Russia?   235
10. A New Global Financial Architecture   265
11. The Global Political Architecture   301
12. The Open Society Alliance   330

Conclusion   360

Index   361

Acknowledgments

This is the first time that the conceptual framework I started developing in my student days has received serious critical attention. It has been a stimulating and in some ways liberating experience. I am grateful to all those who took an interest in either the previous or the current version of this book.

Anatole Kaletsky acted as the de facto editor of *The Crisis of Global Capitalism: Open Society Endangered*, helping me to organize the material and make it more accessible; Roman Frydman was particularly helpful on the conceptual framework; Leon Botstein raised many interesting points and we had several animated discussions; Anthony Giddens commented on more than one version of the manuscript; William Newton-Smith put me right on some philosophical points; and John Gray made me reread Karl Polanyi's *Great Transformation*. Others who made helpful comments include Robert Kuttner, John Simon, Jeffrey Friedman, Mark Malloch Brown, Arminio Fraga, Tom Glaessner, Aryeh Neier, Daniel Kahneman, Byron Wien, and Richard Medley.

In preparing the current version, I had the valuable help of Adam Posen at the Institute for International Economics, although he is in no way responsible for my views. Yehuda Elkana organized a study group at the Central European University in Budapest, and I received written communications from Lóránd Ambrus-Lakatos, Fabrizio Coricelli, John Gray, János Kis, Mária Kovács, Petr Lom, and István Rév. Katie Jamieson summarized the proceedings in her usual lucid style. Les Gelb organized a discussion at the Council on

Foreign Relations in New York from which I learned a lot. It was attended by Elizabeth Colagiuri, Morris Goldstein, Nancy Goodman, Roger Kubarych, Lawrence Korb, Michael Mandelbaum, William Luers, Walter Mead, Peter Osnos, David Phillips, Adam Posen, Gideon Rose, Geoff Shandler, Dimitri Simes, Benn Steil, and Fareed Zakaria. Mort Abramowitz, Martti Ahtisaari, Anthony Lester, Charles W. Maynes, Aryeh Neier, Stewart Paperin, Alex Rondos, Cornelio Sommaruga, and Joseph Stiglitz attended a weekend discussion at my home. Lord Lester raised some important issues with regard to my definition of open society that I did not resolve to his satisfaction. I wish to thank all those who took the trouble to read the manuscript at various stages of its evolution. They are too numerous to list, but I should like to acknowledge Benjamin Barber, Leon Botstein, Bill Clapp, Jacques de Larosière, Jeffrey Friedman, Roman Frydman, Ekaterina Genieva, Anatole Kaletsky, Alex Lupis, Aryeh Neier, Joseph Nye, Andrei Shleifer, John Simon, and F. van Zyl Slabbert, who sent me written communications. Justin Leites made some valuable suggestions at the last minute.

I have been very happy with Peter Osnos and his team at Public-Affairs and I am grateful to Kris Dahl for suggesting him.

Yvonne Sheer has retyped the manuscript innumerable times, checked references, and acted as general manager of the project. I could not have done without her.

Introduction

This is a book of practical philosophy: It offers a conceptual framework that is meant to serve as a guide to action. I have been guided by that framework in both my moneymaking and philanthropic activities, and I believe that it can also apply to society at large: It provides the guiding principles for a global open society. This is an ambitious undertaking. In executing it, I shall have to cover a lot of ground and move on several levels: philosophical and practical, public and personal.

On the practical level, I have established a network of foundations devoted to fostering open societies. This network covers all the countries of the former Soviet empire and it has branched out to other parts of the world: South Africa, the ten countries of Southern Africa, the sixteen countries of Western Africa, Haiti, Guatemala, Burma, and more recently Indonesia. There is also an Open Society Institute in the United States. Each national foundation has its own board and staff who decide their own priorities and take responsibility for the activities of the foundation within their own countries. They support civil society; they also try to work with the central and local governments because a democratic and effective government is an essential part of an open society, but often they are at loggerheads with the government or some of its activities. In some countries, notably in Slovakia and Croatia, the foundations were successful in mobilizing civil society in opposition to repressive regimes. In Belarus and Burma, the foundations are banned and operate from the outside. In Serbia, it is functioning in precarious circumstances. In addition, we have network programs in those program areas where the network is most actively engaged: higher education and general education; youth; the rule of law, the judiciary and law enforcement, including prisons; arts and cultural institutions; libraries, publishing, and the Internet; the media; vulnerable populations such as the mentally disabled; minorities, with special emphasis on Roma peoples (Gypsies); public health, alcohol and drug abuse; and so on.

I enjoy widespread, indeed exaggerated, recognition as some kind of financial guru, but my credentials for holding views on political and security issues are less well recognized. In fact, I am only one of many practitioners in finance; but I am almost unique in practicing crisis prevention in a purposeful and organized way.

In this book I am advocating that the democracies of the world ought to form an alliance with the dual purpose of, first, promoting the development of open societies within individual countries and, second, strengthening international law and the institutions needed for a global open society.

We live in a global economy that is characterized by free trade in goods and services and even more by the free movement of capital. As a result, interest rates, exchange rates, and stock prices in various countries are intimately interrelated, and global financial markets exert tremendous influence on economic conditions everywhere. Financial capital enjoys a privileged position. Capital is more mobile than the other factors of production, and financial capital is even more mobile than other forms of capital. The globalization of financial markets has reduced the ability of individual states to tax and regulate capital because it can move elsewhere. Given the decisive role that international financial capital plays in the fortunes of individual countries, it is not inappropriate to speak of a global capitalist system.

We can speak about the triumph of capitalism in the world, but we cannot yet speak about the triumph of democracy. There is a serious mismatch between the political and the economic conditions that prevail in the world today. We have a global economy, but the political arrangements are still firmly grounded in the sovereignty of the state. How can the needs of a global society be reconciled with the sovereignty of states? That is the crucial problem facing us today.

Capitalism and democracy do not necessarily go hand in hand. There is some correlation: Rising standards of living and the formation of a middle class tend to generate pressure for freedom and democracy; they also tend to support greater political stability. But the connection is far from automatic. Repressive regimes do not relax their grip on power willingly, and they are often aided and abetted by business interests, both foreign and domestic. We can see this in many countries, particularly where natural resources such as oil or diamonds are at stake. Perhaps the greatest threat to freedom and democracy in the world today comes from the formation of unholy alliances between government and business.

This is not a new phenomenon. It used to be called fascism, and it characterized Mussolini's Italy and to various degrees Hitler's Germany, Franco's Spain, and Salazar's Portugal. Today it takes more diverse forms, but it can be detected in Fujimori's Peru, Mugabe's Zimbabwe, the SPDC's Burma, and Mahathir's Malaysia, to mention only a few cases. More disconcerting, the collapse of communism has also led to an unholy alliance between big business and government in many countries, including Russia. The outward appearances of the democratic process are observed, but the powers of the state are diverted to the benefit of private interests. The democratic countries do not pay much heed to the internal political conditions prevailing in other countries: Other priorities usually take precedence. Yet the people living in repressive regimes need outside assistance; often it is their only lifeline.

Capitalism is very successful in creating wealth, but we cannot rely on it to assure freedom, democracy, and the rule of law. Business is motivated by profit; it is not designed to safeguard universal principles. Most businesspeople are upright citizens; but that does not change the fact that business is conducted for private gain and not for the public benefit. The primary responsibility of management is to the owners of the business, not to some nebulous entity called the public interest—although enterprises often try, or at least pretend, to be acting in a public-spirited way because that is good for business. If we care about universal principles such as freedom, democracy, and the rule of law, we cannot leave them to the care of market forces; we must establish some other institutions to safeguard them.

All this is almost too obvious to be stated, yet it needs to be said because there is a widely held creed that the markets will take care of all our needs. It used to be called "laissez-faire" in the nineteenth century, but I have found a better name for it: market fundamentalism. Market fundamentalists hold that the public interest is best served when people are allowed to pursue their own interests. This is an appealing idea, but it is only half true. Markets are eminently suitable for the pursuit of private interests, but they are not designed to take care of the common interest. The preservation of the market mechanism itself is one such common interest. Market participants compete not to preserve competition but to win; if they could, they would eliminate competition.

The protection of the common interest used to be the task of the nation-state. But the powers of the state have shrunk as global capital markets have expanded. When capital is free to move around, it can be taxed and regulated only at the risk of driving it away. Since capital is essential to the creation of wealth, governments must cater to its demands, often to the detriment of other considerations. Chasing away capital can do more harm than taxation and regulation could bring. This point was brought home recently by the spectacular failure of Oscar Lafontaine, the German finance minister, when he tried to increase the burden of taxation on business.

In some ways that is a welcome development. Private enterprise is better at wealth creation than the state, and free competition on a global scale has led to an acceleration in productivity. Moreover, states often abuse their power; globalization offers a degree of individual freedom that no state could provide.

But there is a downside. The capacity of the state to perform the functions that the citizens have come to expect of it has been impaired. This would not be a cause for concern if free markets could be counted on to take care of all needs, but that is manifestly not the case. Some of our collective needs are almost too obvious to need mentioning: peace and security, law and order, human rights, protection of the environment, and some element of social justice. Market values express only what one participant is willing to pay another in free exchange and do not give expression to their common interests. As a result, social values can be served only by social and political arrangements, even if they are less efficient than markets.

Even in the service of individual interests, the market mechanism has certain limitations and imperfections that market fundamentalists ignore. For one thing, financial markets are inherently unstable. The theory of perfect competition takes the supply and demand curves as independently given. Where the twain meet, equilibrium is to be found. But the assumptions upon which the concept of equilibrium is built are rarely met in the real world. In the financial sphere they are unattainable. Financial markets seek to discount a future that is contingent on how it is discounted at present. Given the imperfect understanding of the participants, the outcome is inherently indeterminate. Thus, contrary to the idea of a self-equilibrating mechanism, the stability of financial markets needs to be safeguarded by public policy.

Unfortunately, public policy is also imperfect, and so the history of financial markets is punctuated by periodic crises. Nevertheless, by a process of trial and error, the advanced industrial countries have evolved central banks and elaborate regulatory frameworks that have been remarkably successful in keeping instability within tolerable bounds. The last major breakdown in the advanced industrial countries occurred in the 1930s. Countries at the periphery of the global capitalist system are less well situated: The financial crisis of 1997–1999 wrought as much havoc in some of the emerging markets as the Great Depression of the 1930s in the United States.

The international financial system can no longer be regulated on a national basis. A set of international institutions were established at the end of World War II at Bretton Woods in 1945, but they were designed for a world without the free movement of capital. These institutions have tried valiantly to adapt to changing circumstances, yet they have been unable to keep pace with the recent rapid growth of international financial markets. They failed to stem the contagion in the international financial crisis of 1997–1999. Fortunately, the countries at the center of the global capitalist system remained unaffected (indeed, they even benefited from the distress at the periphery), and the world economy has recovered sooner than could have been expected at the height of the crisis. This remarkable resilience has reinforced the faith in the self-correcting capacity of financial markets, and instead of strengthening the International Monetary Fund (IMF), its power and influence have been allowed to decline. This will leave the world economy more vulnerable in the next crisis, if and when it arises. To think that we shall not have another crisis is to defy history.

The weaknesses in the international financial architecture are exceeded by weaknesses in the international *political* architecture. The tragedy of World War II led to the establishment of the United Nations (UN), designed to preserve peace and security in the world. Unfortunately, the design was not equal to the noble goal. No sooner was the United Nations born than the world broke into two opposing camps, one led by the United States, the other by the Soviet Union. The two sides were locked in mortal combat, both military and ideological; yet each side realized that it had to respect the vital interests of the other, since both possessed the ability to destroy the other with nuclear weapons. This turned the Cold War into an instrument of stability based on the grim yet powerful concept of mutual assured destruction (MAD).

The MAD balance between East and West came to an end with the internal collapse of the Soviet empire. There was a historic moment when the United Nations could have started to function as it was originally designed, yet that opportunity was lost when the Western democracies failed to agree among themselves on how to tackle the Bosnia crisis. The system became unstable.

The experience of two world wars has shown that a system based on the sovereignty of states does not assure peace and stability. Since sovereign states often abuse their powers, a decline in those powers ought to be a welcome development. Up to this point the current promarket, antistate sentiment is fully justified. But the weakening of the sovereign state ought to be matched by the strengthening of international institutions. This is where market fundamentalism, which is opposed to international authority just as much as to state authority, stands in the way.

To be sure, market fundamentalism is not the only culprit; the enduring belief in national sovereignty is another. The United States is even more strongly wedded to its sovereignty than most other states. As the sole remaining military superpower and the strongest economic power, it is willing to enter into arrangements, such as the World Trade Organization, that open markets while providing some protection to vested interests, but it strenuously resists any infringement of its own sovereignty in other spheres. It is willing to interfere in the internal affairs of other countries but is not prepared to submit to the rules it seeks to impose on others.

While the United States views itself as the upholder of lofty principles, others merely see the arrogance of power. It may be shocking to say, but I believe that the current unilateralist posture of the United States constitutes a serious threat to the peace and prosperity of the world. Yet the United States could easily become a powerful force for the good, simply by shifting from a unilateral to a multilateral approach. The world needs some rules and standards of behavior. If the United States were prepared to abide by the rules, it could take the lead in establishing them.

Unfortunately, the aversion of the United States to multilateralism is not without justification. Most international institutions don't work well. That is because they are associations of states and, as Cardinal Richelieu said, states have no principles, only interests. This finds expression in their behavior within international organizations. Whatever the faults of a state bureaucracy, they are multiplied in an international bureaucracy. International institutions such as the United Nations are ill suited to safeguard universal principles. This can be seen in the record of the UN in protecting human rights.

I believe that international institutions can be made to work better only with the help of civil society. It may be true that states have no principles, but democratic states are responsive to the wishes of their citizens. If the citizens have principles, they can impose them on their governments. That is why I advocate an alliance of democratic states: It would have the active engagement of civil society to ensure that governments remained true to the principles of the alliance. That is where the greatest difficulty lies. As the recent demonstrations in Seattle and Washington have shown, civil society can be mobilized in opposition to international institutions; a way must be found to mobilize it in their favor.

The alliance would have two objectives: first, to strengthen international law and international institutions; second, to strengthen democracy within individual countries. The two goals are, of course, connected: The promotion of democracy must be carried out by international institutions. No single state can be entrusted with the protection of universal principles. Whenever there is a conflict between universal principles and self-interest, self-interest is likely to prevail. This point was well understood by the Founding Fathers when they devised the Constitution of the United States.

Yet it is in the interest of all democracies to foster the development of democracies throughout the world. In today's interdependent global society most conflicts occur not between states but within states. Democracies cannot tolerate the large-scale violation of human rights, and sooner or later they are liable to be drawn into such conflicts, as occurred in Yugoslavia. Even if they refuse to be drawn in, they have to face the influx of refugees and various other adverse consequences.

There is something contradictory about imposing democracy from the outside. The contradiction can be avoided only if the intervention brings benefits and is therefore voluntarily accepted. To the greatest possible extent, intervention ought to take the form of incentives and constructive engagement.

Once a conflict has erupted, it is very difficult to deal with it. Crisis prevention cannot start early enough. But in the early stages it is difficult to identify what will lead to a crisis. That is why the best way to prevent crises is to foster the development of what I call open societies. That is what my network of Open Society Foundations has sought to do. By creating open societies, the chances of crises requiring outside intervention can be greatly reduced. And if punitive intervention becomes unavoidable it is more easily justified when it has been preceded by constructive engagement.

At present we rely far too heavily on punitive measures. The only effective alliance of democratic states is a military alliance—the North Atlantic Treaty Organization (NATO). We need to complement NATO with a political alliance. Since the development of open society is closely associated with economic prosperity, the alliance must aim at affirmative action.

These thoughts are particularly relevant today, after the NATO intervention in Kosovo. I believe the intervention was necessary, but it must be justified by ensuring a better future for the region. This can be achieved only if the European Union can bring the countries of the region closer to one another by bringing them closer to Europe. This idea is now widely accepted, and it is given expression in the Stability Pact for Southeastern Europe. Making it work must be a top priority for the European Union. It is certainly a top priority for me.

Going from the particular to the general, I advocate a concerted effort by the developed democracies to foster the development of democracy in the less-advanced parts of the world. It would take the form of technical assistance and economic incentives. Economics and politics cannot be separated. Amartya Sen makes a convincing case that development should be defined in terms of freedom, not in terms of gross national product.*

The membership of the alliance would include the United States, the European Union, and a critical mass of democratic countries from the periphery of the capitalist system—otherwise the alliance could turn into an instrument of domination and exploitation. The most problematic member would be the United States, because at present it is unwilling to abide by the rules it seeks to impose on others. It has nothing to fear from the kind of alliance I have in mind, because such an alliance could not function without U.S. participation; nevertheless, it would require a radical reorientation in U.S. policy from unilateralism to multilateralism.

I realize that my proposal goes against the grain of market fundamentalism. Foreign aid has been a dismal failure in Africa and more recently in the Soviet Union and its successor states, and it threatens to fail also with the Stability Pact. The fact that it doesn't work does not mean that we should abandon the idea. Rather, we must

---

*Amartya Sen, *Development as Freedom* (New York: Alfred A. Knopf, 1999).

examine the reasons for our failure and devise better ways. Foreign aid, as it is administered today, is all too often directed at satisfying the needs of the donors, not the needs of the recipients. I can assert, based on my own experiences in countries such as Russia, that outside assistance can be effective.

The global capitalist system has produced a very uneven playing field. The gap between rich and poor is getting wider. This is dangerous, because a system that does not offer some hope and benefit to the losers is liable to be disrupted by acts of desperation. By contrast, if we offer economic incentives to countries that are eager to take advantage of them we create a powerful tool for crisis prevention. Incentives foster economic and political development; the fact that they can be withdrawn provides leverage that can be used against recalcitrant governments.

Unfortunately, the global financial architecture that prevails today offers practically no support to those who are less fortunate. Current trends go in the opposite direction. After the recent financial crisis, the aim has been to impose greater market discipline. But if markets are inherently unstable, imposing market discipline means imposing instability—and how much instability can societies tolerate?

Now that we have global financial markets, we also need a global central bank and some other international financial institutions whose explicit mission is to keep financial markets on an even keel. But any lender-of-last-resort activity engenders some moral hazard, and the current battle cry of market fundamentalists is to eliminate moral hazard. The result is the downsizing of the IMF. Undoubtedly, that will reduce the danger of excessive lending to emerging markets, but in my opinion the next crisis is likely to come from the opposite direction: from inadequate capital flows to less-developed countries.

The Meltzer Commission established by the United States Congress recommends that the World Bank be converted from a lending agency to a grant-giving agency aimed at the poorest countries of the world. That is a splendid idea, but the way that the Meltzer Commission would go about it is by downsizing the World Bank and returning the unused capital to the shareholders in a major resource transfer from the poor to the rich. I believe that the unused capital ought to be put to more productive use by *increasing* the grant-giving and guarantee-giving activities of the Bank. But that is not what the Meltzer Commission has in mind.

I would urge a similar argument with regard to the World Trade Organization. There is a crying need for labor standards and the protection of the environment. But poor countries can't afford these. Instead of punitive measures, there ought to be incentives that would enable poor countries to comply.

An alliance of democracies could take many different forms. It could try to reform existing institutions such as the World Bank or even the UN, or it could operate more informally and address specific problem areas or problem countries. It would have a better chance of reforming the UN than any previous effort, exactly because it could operate either within the UN or outside it if the other member states refuse to go along. But the alliance could succeed only if its members could agree among themselves. And that means establishing some ground rules for a global open society.

The term *open society* was first introduced by Henri Bergson in 1932 when he published his *Two Sources of Religion and Morality*. According to Bergson, one source of ethics is tribal, the other universal. The former gives rise to closed society, the latter to open society. The concept was further developed by Karl Popper, who argued in his book *Open Society and Its Enemies* that open society is threatened by universal ideologies that claim to be in possession of the ultimate truth. He gave the concept of open society an epistemological foundation—namely, our inherently imperfect understanding. Ideologies that lay claim to the ultimate truth constitute a threat to open society because their claim can be imposed only by compulsion.

Bergson's formulation is useful in understanding ethnic conflicts such as those in Yugoslavia; Popper's formulation is useful in elucidating the threats posed by totalitarian regimes, such as those in Nazi Germany and the Soviet Union. During and after World War II, the concept of open society could be most readily understood by contrasting it with closed societies based on totalitarian ideologies such as fascism and communism. This remained true right up to the collapse of the Soviet empire in 1989.

Since then, the situation has changed. The collapse of communism did not automatically lead to the establishment of open society. The simple dichotomy between open and closed society is no longer applicable. Open society is threatened from an unexpected direction: the unbridled pursuit of self-interest. We have come to think of authority—in the form of a repressive government or an ideology that lays claim to the ultimate truth and seeks to impose itself by repressive measures—as the main obstacle to an open society. The ideology concerned can be either religious or secular in nature. Now it turns out that the lack of authority and the lack of social cohesion can be equally debilitating. The disintegration of the Soviet Union has shown that a weak state can also be a threat to liberty.*

As a student after World War II, I adopted Popper's concept of open society with alacrity. As a Hungarian Jew who first escaped extermination by the Nazis by adopting a false identity and then escaped communism by emigrating, I learned at an early age how important it is what kind of social organization prevails. Popper's dichotomy between open and closed societies seemed to me profoundly important. Not only did it illuminate the fundamental flaw in totalitarian ideologies but it also threw light on some basic philo-

*Stephen Holmes, "What Russia Teaches Us Now: How Weak States Threaten Freedom," *The American Prospect* (July–August 1997): 30–39.

sophical issues. It is his philosophy that guided me in establishing my network of Open Society Foundations.

I was an active participant in the revolution that swept away the Soviet system, and the experience forced me to undertake a thorough reconsideration of the concept of open society. That brings me to the philosophical aspects of the book.

I start this book by examining the relationship between thinking and reality. I don't come down on the side of either realism or idealism; rather, I seek to find the balance between the two. Yes, there is a reality, but it is not fully accessible to our intellect. Our view of the world may approximate the world as it is, but it can never fully correspond to it. Rather than disputing the nature of reality or the ultimate truth, I take it as my starting point that our understanding of the world in which we live is inherently imperfect. We are part of the world we seek to understand, and our imperfect understanding plays an active role in shaping the events in which we participate. There is a two-way interaction between our understanding and these events that introduces an element of uncertainty into both. It ensures that we cannot base our decisions on knowledge and that our actions are liable to have unintended consequences. The two effects feed on each other. I call this two-way feedback mechanism *reflexivity* and it is the cornerstone of my conceptual framework.

The concept of reflexivity is almost too obvious, yet it has implications that have not been generally accepted. It creates a cleavage between the natural and social sciences and it undermines the postulates on which economic theory has been based: rational behavior in general, and rational expectations in particular. It gives rise to a radically different interpretation of how financial markets operate than the one proposed by economic theory. That is one instance where my conceptual framework has practical implications.

In this book I go beyond the criticism of generally accepted ideas. I use the concepts of fallibility and reflexivity to formulate a theory of history. I interpret financial markets as a historical process and I use them as a laboratory for testing my theory. My experiments do not produce determinate results comparable to the equations that define the equilibrium in economic theory. This makes my interpretation unacceptable to economists, but I contend that it is better to accept that financial markets are inherently unpredictable than to abide by a false theory.

I interpret history as a reflexive process in which the participants' biased decisions interact with a reality that is beyond their comprehension. The interaction can be self-reinforcing or self-correcting. A self-reinforcing process cannot go on forever without running into limits set by reality, but it can go on long enough and far enough to bring about substantial changes in the real world. If and when it becomes unsustainable, it may then set into motion a self-reinforcing process going in the opposite direction. Such boom-bust sequences are clearly observable in financial markets, but their extent, duration, and actual course remain uncertain.

When I try to apply the boom-bust model to history in general, my interpretation becomes more idiosyncratic and forced. Nevertheless, it can be illuminating, provided it is not taken too seriously. Unfortunately, I have not always followed my own advice, as the reader will see. More seriously, I try to formulate some ideas on how society ought to be organized. I develop the concept of open society, an association of free individuals respecting one another's rights within a framework of law.*

Market fundamentalism is not diametrically opposed to open society the way totalitarian ideologies such as fascism and communism were; rather, it represents a distortion of the concept, an undue exaggeration of one of its aspects. That does not make it any less dangerous. Market fundamentalism endangers the open society inadvertently by misinterpreting how markets work and giving them an unduly dominant role.

*Bryan Magee, *Confessions of a Philosopher: A Personal Journey Through Western Philosophy from Plato to Popper* (New York: Random House, 1999), p. 119.

Market fundamentalists believe in individual freedom, which is a cornerstone of open society, but they exaggerate the merits of the market mechanism. They believe that efficient markets assure the best allocation of resources and that any intervention, whether it comes from the state or from international institutions, is detrimental. Since market fundamentalism has become so influential, it today constitutes a greater threat to a global open society than communism or socialism, because those ideologies have been thoroughly discredited.

As an advocate of open society, I want to make it clear that I am not opposed to capitalism per se. The concepts of open society and market economy are closely linked, and global capitalism has brought us close to a global open society. But markets are not perfect. They can only cater to individual needs; taking care of social needs is beyond their scope. And even as the allocators of resources, they are less than perfect: Financial markets are inherently unstable. That does not mean we should abolish capitalism; rather, we should endeavor to correct its shortcomings.

Communism sought to abolish the market mechanism and to impose collective control over all economic activities. Market fundamentalism seeks to abolish collective decisionmaking and to impose the supremacy of market values over all political and social values. Both extremes are wrong. We need to recognize that all human constructs are flawed. Perfection is beyond our reach. We must content ourselves with the second-best: an imperfect society that holds itself open to improvement. Global capitalism is badly in need of improvement.

This is not a complete summary of my book. For instance, I have not mentioned the distinction I make between rulemaking and playing by the rules. But enough has been said to indicate that the book seeks to cover a lot of ground—perhaps too much ground. It might have been more effective to concentrate on fewer points, but the conceptual framework does hang together and I found it difficult to make one point without the others. I regard this as a weakness in the construction of the book, because in the light of my working hypothesis of radical fallibility, it is unlikely that all my points are equally persuasive.

The weakness is not inherent in the argument, because the various points are not logically dependent on each other; rather, it is the result of my personal predilection. On a personal level, this book is my life's work. I started working on it as a student and I have still not completed it. I am reluctant to let go of it. Many of the points I am making here I have made before, but I still feel I could have made them better.

I have an uncle by marriage, Tamas Losonczy, who has been an abstract expressionist painter in Hungary all his life. Abstract expressionism was not allowed in Hungary until quite recently. As a result, he felt compelled to repeat his major themes in all his paintings. This made his paintings more cluttered and complex than those of the abstract expressionist masters in the West. I feel about philosophy the way he feels about painting, and I'm afraid I may suffer from the same syndrome: I feel obliged to repeat the arguments I made in previous books, because I do not sense that I got my points across. I may be wrong. My statement that reflexivity is not recognized in economic theory may have been valid in 1987, when I first published *The Alchemy of Finance*, but I have been criticized by some economists who claim it is no longer valid. Yet I can see from their criticism that the main point of reflexivity—namely, that financial markets are inherently unpredictable—is still not generally accepted, since they blame me for not producing a theory that is capable of making valid predictions.

The fact that I have crowded the main ideas of a lifetime into this book does not make for easy reading. I hope, however, that it will be worth the effort. On the level of public discourse, I believe I am making some worthwhile contributions. Apart from the concept of open society and my proposal for an alliance of democracies, I would single out:

- the concept of reflexivity;

- the working hypothesis of radical fallibility;

- the assessment of the cleavage between natural and social sciences;

- the critique of equilibrium theory in economics and the outlines of a new paradigm;

- the discussion of the ways market values penetrate into areas where they do not properly belong;

- the critique of market fundamentalism;

- the concept of far-from-equilibrium situations;

- the concept of fertile fallacies;

- the interpretation of financial markets as a historical process in which outcomes diverge from expectations;

- the distinction between rulemaking and playing by the rules and the proposition that in political participation (as distinct from market participation) we ought to be guided by our conception of the common interest *even if others are not*;

- the exploration of the difference between center and periphery in the global capitalist system;

- the examination of the new global financial and political architecture.

The difficulties presented by this book are compounded by the way it came to be written. It has its origin in an article I published in the February 1997 issue of *The Atlantic Monthly* under the title "The Capitalist Threat." The fact that a prototypical capitalist was critical of capitalism created considerable stir, and I decided to expand the article into a book. As I was writing, a major international financial crisis of the kind I was warning against erupted in July 1997, and I felt I had something urgent and important to say on the subject. When Russia defaulted on its internal debt in August 1998, I thought the global financial system was about to come apart at the seams, and so I decided to rush the book into print.

The book was published in November 1998 under the title *The Crisis of Global Capitalism: Open Society Endangered*. When the time came to prepare a paperback edition, I started revising it, and the revision soon became so substantial that it qualified as a new book. I make the point by publishing it under a new title.

In retrospect, I was wrong to predict disaster, and now I have some egg on my face. Looking back from the perspective of 2000, it appears that I made two major miscalculations. One was to underestimate the capacity of the financial authorities to prevent a disaster when it threatened the center of the global capitalist system. After all, I was emphasizing the disparity between center and periphery. The fact that the Federal Reserve was successful in protecting the U.S. economy while the International Monetary Fund failed to protect the economies at the periphery was a demonstration of that disparity. I should have been able to anticipate it.

The second miscalculation was to ignore the impact of the technological revolution. Clearly, it was a major factor in enabling the center to shake off the troubles at the periphery. There was an Internet boom concurrent to the bust in emerging markets. How could I ignore that? I was misled by the fact that similar technological advances—railroads, electricity, telephone—had taken place in the nineteenth century, which was itself a period of global capitalism. Yet technologies caused booms and busts in those days as well. This was a major error in my analysis, one that I shall not be able to erase without falsifying the historical record. I can, however, acknowledge it.

In spite of these mistakes, I feel that there is enough validity in my approach to justify revising the book. For the first time in my life, my ideas received serious critical attention, and I have greatly benefited from it. Since recognizing mistakes is at the heart of my approach, I incorporated all of the criticisms that I considered valid. I also shifted the emphasis from the financial to the political. *The Crisis of Global Capitalism* attracted attention mainly for what I had to say about the financial crisis. This is understandable in view of the then-prevailing conditions and my notoriety as a financial spec-ulator. My discussion of what I call the "nonmarket sector" elicited much less response. As I was revising the book, I felt a great sense of urgency to elaborate my ideas on the global political and security architectures in much greater depth.

The revision posed a problem: If I revised my original analysis of the crisis of 1997–1999, I would falsify the historical record. Accordingly, in that part of the book which deals with the crisis of 1997–1999, I decided to leave the original text intact and indicate where I had made revisions. This solution has made the structure of the book more cumbersome.

To make up for this, I should like to provide a simplified road map. In Chapter 1 I begin with reflexivity and fallibility. This leads me to a discussion of scientific method in Chapter 2.

In Chapter 3 I test the validity and relevance of reflexivity in the laboratory of the financial markets, relying largely on material drawn from my previous book, *The Alchemy of Finance*.

In Chapter 4 I try to develop a theory of history based on the reflexive relationship between participants' thinking and the events in which they participate. Fallibility renders equilibrium impossi-ble, leaving three possibilities: the near-equilibrium of open society; the static disequilibrium of closed society; and the dynamic disequi-librium of revolutionary regime change. This leads to a discussion of open society as an ideal in Chapter 5. In Chapter 6 I tackle the problem of social values and introduce the distinction between rule-making and playing by the rules. This completes the theoretical framework.

Part II applies the theoretical framework to the present moment in history. But time does not stand still. As I mentioned earlier, I had started writing *The Crisis of Global Capitalism* before the financial crisis of 1997–1999 erupted; I rushed the book into print just as the crisis climaxed and have thoroughly rethought and revised it since then: All this is reflected in the text. Chapter 7 provides an analytical overview of the global capitalist system. Chapter 8 addresses the financial crisis of 1997–1999. Chapter 9 reviews the failure of Russia to make the transition from closed to open society. Chapter 10 examines the global financial architecture and makes some suggestions regarding possible improvements. Chapter 11 addresses the global political architecture in the context of a test case: the disintegration of Yugoslavia. And Chapter 12 examines the prospects for a global open society.

For the sake of historical accuracy, I kept the text of Chapters 7 and 8 largely unchanged, pointing out where my views have changed. The remaining chapters express my current views.

Where the text has remained the same, it is because I could not improve on it. I remain open to criticism, however, and am ready to make further revisions. I should have liked to continue working on the book, but in the end another deadline loomed and I have had to rush it into print once again. As I said before, I consider this book my life's work and I shall continue working on it as long as I am alive.

PART I

Conceptual Framework

CHAPTER 1

Thinking and Reality

The concept of open society is based on the recognition that our understanding of the world is inherently imperfect. Those who claim to be in possession of the ultimate truth are making a false claim, and they can enforce it only by imposing their views on those who differ. The result of such intimidation is a closed society, in which freedom of thought and expression is suppressed. By contrast, if we recognize our fallibility, we can gain a better understanding of reality without ever attaining perfect knowledge. Acting on that understanding, we can create a society that is open to never-ending improvement. Open society falls short of perfection, but it has the great merit of assuring freedom of thought and speech and giving ample scope to experimentation and creativity.

To explain the concept of open society, I must begin with the relationship between thinking and reality, particularly as it relates to social affairs. I need to show what it is that renders our understanding inherently imperfect. Knowledge is not beyond our reach, but when it comes to situations in which we are active participants we cannot base our decisions on knowledge alone. Knowledge relates to facts, but the events to which our decisions relate are not facts. They lie in the future and they are contingent on our decisions in the present. Even after they have occurred, they are different from the facts that form the subject matter of natural science because they will have been influenced by what we think. What we think is part of what we have to think about; that is the source of our difficulties.

The relationship between thinking and reality is a subject that has preoccupied philosophers since the beginning of philosophy, but it is still not properly understood. It is in the nature of philosophical questions that they do not have final, incontrovertible answers, or, more exactly, that every answer raises new questions. I cannot expect to do any better, yet I feel I have something important to say.

The central point I want to make is that the relationship between thinking and reality is reflexive—that is, what we think has a way of affecting what we think about. Obviously, this is not true of every aspect of reality. Natural phenomena follow their course irrespective of what we think. It is only in the social sphere that reflexivity is relevant, but that is the subject that interests us here. I shall try to show that reflexivity introduces an element of uncertainty both into the participants' understanding and into the events in which they participate. Reflexivity is not the only source of uncertainty, either in our thinking or in reality, but when it occurs, it constitutes an *additional* source of uncertainty.

I enter the discussion with trepidation. Philosophical arguments tend to be never-ending, and reflexivity, in particular, rests on a circular argument: The participants' understanding is imperfect because their imperfect understanding introduces an unpredictable element into the situation in which they participate. I also have some personal difficulties in dealing with the subject. Once, in the early 1960s, I spent three years exploring it until one day I could not understand what I had written the day before and decided to quit. Now I am reentering the same arena. I have been fortified by my success in applying my conceptual framework in the real world.

The Correspondence Theory of Truth

In order to attain knowledge, it is necessary to distinguish between thinking and reality. Knowledge consists of true statements and, according to the correspondence theory of truth, statements are true if, and only if, they correspond to the facts. To be able to determine whether statements are true, the facts must be independent of the statements that refer to them; there must be a watertight separation between statements and facts: facts on one side, statements on the other. The facts can then serve as the criterion by which the truth of statements are judged.

It does not follow, however, that the facts are always separate and independent of the statements that relate to them. All that has been asserted is that the separation is necessary for the acquisition of knowledge. Sometimes the necessary separation prevails, at other times not; in the latter case, the participants' understanding falls short of knowledge.

In primitive societies, people fail to distinguish between their own thoughts and the world to which those thoughts relate. They form beliefs that are treated as reality. For instance, they endow objects with spirits and they accept the existence of those spirits. Once the distinction between thinking and reality is recognized, this view of the world can be seen to be false. True statements can be distinguished from false ones and the way is opened to the development of knowledge. Animism and primitive religion lose their appeal; philosophy and science come into their own.

When philosophers started to discuss the relationship between thinking and reality, their main concerns were to establish the nature and existence of reality (ontology) and to explain how it can be known (epistemology). This led them to think in terms of a one-directional relationship in which reason is actively seeking for knowledge while reality is passively waiting to be discovered. This way of looking at the relationship was reinforced by the success of science. Scientific method has gone to great lengths to protect the subject matter from getting contaminated by the thoughts and actions of the scientific observers.

But the relationship between thinking and reality is not a one-way street. Situations that have thinking participants do not inertly wait to be studied; they are actively shaped by the participants' decisions.

There are, of course, events that occur independently of what anybody thinks; these phenomena, such as the movement of planets, form the subject matter of natural science. Here thinking plays the simple, one-way role assigned to it: It serves to understand reality. Scientific statements may or may not correspond to the facts of the physical world, but in either case the facts are separate and independent of the statements that refer to them. That is why the natural sciences have been able to produce such impressive results.

Social events are different, for they have thinking participants. Here the relationship between thinking and reality is more complicated. Our thinking guides us in our actions, and our actions have an impact on what happens. Where many different people are involved, it cannot be assumed that everyone facing the same situation will think alike. The outcome is a fact, but it does not qualify as an independent criterion by which the truth or validity of the participants' thinking can be judged, because it is contingent on what the participants think and do. In the absence of an independent criterion, the participants' thinking cannot qualify as knowledge. Even if there is a correspondence between what the participants think and what actually happens, it may have been brought about by the impact of the participants' decisions; therefore, the correspondence does not provide the kind of evidence about the truth of statements that would be available if statements and facts were truly independent of one another. Instead of the one-way relationship that is the basis of knowledge, thinking plays a dual role.

On the one hand, the thinking participants seek to understand the situation in which they participate. I call this the passive or cognitive function. On the other hand, they participate in the situation that they seek to understand. I call this the active or participating function. Instead of a one-way street, there is a two-way interaction between the participants and the situation. The two functions work in the opposite direction, and they may come in conflict with each other. The independent variable of one function is the dependent variable of the other. If both functions connect the same variables at the same time, one function may deprive the other of an independent variable. The interference introduces an element of indeterminacy into both functions that would be absent if the two functions operated independently of each other. That is what I call *reflexivity*. I have taken the word from French grammar, which calls a verb reflexive when its subject and object are the same, as in *je me lave* (I wash myself).

The Theory of Reflexivity

Reflexivity can be stated in the form of two recursive functions:

$x = f(y)$ cognitive function
$y = ö(x)$ participating function

where x represents the participants' view of the situation y. Both functions have some value so that x cannot be identical with y.

Moreover, both functions involve the passage of time, which we can denote using the notation x_{t1}, x_{t2} and y_{t1}, y_{t2}.

Each function on its own would yield a determinate result: In the case of the cognitive function, the situation would determine the participants' views; in the case of the participating function, the participants' views, translated into action, would determine the outcome. But neither function operates in splendid isolation. The independent variable of one function—y in the case of f and x in the case of $\ddot{o}$—is the dependent variable of the other function. In terms of our notation,

$$y_{t2} = f\,[\ddot{o}\,y_{t1}] \text{ and}$$
$$x_{t2} = \ddot{o}\,[f\,x_{t1}].$$

As long as the two functions have a value other than 1 and both functions are operating, neither the participants' views nor the actual state of affairs remains the same with the passage of time and neither is determined by what preceded it. Both functions yield indeterminate results, and the element of indeterminacy in one function can be attributed to its dependence on the other.

This is, of course, a simplified presentation. Most situations have more than one participant, so that instead of simply x we ought to list $x_{1,2,3,\,\ldots}$ ^{n} And the situation itself contains many variables besides simply the participants' actions, so that the formula ought to read

$$y = a,b,c \ldots \ddot{o}\,(x_{1,2,3,\,\ldots}{}^{n}).$$

But that does not change the basic argument: When the two functions connect the same variables at the same time, their interaction introduces an element of uncertainty into both. The participants' views cannot be determined by the situation because the situation is contingent on the participants' views, and the situation cannot be determined by the participants' decisions because the participants act on the basis of inadequate knowledge. There is *a lack of correspondence* between the participants' views and the actual state of affairs on the one hand and the participants' intentions and the actual outcome on the other.

Reflexivity operates within a rather narrow range. Reality contains vast areas that are not affected by the participants' thinking, and people's thinking relates to many subjects other than the situation in which they participate: They can dream, indulge in fantasies, or become immersed in philosophical speculations or scientific investigations. Moreover, reflexivity is not the *only* source of uncertainty, either in reality or in the participants' thinking, but within the narrow range where it operates, it is an *additional* source of uncertainty. That narrow range happens to be particularly important to us as thinking participants, because that is where we live our lives.

Participant Versus Observer

It is worthwhile to contrast the position of the participant with that of a natural scientist. This is not a comparison that is normally made, but in this case it will be illuminating. Natural scientists think about a universe that is independent of their thinking. Their statements belong to one universe, the facts to which they refer to another. Only a one-way correspondence between statements and facts is possible.

That is the key characteristic that renders the facts suitable to serve as the criterion by which the truth or validity of scientific statements can be judged. It also renders the facts immune to being manipulated by making statements about them. If the scientist wants to successfully manipulate reality, she must first gain knowledge of it.

Not so in the case of thinking participants. They can manipulate reality more directly by formulating ideas and arguments that will influence their own and other participants' decisions. These ideas need not correspond to the facts of the situation; indeed, they cannot do so because of the lack of correspondence that characterizes the participants' thinking. Nevertheless, they will make an impact on the situation—although, on account of their imperfect understanding, the outcome is liable to diverge from expectations. There is a two-way feedback mechanism at work that leaves neither the participants' views nor the actual course of events unaffected. A process that changes both thinking and reality qualifies as historical.

A Historical Process

The two-way feedback mechanism does not necessarily give rise to a historical process. It merely has the potential to do so. There are many cases in which the outcome does not diverge from expectations or the divergence does not trigger a change in the participants' expectations. But obviously those cases that set in motion a dynamic process are more interesting.

The key to understanding such dynamics is to be found in the element of judgment or bias that the participants must bring to bear on their decisions. We have seen that they cannot do without introducing such a bias. In turn, the divergence between outcomes and expectations is liable to affect the bias. The feedback can then be positive or negative. A positive feedback would reinforce the initial bias, which may in turn produce further positive feedback, but the process cannot continue indefinitely because eventually the bias is bound to become so pronounced that reality cannot possibly live up to expectations.

Different participants have different biases, but in many situations—particularly in financial markets—it is possible to speak of a "prevailing" bias. Initially, the outcome may validate the prevailing bias, but as the bias becomes more exaggerated its ability to influence the course of events may no longer be sufficient to ensure that outcomes reinforce expectations. As the gap between outcomes and expectations grows, the prevailing bias becomes increasingly difficult to maintain. If and when the participants question or abandon their bias, a self-reinforcing process may be set in motion in the opposite direction. The more a prevailing bias depends on a self-validating process and the greater the gap between outcomes and expectations, the greater the probability that such a reversal will occur. I shall give some examples of reflexivity in financial markets in Chapter 3.

The reflexive process unfolds over time. At a given moment, people are guided by one set of expectations that through their decisions leads to certain outcomes; the outcomes may alter peoples' expectations, which may alter the next set of decisions creating new outcomes, and so on, but the interaction takes time.

It may be argued that the cognitive and participating functions do not really interfere with each other because they are insulated from each other by the passage of time. At any moment the participants' bias is given; it is only at the subsequent moment that it can be affected by an unexpected outcome.

This argument is invalidated by the fact that the participants' thinking is not confined to events in the outside world and changes in their thinking are not necessarily triggered by outside events. Especially when people think about themselves or one another, the two functions operate simultaneously. Consider statements such as "I love you" or "He is my enemy." These statements affect the person to whom they are addressed at the time they are uttered. When a person alters her self-perception, the effect is even more instantaneous. The insulation provided by the passage of time is missing, and there is a genuine short circuit between the two functions. When people change their mind, they also change their behavior, and the change is not determined by external circumstances.

When such a change occurs, it affects the participants' thinking directly but the outside world only indirectly. The effect of reflexivity in shaping the participants' self-image, their values, and their expectations is much more pervasive than its effect on the course of events. To a large extent, peoples' identity and character are built in a reflexive fashion. The initially self-reinforcing but eventually self-defeating sequence I described earlier occurs less frequently, but when it occurs it takes on historic significance.

The genuine uncertainty in the participants' view of themselves or one another also introduces an element of uncertainty into the course of events. Take marriage: It has two thinking participants, but their thinking is not directed at a reality that is separate and independent of what they think and feel. One partner's thoughts and feelings affect the behavior of the other, and vice versa. Both feelings and behavior can change out of all recognition as the marriage evolves.

Even when thinking is directed at events in the outside world, those events do not actually have to occur for the participants' thinking to change. Consider the financial markets: The essence of investment decisions is to anticipate, or "discount," the future. But the future is uncertain because the price investors are willing to pay for a stock today may influence the fortunes of the company in many different ways. In other words, changes in current expectations can affect the future they discount. This renders prices in financial markets genuinely uncertain.

Not all social phenomena qualify as reflexive, but most historical processes do. Indeed, it could be argued that it is reflexivity that renders events truly historic. We can distinguish between humdrum, everyday events, where the two functions do not interact with each other in any significant way, and historic events, where they do. To take an example: Driving to work is a humdrum event, but Nikita Khrushchev's speech to the Twentieth Congress of the Communist Party of the Soviet Union was a historic one. A truly historic event does not just change the world; it also changes our understanding of the world—and that new understanding, in turn, has a new and unpredictable impact on the course of events.

The distinction between humdrum and historic events is, of course, tautological, but tautologies can be illuminating. Party congresses in the Soviet Union were rather humdrum, predictable affairs, but Khrushchev's speech to the Twentieth Congress was different. By exposing and repudiating Stalin's crimes, Khrushchev changed people's perceptions, and even if the communist regime did not change immediately, the speech had unpredictable consequences: The outlook of those at the forefront of glasnost three decades later had been shaped in their youth by Khrushchev's revelations.

Indeterminacy

Although it is perhaps an obvious point, it needs to be emphasized that the element of uncertainty I speak about is not produced by reflexivity on its own; reflexivity must be accompanied by imperfect understanding. If by some fluke people were endowed with perfect knowledge, the interaction between their thoughts and the outside world could be ignored. The outcome of their actions would perfectly correspond to their expectations because the true state of the world would be perfectly reflected in their views. Similarly, if the participants' thinking were fully determined by external circumstances or internal impulses, the element of uncertainty would be eliminated. This state of affairs is unrealistic, yet it has been seriously proposed. Karl Marx claimed that the material conditions of production determined the ideological superstructure; Sigmund Freud claimed that human behavior was dictated by the unconscious; and classical economic theory was based on the assumption of perfect knowledge. In each case, the impulse was the same: to provide a scientific explanation of human behavior. In accordance with the standards prevailing in the nineteenth century, the explanation had to be deterministic in order to qualify as scientific.

Reflexivity in Context

The concept of reflexivity is so fundamental that it would be hard to believe that I am the first to discover it. Indeed, I am not. Reflexivity is merely a new label for the two-way interaction between thinking and reality that is deeply ingrained in our common sense. If we look outside the realm of social science, we find a widespread awareness of reflexivity. The utterances of the Delphic oracle were reflexive, and so were Greek dramas, in the sense that prophecies were validated by the impact they made.

Even in social science, there were occasional acknowledgments: Machiavelli introduced an element of indeterminacy into his analysis and called it fate; Robert Merton drew attention to self-fulfilling prophecies and the bandwagon effect; and a concept akin to reflexivity was introduced into sociology by Alfred Schutz under the name "intersubjectivity." Sociologists such as Anthony Giddens have been using the term *reflexivity* in very much the same sense as I do.

More recently, a whole new science, evolutionary systems theory, has grown up to study the two-way interaction between predator and prey, or more generally between participant and environment. The participant is not necessarily human and its behavior is not necessarily guided by imperfect understanding, but the relationship is similar insofar as it involves a two-way interaction. Evolutionary systems theory has developed algorithms for studying the relationship. Game theory has also become evolutionary. It started out with the assumption of rationality, but the assumption was gradually abandoned and the study of rational behavior was replaced by that of "adaptive behavior." Reflexivity is no longer a stranger even to economic theory.

These are relatively recent developments. It is easy to forget that until recently social scientists, particularly economists, have gone out of their way to banish reflexivity from their subject matter. Why that should be so will be discussed in Chapter 3.

I started thinking in terms of reflexivity nearly fifty years ago. It may be interesting to recall how I arrived at the idea. It was through the footnotes of Karl Popper's *Open Society and Its Enemies*. These footnotes dealt with the problem of self-reference. Self-reference is only distantly related to reflexivity. Self-reference is a property of statements; it belongs entirely in the realm of thinking. Reflexivity connects thinking with reality; it belongs to both realms. But the two concepts have something in common: an element of indeterminacy.

The fact that statements may affect the subject matter to which they refer was first established by Epimenides the Cretan when he posed the paradox of the liar. Cretans always lie, he said, and by saying it he brought into question the truth of his statement. Being a Cretan, if the meaning of what he said was true, then his statement had to be false; conversely, if his statement was true, then the meaning it conveyed would have to be false.*

The paradox of the liar was for the longest time treated as an intellectual curiosity and was neglected because it interfered with the otherwise successful pursuit of truth. Truth was defined as the correspondence of statements to external facts. The so-called correspondence theory of truth came to be generally accepted at the beginning of the twentieth century. That was a time when the study of facts yielded impressive results and science enjoyed widespread admiration.

Emboldened by the success of science, Bertrand Russell tackled the paradox of the liar head-on. His solution was to distinguish between two classes of statements: a class that included statements that referred to themselves, and a class that excluded such statements. Only statements belonging to the latter class could be considered well formed in the sense of having a determinate truth value. In the case of self-referent statements, it may not be possible to establish whether they are true or false.

*The paradox of the liar can be interpreted as a case of negative feedback. If the question (that is, whether Epimenides' statement is true) is fed into a computer, the answer is "No, Yes, No, Yes, No, Yes" in an infinite series.

Logical positivists carried Bertrand Russell's argument to its logical conclusion and declared that statements whose truth value cannot be determined either by empirical facts or by their logical form are meaningless. Remember, that was a time when science was providing deterministic explanations for an ever-expanding range of phenomena while philosophy had become ever more removed from reality. Logical positivism was a dogma that outlawed metaphysics and exalted scientific knowledge as the sole form of understanding worthy of the name. "Those who have understood my argument," said Ludwig Wittgenstein in the conclusion of his *Tractatus Logico-Philosophicus*, "must realize that everything I have said in the book is meaningless." It seemed to be the end of the road for metaphysical speculations and the total victory of the fact-based, deterministic knowledge that characterized science.

Soon thereafter, however, the tide turned. Wittgenstein realized that his judgment had been too severe, and he embarked on the analysis of everyday language. Meanwhile, even natural science was becoming less deterministic. It encountered boundaries beyond which observations could not be kept apart from their subject matter. Scientists managed to penetrate the barrier, first with Einstein's theory of relativity, then with Heisenberg's uncertainty principle. More recently, investigators using evolutionary systems theory started exploring complex physical phenomena whose course cannot be determined by timelessly valid laws. Events follow an irreversible path in which even slight disturbances become magnified with the passage of time. Chaos theory was built on this recognition and was able to shed light on many complex phenomena, such as the weather, that had previously proved impervious to scientific treatment. These advances have made the idea of a path-dependent rather than deterministic universe, where events follow a unique, irreversible course, more acceptable. Gradually the idea has made its way into the social sciences, where it really belongs because it characterizes the path that reflexive phenomena follow.

I started to apply the concept of reflexivity to the understanding of social affairs, and particularly of financial markets, in the early 1960s before evolutionary systems theory was born. By introducing the concept, I was hoping to set logical positivism on its head. Logical positivism outlawed self-referent statements as meaningless. I claimed that statements whose truth value is indeterminate are, far from being meaningless, even more significant than statements whose truth value is known. The latter constitute knowledge: They help us understand the world as it is. But the former—expressions of our inherently imperfect understanding—help to shape the world in which we live.

At the time I reached this conclusion, I considered it a great insight. The concept of reflexivity and the uncertainty associated with it seemed to fly in the face of the generally accepted wisdom. Even as physics was abandoning a deterministic point of view, the social sciences in general and economics in particular were desperately clinging to it.

How times have changed! Logical positivism has fallen out of favor to such an extent that I feel as if I were beating a dead horse. Evolutionary systems theory has made great inroads not only in the physical and biological sciences but also in the social sciences. While rational expectations and rational choice are still going strong, many economists have abandoned the assumption of rationality and begun to explore alternative ways of looking at economic behavior.

As one would expect in a reflexive world, the changes have not been confined to thinking; they have also affected reality. In a way, the computer has breached the separation between thinking and reality, because the contents and the operating instructions are contained in the same message. This has spawned a new way of looking at the world in which thinking and reality are interactive rather than forming separate categories. It has also revealed the importance of information. Many aspects of reality, such as organic growth, that were previously interpreted in terms of energy could be understood much better in terms of information. Previously nonexistent forms of information and communication, such as computer imaging, biotechnology, the decoding of the human genome, the Internet, and various forms of virtual reality, play an increasingly important role in our lives.

The idea that reality is somehow separate and independent from thinking has become outmoded. This change in the perception of reality has accelerated in recent years to the point where it amounts to a veritable revolution. Feedback and reflexivity are recognized as real-life phenomena. Reflexivity may not be acknowledged as a concept, but that may no longer be due to the fact that it contradicts the prevailing wisdom; rather, it may be ignored because it has become too obvious.

This revolutionary transformation has caught me somewhat unprepared. That is understandable: It is the characteristic of revolutions that the rate of change outpaces our comprehension. If I started afresh, I would probably not feel the need to dwell on the concept of reflexivity and its affinity to self-reference. But I believe there is something to be gained from my approach: People today may be willing to take reflexivity for granted, but they may not be fully aware of all its implications. And I may not be the only one who finds it difficult to adjust to the radical shift in attitudes. In fact, most people may not be aware that a radical transformation has occurred—the young because they have little understanding of how people thought fifty years ago, the old because they have failed to adjust their thinking and so feel perplexed by the current environment.

We forget that logical positivism was very influential earlier in this century; it effectively outlawed reflexivity by declaring that statements whose truth value cannot be unequivocally determined are meaningless. It is worth remembering this, because it reminds us how poorly the limitations of our understanding were under-

stood. We all know that we are fallible, yet we do not really understand why. It is the fact that we are *participants* that limits our powers as observers. We cannot avoid relying on beliefs that can affect
their own validity, and we cannot attain the kind of certainty that is
available in those areas where the truth can be established on the
basis of the facts. Take death and dying: We can study it scientifically, but when it comes to our own death, science does not provide
the answer; we must make up our own.

There are many ways to reconcile being observer and participant
at the same time, but none is entirely satisfactory. Logical positivism has done this by outlawing self-referent statements and in so
doing has simply sidestepped the quandary of being a thinking participant. Logical positivism has merely carried the Enlightenment
idea of reason as something separate from reality to its logical conclusion. "I think, therefore I am," Descartes said. The Enlightenment idea that reason is capable of explaining and predicting reality
remains deeply ingrained in our way of thinking. In economics, for
instance, it is embedded in the theory of perfect competition and
rational expectations that, as we shall see, provide the scientific justification for the prevailing creed of market fundamentalism.
Expectations cannot be rational when they relate to something that
is contingent on itself. The concept of equilibrium in economics is
based on the old-fashioned perception of reality and reason as separate categories.

Currently, the cutting edge of intellectual fashion has swung to
the opposite extreme: The deconstruction of reality into the subjective views and prejudices of the participants has become all the rage
in the humanities. The very basis upon which differing views can be
judged—namely, the objective truth—is being questioned. I have
little sympathy with those who seek to deconstruct reality. I consider this other extreme equally misguided, and the concept of
reflexivity should help me to make my point.

Reflexivity is based on the recognition that there is a reality and we are part of that reality: That is why our understanding is inherently imperfect. Reality is unique and uniquely important. It cannot be reduced or broken down into the views and beliefs of the participants, exactly because there is a *lack of correspondence* between what people think and what actually happens. In other words, there is more to reality than the participants' views.

The lack of correspondence also thwarts the prediction of events on the basis of universally valid generalizations. There is a reality, even if it is unpredictable. This may be difficult to accept, but it is futile, even downright dangerous, to deny it—as any participant in the financial markets who has lost money can testify. Markets rarely gratify one's expectations, yet their verdict is real enough to cause anguish and loss—and there is no appeal.

It may strike readers as strange that I should present financial markets as an example of reality; to most people they seem unreal. But that only goes to show that our understanding of reality is somehow warped. We think of reality as something independent of human foibles, whereas our imperfect understanding is very much part of reality. Financial markets reflect the biased views of the participants; they also play an important role in shaping the course of events. The course of events cannot be understood simply by studying the participants' views; we must also study how the actual course of events differs from those views. Otherwise we would leave out of account the divergence between expectations and outcomes—and that would be a significant distortion of reality.

I seek to reconcile the contradictions inherent in being participant and observer at the same time by taking our fallibility as my starting point. To rephrase Descartes, *I am part of the world I seek to understand, therefore my understanding is inherently imperfect.* This applies with particular force to those aspects of reality that have thinking participants. It renders both our understanding and the course of events uncertain. Since the uncertainty cannot be removed, we had better take it as our starting point. Doing so does not rule out speculating either on the nature of reality or on the nature of knowledge, but it offers a firmer basis for understanding the world in which we live than either on its own. And it will lead to the concept of open society as a desirable form of social organization.

While we have become familiar with reflexivity as a phenomenon, we have not yet learned to appreciate its implications. We must recognize that reality is not something separate and independent of our thinking. Perfect knowledge is unattainable, but even with our imperfect understanding we are capable of having an impact on the world in which we live. We should remember, however, that our fallibility is liable to create a gap between intentions and outcomes. Instead of the futile pursuit of the perfect design—whether in the form of communism or in the form of markets that tend toward equilibrium—we should content ourselves with the next best thing: a society that holds itself open to change and improvement. That is the concept of open society.

A Reflexive Concept of Truth

Logical positivism sought to outlaw self-referential statements as meaningless. The scheme is eminently suitable to a universe that is separate and independent of the statements that refer to it, but it is quite inadequate for understanding the world of thinking agents.

It was always possible to attack the logical positivist position at the margin by conjuring up certain statements whose truth value was indeterminate—for instance, "The present king of France is bald." But such statements are either nonsensical or contrived; either way, we can live without them. By contrast, reflexive statements are indispensable to a proper understanding of human affairs. We cannot do without reflexive statements because we cannot avoid decisions that have a bearing on our fate; and we cannot reach those decisions without relying on theories and predictions that can affect the subject matter to which they refer. To ignore our use of reflexive statements when we all do use them, or to force them into the categories of "true" and "false," misinterprets the role of thinking in human affairs. Instead of categorizing statements solely as true or false, it may be useful to introduce a third category: reflexive statements whose truth value is contingent on their impact.

All value statements are reflexive in character: "Blessed are the poor, for theirs is the kingdom of heaven." If this statement is believed, then the poor may indeed be blessed with the ability to ignore their travails in this world but they will be less motivated to get themselves out of their misery. By the same token, if the poor are held to be guilty of their own misery, then they are less likely to receive any relief and will have less reason to consider themselves blessed. Most generalizations about history and society are similarly reflexive in character: "The proletarians of the world have nothing to lose but their chains" or "The common interest is best served by allowing people to pursue their own interests." It may be appropriate to assert that such statements have no determinate truth value, but it would be misleading (and historically it has been very dangerous) to treat them as meaningless. To the extent they are believed, they affect the situation to which they refer.

I am not claiming that a third category of truth is indispensable for dealing with reflexive phenomena. The time-hallowed distinction between true and false may suffice, provided we recognize that statements need not be true or false in order to be meaningful. Predictions relating to singular events are true or false depending on whether or not they come to pass. It is only when it comes to predictive *theories* that the uncertainty connected with reflexivity comes into play. Perhaps it is best dealt with at the level of theories rather than at the level of statements. The crucial point is that in reflexive situations the facts do not necessarily provide an independent criterion by which the truth or validity of our theories can be judged. We have come to treat correspondence as the hallmark of truth. But correspondence can be brought about in two ways: either by making statements that correspond to the facts, or by making facts correspond to the statements. Only in the first case is correspondence the guarantor of truth; in the second case the correspondence may bear testimony to the impact of a belief rather than to its truth or validity. This caveat applies to most political pronouncements and many social theories. Instead of being true or false, they are contingent on being believed.

I hardly need emphasize the profound significance of this proposition: Nothing is more fundamental to our thinking than our concept of truth. We are accustomed to thinking about situations that have thinking participants in the same way as we do about natural phenomena, but the relationship between facts and statements is different: Instead of a one-way street, we find a two-way feedback mechanism—reflexivity. Therefore we must thoroughly revise the way we think about the world of human and social affairs.

An Interactive View of the World

In the social realm we may draw a distinction between statements and facts, between thoughts and reality, but we must recognize that this distinction has been introduced *by us* in an attempt to make sense of the world in which we live; it does not prevail in that world. Our thinking belongs in the same universe that we are thinking about. This gives rise to innumerable difficulties that are absent when dealing with aspects of reality where thinking and reality can be separated into watertight compartments (as in natural science). Instead of separate categories, we must treat thinking as part of reality. Incidentally, similar difficulties arise when we try to comprehend reality as a whole (because we are part of it), but that is not the primary focus of the current discussion.

It is impossible to form a picture of the world in which we live without distortion. In a literal sense, when the human eye forms a visual image we have a blind spot where the optic nerve is attached to the nerve stem. The image made in our brain replicates the outside world remarkably well, and we can even fill in the blind spot by extrapolating from the rest of the picture, though we cannot actually see what is in the area covered by the blind spot. This is a useful metaphor for the problem we confront. The fact that I rely on a metaphor to explain the problem is perhaps an even better metaphor.

The world in which we live is extremely complicated. To form a view of the world that can serve as a basis for decisions, we must simplify. Using generalizations, metaphors, analogies, comparisons, dichotomies, and other mental constructs serves to introduce some order into an otherwise confusing universe. But every mental construct to some extent distorts what it represents, and every distortion adds something to the world that we need to understand. Ideas have a way of taking on a life of their own. I shall give a practical demonstration of this in connection with the concept of open society (see Chapter 5). The more we think, the more we have to think about. That is because reality is not a given. It is formed in the same process as the participants' thinking: The more complex the thinking, the more complicated reality becomes. Thinking can never quite catch up with reality, for reality is always richer than our comprehension. Reality has the power to surprise thinkers, and thinking has the power to create reality.

This point was brought home to me by Gödel's theorem. Gödel proved mathematically that there are always more laws in mathematics than the ones that can be proved mathematically. The technique he used was to denote the laws of mathematics by so-called Gödel numbers. Since the number of integers is infinite, it is always possible to add a number to the universe to which these numbers belong, namely, the laws of mathematics. In this way, Gödel was able to prove not only that the number of laws is infinite but also that it exceeds the number of laws that can be known because there are laws about laws about laws ad infinitum; what is to be known expands in step with our knowledge.

The same line of reasoning can be applied to situations that have thinking participants. To understand this, we need to construct a model that contains the views of all the participants. Those views themselves also constitute models that must contain the views of all the participants. So we need models of model builders whose models incorporate the models of model builders, and so on, ad infinitum. The more levels the models recognize, the more levels there are to be recognized—and if the models fail to recognize them, as they must sooner or later—they no longer reproduce reality. If I had Gödel's mathematical skills, I ought to be able to prove along these lines that the participants' views cannot correspond to reality.*

This is not the place to discuss the many different ways in which thinking both distorts and alters reality. For now we can lump them together under the name "fallibility." There are problems that have no ultimate solutions, and the attempts to find solutions can compound the problems. A thinking participant seeking to obtain knowledge or trying to cope with the prospect of her own death confronts insoluble problems. I refer to these sorts of problems as "the human condition." Still, insoluble problems are not confined to the human condition. We run up against them in many contexts: Designing an exchange-rate system, tackling drug abuse, preserving the stability of financial markets—all of these present insoluble problems, where the solution adopted is bound to raise new problems.

---

*It has been pointed out to me by William Newton-Smith that my interpretation of Gödel numbers differs from Gödel's own. Apparently Gödel envisaged a Platonic universe in which Gödel numbers existed before he discovered them, whereas I think that Gödel numbers were invented by him, thereby enlarging the universe in which he was operating. In that case, my interpretation of Gödel's theorem may serve as a "fertile fallacy." (This concept will be explained later in this chapter.)

Two Versions of Fallibility

I submit for discussion two versions of fallibility: first, a more moderate, better-substantiated "formal" version that is inherent in the concept of reflexivity and justifies a critical mode of thinking; second, a more radical, personal, and idiosyncratic version that has actually guided me through life and forms the basis of my theory of history.

The formal, moderate version of fallibility has already been discussed. Fallibility means that there is a lack of correspondence between the participants' thinking and the actual state of affairs; as a result, actions have unintended consequences. Outcomes do not necessarily diverge from intentions, but they are liable to do so. There are many humdrum, everyday events that play out exactly as intended, but those events that show a divergence are more interesting. They may alter peoples' view of the world and set in motion a reflexive process that is initially self-validating and self-reinforcing but eventually becomes self-defeating. When it occurs, such a process can drive prevailing views and the actual state of affairs quite far apart from each other without any assurance that they will ever be brought back together again. Normally, mistakes tend to get corrected, but when views are self-validating it does not become apparent that they are mistaken until much later in the process— and by that time, the underlying reality has also changed.

Fallibility has a negative sound, but it has a positive aspect that is in many ways more important. What is imperfect can be improved. The fact that our understanding is inherently imperfect makes it possible to learn and to enhance our understanding. All that is needed is to recognize our fallibility and establish error-correcting mechanisms. This opens the way to critical thinking, and there is no limit to how far our insights may go. The scope for improvement is infinite precisely because perfection is unattainable.

This is true not only for our thinking but also for our society.

Perfection eludes us; whatever design we choose, it is bound to be defective. We must therefore content ourselves with the next best thing: a form of social organization that falls short of perfection but holds itself open to improvement. This is the concept of open society—a society open to improvement. Therein lies its superiority over closed society, which seeks to deny its own imperfection even as the world around it changes. Recognition of our fallibility is the key to progress.

Radical Fallibility

At this point, I shall change my tack. Instead of discussing fallibility in general terms, I shall try to explain what it means to me personally. It is the cornerstone not only of my view of the world but also of my personal identity, and as such it is reflected in my behavior. It has guided my actions both as a participant in financial markets and as a philanthropist, and it is the foundation of my theory of history. If there is anything original in my thinking, it is this "radical" version of fallibility.

I take a more stringent view of fallibility than my previous theoretical arguments would justify. I contend that all the constructs of the human mind—whether confined to the inner recesses of our thinking or expressed in the outside world in the form of disciplines, ideologies, and institutions—are deficient in one way or another. The flaws may manifest themselves in the form of internal inconsistencies or inconsistencies with the external world or inconsistencies with the purpose for which they were designed.

This proposition is, of course, much stronger than the recognition that all our constructs *may* be wrong. I am not speaking of a mere lack of correspondence but of an actual defect in our thinking or an actual divergence between intentions and outcomes. As I explained earlier, this proposition applies only to historic events where the divergence sets in motion an initially self-reinforcing but eventually self-defeating process. In normal, humdrum situations, mistakes get corrected. That is why the radical version of fallibility can serve as the basis for a theory of history.

The contention that all human constructs are flawed sounds bleak and pessimistic, yet it is no cause for despair. Fallibility sounds negative only because we cherish false hopes of perfection, permanence, and the ultimate truth—with immortality thrown in for good measure. Judged by those standards, the human condition is bound to be unsatisfactory. In fact, perfection and immortality elude us, and permanence can only be found in death. But life gives us a chance to improve our understanding exactly because it is imperfect, and open society gives us a chance to improve the world in which we live exactly because it admits its own imperfection. In a perfect world, there would be nothing left to strive for.

There are two ways to deal with the realization that all constructs are deficient: look for an escape, or look for improvements that fall short of perfection. A closed society pursues the delusion of perfection and permanence; an open society accepts the human condition. When all constructs are imperfect, some alternatives are better than others, and it makes all the difference which alternative we choose. There is much to be gained from recognizing our fallibility. Open society ought to be preferable to a closed one.

Still, my contention that all human and social constructs are defective does not qualify as a scientific hypothesis because it cannot be properly tested. Though I can claim that the participants' views always diverge from reality, I cannot prove it because we can never know what reality would look like in the absence of our biased views. I could wait for events to show a divergence from expectations, but, as I have indicated, subsequent events do not serve as an independent criterion for deciding what the correct expectations would have been, because different expectations would have led to different outcomes.

Similarly, I can claim that all human constructs are defective, but I cannot specify what the flaws are until after the fact, and even then the subject can be endlessly debated. The flaws usually manifest themselves at some future date, but that is no evidence that the constructs were flawed at the time they were formed. The shortcomings of dominant ideas and institutional arrangements become apparent only with the passage of time, and the concept of reflexivity justifies only the claim that all human constructs are *potentially* flawed. That is why I present my proposition as a working assumption, without logical proof or scientific status.

I call it a "working assumption" because it has worked for me as an investor. It has encouraged me to look for the flaws in every investment thesis and, when I found these flaws, to take advantage of the insight. When I formulated an investment thesis, I recognized that my interpretation of the situation was bound to be distorted. This did not discourage me from having a view; on the contrary, I sought out situations where my interpretation was at loggerheads with the prevailing wisdom, because that is what offered an opportunity for profit. But I was always on the lookout for my error; when I discovered it, I grasped it with alacrity. The discovery of error would allow me to take whatever profits I had made from my flawed initial insight—or to cut my losses if the insight had not yielded even a temporary profit.

Most people are reluctant to admit that they are wrong; I derived actual pleasure from discovering a mistake, because I knew it would save me from financial grief. Since I assumed that every investment thesis is bound to be flawed, I preferred to know what the flaws were. This did not stop me from investing; on the contrary, I felt much safer when I knew the potential danger points because that told me what signs to look for to avoid losses. No investment can offer superior returns indefinitely. Even if a company has a strong market position, outstanding management, and exceptional profit margins, the stock can become overvalued, management can become complacent, and the competitive or regulatory environment can change. It is wise to look for the fly in the ointment; when you know what it is, you are ahead of the game.

I developed my own variant of Popper's model of scientific method (which I shall describe in the next chapter) for use in financial markets. I would formulate a hypothesis on the basis of which I would invest. The hypothesis had to differ from the accepted wisdom; the bigger the difference, the greater the potential profit. If there was no difference, there was no point in taking a position. This corresponded to Popper's contention—much criticized by philosophers of science—that the more severe the test, the more valuable the hypothesis that survives it. In science, the value of a hypothesis is intangible; in financial markets, it can be readily measured in money. In contrast to scientific hypotheses, a financial hypothesis does not have to be true to be profitable because of its reflexive character; it is enough that it should come to be generally accepted. But a false hypothesis cannot prevail forever. That is why I liked to invest in flawed hypotheses that had a chance of becoming generally accepted, provided I knew their flaws. This approach allowed me to sell in time. For instance, I participated in the conglomerate boom exactly because I knew what the weak points were (see Chapter 2 for an explanation). I called my flawed hypotheses "fertile fallacies," and I built my theory of history, as well as my success in financial markets, around them.

My working hypothesis—that *all* human constructs are flawed—not only is unscientific but also has a more radical defect: It is actually untrue. As we have seen, it is possible to make true statements and to construct valid theories. Natural science stands as a monument of what the human mind is capable of constructing. Yet the hypothesis works in practice. Valid constructs are so scarce that when we find one we tend to overburden it or extend it beyond its proper limits. Scientific method is a good example: It worked for nature; therefore we want to apply it to society. The market mechanism is another case in point: It works well in allocating resources among private needs; therefore we are tempted to rely on it for fulfilling public needs. Similarly with institutions: Once they are established we tend to rely on them even after they have lost their vitality or justification. Every institution develops weaknesses with the passage of time, but this does not mean that it was inappropriate or ineffective at the time it was constructed.

The creation of institutions, like other actions, has unintended consequences; such consequences cannot be properly anticipated at the time of their creation. Even if they could be, one might still go forward, because the unintended consequences would arise in the future and in the meantime the institution could fill a current need. So my working hypothesis is not incompatible with the idea that one course of action is better than another, that there is indeed an optimal course of action at a given time and place. It does imply, however, that the optimum applies only to a particular moment in history; what is optimal at one moment may cease to be so at the next. This is a difficult concept to work with, particularly for institutions that cannot avoid some degree of inertia. The longer any form of taxation is in effect, for example, the more likely it is that it will be evaded; that may be a good reason for changing the form of taxation after a while but not a good reason for having no taxation. To take another example, the Catholic Church has evolved into something quite different from what Jesus had in mind, but that is not sufficient ground for dismissing his teachings. We can call human constructs flawed only if we expect them to be timelessly valid, like the laws of science.

In other words, defective theories and policies can be temporarily useful at a certain point in history. These fertile fallacies are flawed constructs with initially beneficial effects. How long the beneficial effects endure depends on whether the flaws are recognized and corrected in time. In this way, constructs may become increasingly sophisticated (the evolution of central banking is a good example). But no fertile fallacy is likely to last forever; eventually, the scope for refining it and developing it will be exhausted, and a new fertile fallacy will capture people's imagination. What I am about to say may be a fertile fallacy, but I am inclined to interpret the history of ideas as composed of fertile fallacies. Other people might refer to them as "paradigms."*

The combination of these two ideas—that even though all mental constructs are flawed, some of them are fertile—lies at the core of my own, radical version of fallibility. My working assumption allows me to operate with fertile fallacies. I apply them to the outside world and to my own activities with equal vigor, and they have served me well both as a fund manager and, more recently, as a philanthropist. Whether these ideas will also serve me well as a thinker is being tested right now, because radical fallibility serves as the foundation for the interpretation of financial markets and the theory of history that I lay out in this book.

A Personal Postscript

Radical fallibility is for me not only an abstract theory but also a matter of deep personal conviction. As a fund manager, I depended a great deal on my feelings, because I was aware of the inadequacies of my knowledge. The predominant feelings I operated with were uncertainty and fear. I had moments of hope, even euphoria, but those emotions made me insecure; worrying made me feel safer. So the only genuine joy I experienced was when I discovered what it was that I had to worry about. By and large, I found managing a hedge fund† extremely painful. I could never acknowledge my success—it might stop me from worrying—but I had no trouble acknowledging my mistakes.

*Kuhn, *The Structure of Scientific Revolutions*.
†Hedge funds engage in a variety of investment activities. They cater to sophisticated investors and are not subject to the regulations that apply to mutual funds geared toward the general public. Fund managers are compensated on the basis of performance rather than as a fixed percentage of assets. "Performance funds" would be a more accurate description.

It has only recently dawned on me how unusual this self-critical attitude is. It has surprised me that other people were surprised by my way of thinking. Discovering an error in my thinking or my investment positions was a source of joy rather than regret. That made so much sense to me that I thought it ought to make sense to others as well; but that is not the case. Most people go to great lengths to deny or cover up their mistakes. Indeed, their misconceptions and misdeeds become an integral part of their personality. I shall never forget an experience I had when I visited Argentina in 1982 to look at the mountain of debt that the country had accumulated. I sought out a number of politicians who had served in previous governments and asked them how they would handle the situation. To a man, they said they would apply the same policies they had followed when they were in power. Rarely had I met so many people who had learned so little from experience.

I must not overstate the case for a self-critical attitude. It cannot work by itself. It must be associated with some degree of success in order to yield positive results. A self-critical attitude is part of a reflexive process which can be self-reinforcing in either direction. Being aware of one's limitations does not, by itself, help to overcome them; on the contrary, self-doubt can easily become self-validating by undermining one's self-confidence. By contrast, the ability to correct mistakes enhances performance and a strong performance puts one in a strong position to recognize and correct mistakes. I know whereof I speak because I have gone through both experiences. My self-critical attitude predates my involvement in the stock market. I was fortunate to have landed in the investment business where I could put that attitude to good use. I am not sure whether the same attitude will prove to be equally rewarding in writing this book. I have no hesitation in admitting my mistakes but that may not make me as successful as I was in the stock market.

I have carried this critical attitude into my philanthropic activities. I found that philanthropy is riddled with paradoxes and unintended consequences. For instance, charity may turn the recipients into objects of charity. Giving is supposed to help others, but in reality it often merely serves the ego gratification of the giver. Worse yet, people frequently engage in philanthropy because they want to feel good, not because they want to do good.

Holding these views, I felt obliged to follow a different path. I found myself behaving in much the same way as I do in business. For instance, in business I had no compunctions about hurting the feelings of my investment team when the performance of my investment fund was at stake; similarly, I gave precedence to the mission of the foundation over the interests of the foundation personnel or of the individual applicants. I used to joke that ours is the only misanthropic foundation in the world. I remember explaining my views about foundations at a staff meeting in Karlovi Vari, Czechoslovakia, around 1991, and I am sure those who were present will never forget it. I explained that foundations ought to put their mission ahead of their self-interest in order to justify their existence, but that goes against human nature. As a result they are rife with corruption, and the lack of clarity about their objectives leads to inefficiencies. I had no interest in having such a foundation, and I would consider it a greater accomplishment to wind up a foundation that was failing than to set up a new one.

I must confess that I have mellowed with the passage of time. Having a foundation is very different from running a hedge fund. The external pressures are largely absent, and it is only internal discipline that keeps a critical attitude alive. Moreover, heading a large foundation requires managing people rather than managing money. People do not like to hear critical remarks—they want praise and encouragement. Not many people share my predilection for identifying error, and even fewer share my joy in finding it in themselves. To be an effective leader, one has to gratify people. I am learning the hard way what seems to come naturally to politicians and heads of corporations.

There is another influence at work as well. I have to make public appearances, and when I do I am expected to exude confidence. In reality, I am consumed by self-doubt, and I cherish the feeling. I would hate to lose it. There is a wide gap between my public persona and what I consider my real self, but I am aware of a reflexive connection between the two. I have been watching with amazement how the development of a public persona has affected me. I have become a "charismatic" personality. Fortunately, I do not quite believe in myself as others do. I try to remember my limitations, even if I do not feel them as acutely as I used to. But other charismatic personalities have not arrived at their leadership position following the same route. They do not have the same memories. They probably remember that they always tried to get others to believe in them, and eventually they succeeded. They are not consumed by self-doubt, and they do not need to repress the urge to express it. No wonder that their attitude toward their own fallibility is different. Moreover, if they admitted their shortcomings they could not retain their leadership position. People do not want their leaders to be fallible. That is one of the worst defects of our contemporary democracies: Our leaders are held to standards that they cannot possibly meet.

It is fascinating to consider how my newly acquired public personality relates to my previous self as fund manager. When I was an active fund manager, I shunned publicity; I considered it the kiss of death to be on the cover of a financial magazine. This amounted to a superstition, but it was well supported by experience. It is easy to see why. The publicity would engender a feeling of euphoria, and even if I tried to suppress it, it would throw me off my stride. And if I expressed a market view in public, I would find it more difficult to change my mind.

In my new incarnation, public opinion—what other people think of me—plays a more important role. It qualifies me to make deals, even to manipulate markets, yet it disqualifies me from managing money. My utterances can move markets, although I make great efforts not to abuse that power. At the same time, I have lost the ability to be a successful money manager. I have dismantled the mechanism of pain and anxiety that used to guide me, and at the same time the glare of publicity makes it practically impossible for me to operate as a more or less anonymous participant.

It can be seen that operating in the financial markets requires a different mind-set from that required for operating in a social, political, or organizational setting—or indeed for acting like a normal human being. For a money manager, only one thing counts: performance. All other considerations must be subordinated to it. The market is a hard taskmaster: It does not allow either self-indulgence or consideration for others. What others think of you matters, but the results—measured by an objective criterion, money—matter more. Having an objective criterion encourages objective performance. That is what makes financial markets so efficient: They turn people into profit-making machines. That has its merits, but a society dominated by financial markets could easily become inhuman. This is not a flight of fancy but a present danger.

The radical version of fallibility I have adopted as a working assumption certainly proved effective in the financial markets. My performance exceeded what would be permitted by the random-walk hypothesis* by a convincing margin. Does it also apply to other aspects of human existence? That depends on what our goal is. If we want to understand reality, I believe it is helpful; but if our aim is to manipulate reality, it does not work so well. Charisma works much better.

Coming back to my personal feelings, I have learned to adjust to the new reality in which I am operating. I used to find public

---

*The random-walk hypothesis assumes that financial markets make available all information to all participants. It claims, on the basis of rational expectations in an efficient market, that no one can consistently beat the market.

expressions of praise and gratitude positively disturbing, but I have come to realize that this is a reflex left over from the days when I was actively managing money; I had to be guided by the results of my actions, not by what other people thought of them. I am still embarrassed by gratitude, and I still believe that philanthropy—if it is deserving of praise—should put the achievements of its mission ahead of ego gratification. Still, I am willing to accept praise, because my philanthropy has in fact met this condition. Whether it can continue to do so in the light of my changed attitude toward praise is a question that troubles me, but as long as I am troubled the answer will probably remain in the affirmative.

CHAPTER 2

A Critique of Economics

Fallibility and reflexivity pose serious problems for the social sciences in general and for economic theory in particular. I want to examine these problems in some detail, even if it obliges us to dwell longer in the rarefied realm of abstractions. When I say that the implications of reflexivity have not been properly understood, I have mainly these problems in mind. We need to understand them better in order to lay the theoretical foundations for what I call a global open society.

The problems can be grouped under two headings. One relates to the subject matter, the other to the observer. I shall discuss them in this order, although the two problem areas are interrelated.

Reflexivity in Social Phenomena

We need a basic understanding how scientific method operates. For the purposes of this discussion, I shall invoke Karl Popper's theory of scientific method. Popper's simple and elegant model shows how specific phenomena can be made to yield universally valid generalizations that in turn can be used to explain and predict specific phenomena. The model contains three components and three operations. The three components are specific initial conditions, specific final conditions, and generalizations of a hypothetical character. The initial and final conditions can be verified by direct observation; the hypotheses cannot be verified, only falsified. The three basic scientific operations are prediction, explanation, and testing. A hypothetical generalization can be combined with known initial conditions to provide a specific prediction. It can be combined with specific final conditions to provide an explanation. Since the hypothesis is timelessly valid, the two operations—prediction and explanation—are reversible. This allows testing, which involves comparing any number of specific initial and final conditions to establish whether they conform to the hypothesis. No amount of testing will verify a hypothesis, but as long as a hypothesis has not been falsified it can be accepted as provisionally valid.

The model does not claim to describe how scientists work in practice; it shows how, in theory, generalizations capable of predicting and explaining singular facts can be established. A generalization cannot be verified; it is enough if it has not been falsified, provided that it *can be* falsified by testing. The main merit of this construction is that it avoids the pitfalls of inductive reasoning. We do not need to insist that the sun will always rise in the east just because it has done so every day; it is enough if we accept the hypothesis provisionally—that is, until it is falsified. This is an elegant solution to what would be an otherwise insuperable logical problem. The trick is to distinguish between verification and falsification. It allows hypotheses to provide predictions and explanations without insisting on verification. The predictions and explanations themselves can be either deterministic or probabilistic, depending on the nature of the hypothesis.

Recognizing the asymmetry between verification and falsification is, in my opinion, Popper's greatest contribution not only to the philosophy of science but also to our understanding of the world in which we live. It reconciles the achievements of science with the idea that the ultimate truth is beyond our reach.

It has perhaps not been sufficiently emphasized that hypotheses must be timelessly valid to make testing possible. If a particular result cannot be replicated, then the test cannot be considered conclusive. But reflexivity gives rise to irreversible, historical processes; therefore it does not lend itself to timelessly valid generalizations. More exactly, the generalizations that can be made about reflexive events cannot be tested, because the initial and final conditions cannot be replicated. They may even yield high-probability predictions and explanations, but their probability cannot be measured in the same way as in the case of a testable hypothesis. The fact that a certain sequence of events prevailed in the past with a certain frequency does not imply that its probability will be the same in the future. On the contrary, the discovery of the probability distribution is liable to alter it.* There is a certain similarity here with Heisenberg's uncertainty principle, but there is an important difference: In quantum mechanics, it is an act—namely, measurement—that interferes; in financial markets and other reflexive situations, it is a thought or belief that affects the subject matter to which it refers.

The point I have just made does not invalidate Popper's elegant model of scientific method in any way. The model remains valid; it merely fails to apply to reflexive phenomena. This qualification does draw attention, however, to an important cleavage between natural and social science, because reflexivity occurs only when a situation has thinking participants. It is a cleavage that Popper himself refused to recognize. He propounded the doctrine of the unity of science, which holds that the same methods and criteria apply to

*I offer a specific example in connection with Long Term Capital Management in Chapter 10.

both the natural and social sciences. This doctrine allowed him to demonstrate that theories such as Marxism do not qualify as scientific because they cannot be falsified. I take a somewhat different view. I contend that reflexive phenomena in general do not fit into Popper's model of scientific method—and that it is not only Marxism that is unscientific. Market fundamentalism, which derives its scientific justification from mainstream economics, is just as spurious an ideology as Marxism.

There is a fundamental difference between the natural and the social sciences that has yet to be properly recognized. To understand it better, we must consider the second problem: the scientific observers' relation to their subject matter.

Reflexivity and Social Scientists

Science is a social process, and as such it is potentially reflexive. Scientists are linked to their subject matter both as participants and as observers, but the distinctive feature of scientific method—as exemplified in Popper's model—is that the participating function is not allowed to interfere with the cognitive function. Science is devoted to the understanding of reality, and to this end the facts are kept rigorously segregated from the scientific statements that refer to them. The facts belong to one universe, the statements to another. In this way, the facts can serve as an independent criterion by which the truth or validity of statements can be judged. Scientists participate in experiments, but they go to great lengths not to influence the outcome. Experiments must be replicable by others in order to qualify as scientific.

In practice, these ideal conditions do not prevail, even in natural science. The selection of the theories also influences the selection of the facts that are used to test them; as a consequence, the universe in which a science operates is not necessarily the same as the universe it claims to describe. Nevertheless, the separation between the universe of facts and the universe of statements remains inviolate, and the facts continue to provide an independent criterion for judging the truth of statements. All that happens when a science fastens on to a particular set of facts is that the universe constituted by its statements is not coterminous with the world in which we live. When the discrepancy between the two becomes too glaring, the pressure mounts for a paradigm shift. This is an important feature of the history of science.

Science does have a history, and that history is reflexive. Hypotheses that lead to valuable discoveries and inventions receive a boost; when their potential is exhausted, they tend to lose their hold on peoples' minds and there is more receptivity for other ways of looking at things. That is how paradigm shifts come about. Popper himself was fully aware of this: He advised me to read Thomas Kuhn and Paul Feyerabend. Thomas Kuhn is, of course, the originator of the expression "paradigm shift."

The social sciences are even further removed from the ideal conditions postulated by Popper's model than are the natural sciences. That is because the facts studied by the social sciences include ideas and beliefs; the built-in separation between statements and facts that characterizes the natural sciences does not prevail. It may be possible to keep the statements of scientists and the statements that belong to the subject matter segregated, but that requires a conscious effort. The effort is needed in order to make it possible to establish the truth of scientific statements. This raises a question that in the case of natural science hardly needs to be asked: What is the purpose of science? Is it to understand reality or to turn it to our advantage?

In natural science, the facts (as distinct from the selection of facts) cannot be changed by making statements about them. Reality cannot be turned to our advantage without first understanding it. Experiments can be forged, but the forgery is liable to be detected because experiments must be capable of being replicated by others. Therefore it does not make sense to cheat. It is possible to *select* the facts that are subjected to scientific examination, but even in this regard it pays to get as close to reality as possible, because we can benefit from our understanding much better if it relates to reality rather than to some artificial universe.

Not so in the social sciences. When the universe of facts also contains statements, statements and facts may interact reflexively, which means that statements may alter the facts via the participants' decisions. This holds true for social scientists as well as for the people whom they study, because there is no built-in separation between statements and facts, as in the case of natural science. Scientists must make a special effort to keep their statements from affecting the subject matter to which they refer. That is where the question about the purpose of science comes into play.

As long as the separation between statements and facts remains watertight, there can be no doubt about the purpose of science: It is to acquire knowledge. The goals of individual participants may differ. Some may pursue knowledge for its own sake, others for the benefits it may bring to humanity, yet others for personal advancement. Whatever the motivation, however, the yardstick of success is knowledge, and it is an objective criterion. Those who are seeking personal advancement can do so only by making true statements; if they falsify experiments, they are liable to be found out. Those who are trying to bend nature to their will can do so only by acquiring knowledge first. Nature follows its course irrespective of any theory that relates to it; therefore we can make nature serve our needs only by understanding the laws that govern its behavior. There are no shortcuts.

Recognition of this fundamental principle was a long time in coming. For thousands of years, people have tried every form of magic, ritual, and wishful thinking to influence nature more directly; they were reluctant to accept the harsh discipline that scientific method imposed. The conventions of scientific method took a long time to prove their superiority, but eventually, as science continued to produce powerful discoveries, it attained a status that equaled that of magic in earlier times. The agreement on purpose, the acceptance of certain conventions, the availability of an objective criterion, the possibility of establishing timelessly valid generalizations—all these combined to make science successful. It is recognized today as the crowning achievement of the human intellect.

This beautiful combination is disrupted when the subject matter is reflexive. For one thing, positive results are more difficult to attain, because the subject matter does not readily lend itself to the discovery of timelessly valid (and therefore testable) hypotheses that carry the authority of scientific laws. Looking at the evidence, we can see that the achievements of the social sciences do not compare well with those of the natural sciences. For another thing, the independence of the objective criterion—namely, the facts—is impaired. This renders the conventions of science difficult to enforce. Facts can be influenced by forming beliefs or propounding theories about them. This is true not only for the participants but also for the scientists. Reflexivity implies a short circuit between statements and facts, and that short circuit is available to scientists as well as participants.

This is an important point. Let me illuminate it by comparing the indeterminacy involved in reflexivity with the indeterminacy observed in the behavior of quantum particles. The indeterminacy is similar, but the relation of the observer to the subject matter is not. The behavior of quantum particles is the same whether Heisenberg's uncertainty principle is recognized or not. But the behavior of human beings can be influenced by scientific theories just as it can be influenced by other beliefs. For instance, the scope of the market economy has expanded because people believe in the magic of the marketplace. In natural science, theories cannot change the phenomena to which they relate; in social science, they can. This gives rise to an additional element of uncertainty, which is absent from the Heisenberg principle. This additional element of uncertainty concerns the role of the scientific observer and the impact of scientific theories.

Admittedly, scientists could take special precautions to insulate their statements from their subject matter—for instance, by keeping their predictions secret. But why should they? Is the purpose of science to acquire knowledge for its own sake or for some other benefits? In natural science, the question does not arise because the benefits can be realized only by first attaining knowledge. Not so in social science: Reflexivity offers a shortcut. A theory does not need to be true to affect human behavior. At the same time, the reliability of the facts as an independent criterion is compromised. In this way, it is possible to propound self-fulfilling prophecies.

Given the respect science commands, propounding a theory that claims to be scientific can be an effective way to influence reality; the more it affects the subject matter to which it refers, the better. Karl Marx did that consciously, and his interpretation of history was difficult to disprove. Indeed, Karl Popper had to develop an elaborate argument to discredit Marxist theory by showing that it is not scientific. I subscribe to Popper's argument, but I want to carry it one step further: I contend that the misuse of scientific theories for political purposes is not confined to totalitarian ideologies; it applies to market fundamentalism with equal force. Classical economic theory is as easily misused for political purposes as is (or was) Marxist theory.

I am particularly suspicious of the concept of equilibrium. It implies a desirable state of affairs, a resting point that cannot be improved. Market fundamentalists claim that markets tend toward equilibrium and that any political interference is harmful. It has been shown that in many cases there is no uniquely determined equilibrium point. John Maynard Keynes demonstrated that the economy may reach equilibrium short of full employment. In modern economic theory, the possibility of multiple equilibria is widely recognized. Still, the idea that markets tend toward equilibrium persists and serves as a purportedly scientific basis for market fundamentalism.*

The classic example of pseudoscientists trying to impose their will upon their subject matter was the attempt to convert base metal into gold. Alchemists toiled at the alembic until finally persuaded to abandon the enterprise by their lack of success. Their failure was inevitable because the behavior of base metals is governed by laws of universal validity that cannot be modified by any statements, incantations, or rituals. Medieval alchemists were barking up the wrong tree. Base metals cannot be turned into gold by incantation, but people can become wealthy in financial markets and powerful in politics by propounding false theories and self-fulfilling prophecies. Moreover, their chances of success are increased if they can cloak themselves in scientific guise. It is noteworthy that both Marx and Sigmund Freud were vocal in claiming scientific status for their theories and based many of their conclusions on the authority they derived from being "scientific." Once this point sinks in, the very expression "social science" becomes suspect; it becomes a magic phrase employed by social alchemists to impose their will upon their subject matter through learned incantations.

Social scientists have tried very hard to imitate the natural sciences but with remarkably little success. Their endeavors often yielded little more than a parody of natural science. Only when they abandoned the false analogy and pursued their subject matter wherever it would lead did they produce worthwhile results. Some of the best work is set in a historical context instead of aiming at universal

*I should point out, however, that even though most economists espouse the concept of equilibrium, they are not necessarily market fundamentalists. Moreover, the concept of reflexivity is increasingly recognized in contemporary economic theory. See, for example, Maurice Obstfeld, "Models of Currency Crises with Self-Fulfilling Features," *European Economic Review* (April 1996).

validity, but it still does not meet the requirements of Popper's model. Valid theories that fit that mold are few and far between.

The slavish imitation of natural science fits in well with my concept of radical fallibility. Radical fallibility rests on the admittedly exaggerated claim that *all* human constructs are flawed. Scientific method undermines that claim by producing generalizations that predict and explain the markings of nature. Yet, exactly because natural science has been so amazingly successful, social science is expected to be able to do the same for society. A method that works in one area is extended to another where it is less appropriate. There is a parallel here with the exaggerated claims made for the market mechanism. Just because markets have been so useful in organizing economic activity, they are now expected to provide the answer to all the problems of social organization.

There is a crucial difference between the failures of social scientists and the failures of alchemists. Although the failure of the alchemists was well-nigh total, social scientists usurping the authority of natural science have managed to make their mark on society. The behavior of people—exactly because it is not governed by reality—is easily influenced by theories. In the field of natural phenomena, scientific method is effective only when theories are valid; but in social, political, and economic matters, theories can be effective without being valid. Although alchemy failed as science, social science can succeed as alchemy.

Karl Popper saw the danger of political ideologies exploiting the prestige of science to influence the course of history; the danger became particularly potent in the case of Marxism. To protect scientific method against this kind of abuse, he proclaimed that theories that cannot be falsified do not qualify as scientific. But if we use Popper's model of scientific method as our yardstick, very few social theories measure up. Reflexivity gives rise to a unique, irreversible pattern that does not lend itself to replication and testing. Economic theory has gone to great lengths to avoid reflexivity in order to qualify as scientific, and it became rather far removed from reality in the process; even so, it could not avoid being exploited for political purposes. For instance, economists have gone out of their way to avoid introducing value judgments, but because of that very fact their theories have been appropriated by the advocates of laissez-faire and used as the basis for the most pervasive value judgment imaginable: that no better social outcomes than those available under market competition can ever be achieved.

In my opinion, there is a better way to protect scientific method than the one Popper suggests. All we need to do is to declare that the social sciences are not entitled to the status that we accord the natural sciences. This would stop pseudoscientific social theories from masquerading in a borrowed suit of armor; it would also discourage the slavish imitation of natural science in areas where that is not appropriate. It would not prohibit the scientific study of human behavior, but it would help to scale down our expectations about the results. My suggestion would also constitute a major loss of status for social scientists, so it is unlikely to be very popular among them.

The convention I propose—depriving the social sciences of their scientific status—would have the benefit of allowing us to come to terms with the limitations of our knowledge. It would release social science from the straitjacket into which it has been forced by the pursuit of scientific status. That is what I advocated in *The Alchemy of Finance* when I suggested that social science is a false metaphor. Popper's model works with timelessly valid generalizations. Reflexivity is a time-bound, irreversible process—why should it fit Popper's model? There may be better ways of understanding social phenomena than by proposing theories of universal validity. A particularly promising approach has emerged in recent years: the study of irreversible evolutionary processes and the design of nonlinear models to represent them. These models do not fit Popper's model of scientific method—they do not allow the testing of universal laws—but they do provide algorithms that can be useful.

Recognizing the limitations of social science does not mean that we must give up the pursuit of truth in exploring social phenomena. It means only that the pursuit of truth requires us to recognize that some aspects of human behavior are not governed by timelessly valid laws. This should encourage us to explore other avenues to understanding, as I do in this book. The pursuit of truth should also force us to recognize that social phenomena may be influenced by the theories put forward to explain them. As a consequence, the study of social phenomena may be motivated by objectives other than the pursuit of truth. That is the truth underlying the convention I have proposed. The best way to guard against the abuse of scientific method is to recognize that social theories do not deserve the status accorded to natural science. This would not prevent individual theories from establishing scientific status on their own merit, but it would hinder ideologues from cloaking themselves with the veil of science.

Looking at history, it is difficult to escape the conclusion that there must be a fundamental difference between natural and social science. Humankind's power over nature has increased by leaps and bounds, but there has been no corresponding progress in resolving political and social problems. Most advances in social conditions, such as improvements in living standards or life expectancy, can be attributed to natural science, not to social science. Indeed, social conflicts have become more destructive because of the increased control we enjoy over the forces of nature. Our ability to kill one another has been greatly enhanced. It is high time we recognize that and look for new ways to resolve and contain conflicts.

A Critique of Economic Theory

Economic theory is the most far-reaching attempt to emulate the natural sciences, and it is by far the most successful. Classical economists were inspired by Newtonian physics. They aimed at establishing universally valid laws that could be used to explain and predict economic behavior and hoped to achieve that goal by relying on the concept of equilibrium. Equilibrium is the price at which demand and supply are brought into balance and there are no unsatisfied buyers or sellers left. It is an eminently sensible concept in a market where buyers and sellers come together to engage in a free exchange. It allows economic analysis to focus on the ultimate outcome and to disregard temporary disturbances. This prepares the ground for timelessly valid rules about the equilibrating role of markets.

The concept of equilibrium is quite deceptive. It has the aura of something empirical, but that impression is not justified. Equilibrium itself has rarely been observed in real life (market prices have the nasty habit of fluctuating). The process that can be observed is supposed to move toward equilibrium, yet equilibrium may never be reached. It is true that market participants adjust to market prices, but they may be adjusting to a constantly moving target. In that case, speaking of an "adjustment process" may be a misnomer.

Equilibrium is the product of an axiomatic system. Economic theory is constructed like logic or mathematics: It is based on certain postulates, and all of its conclusions are derived from them by logical manipulation. Its great merit is that it lends itself to mathematical treatment: Equilibrium can be expressed in the form of equations.

The possibility that equilibrium may never be reached does not invalidate the logical construction. Only when a hypothetical equilibrium is presented as a model of reality is a significant distortion introduced. Geometry and astronomy are perfectly valid axiomatic systems, yet they gave rise to false interpretations of reality, such as the belief that the earth was flat or that it was the center of the universe (and we know what happened to those who questioned such truths).

Economic theory starts by taking the demand and supply curves as separately given; the intersection of the demand and supply curves then determines the equilibrium point. This construction presumes that demand and supply are definite and separately measurable quantities. They go on opposite sides of the scale, and an adjustment process brings them into balance. When sellers know how much they are willing to supply at each price and buyers know how much they are willing to buy, all that needs to happen to achieve equilibrium is for the market to find the unique price that matches demand and supply. But what if price movements themselves change the willingness of buyers and sellers to trade their goods at given prices, for example, because a fall in prices makes them expect prices to fall even further in the near future? This possibility, which is the dominant fact of life in financial markets as well as in industries with rapidly advancing technologies, is simply assumed away.

Classical economic theory is the child of the Enlightenment. We have seen that the Enlightenment sought to establish the authority of reason by treating reality as something passively waiting to be understood. Reason could then gain knowledge by making statements that corresponded to the facts. The outstanding scientific accomplishment of the Enlightenment was Newtonian physics, and economic theory sought to imitate it. Equilibrium was a Newtonian concept, and economic theory adopted it with alacrity. If thinking could be separated from reality, then so could demand, which was largely a subjective factor, from supply, which was mainly an objective one. Aggregating the behavior of various participants presented difficulties, but these could be overcome by postulating perfect knowledge. The theory of perfect competition assumed perfect knowledge. The assumption fitted in well with the Enlightenment view of the world, but it did not survive critical examination. Perfect knowledge could be seen to be too ambitious an assumption, and it was replaced by perfect information. Perfect information on its own, however, was not sufficient to support the theory of perfect competition, so it had to be reinforced by what Lionel Robbins* called a "methodological convention": The conditions of supply and demand were treated as if they were independently determined. The task of economic theory, Robbins argued, was to study not the conditions of supply and demand but the relationship between them. Therefore economic theory could take the conditions of supply and demand as a given and show, with the help of equations, how the market could allocate limited resources among unlimited ends and bring supply and demand into equilibrium.

Lionel Robbins's argument, which was influential fifty years ago when I studied economics under him, has been largely forgotten, but the watertight separation between demand and supply remained ingrained in economic analysis. As a student, I found Robbins's solution objectionable because it eliminated reflexive feedback by a methodological subterfuge. It allowed economists to continue treating markets as a purely passive mechanism whose sole role is to reflect the forces of demand and supply. The possibility that movements in market prices can alter the shape of the demand and supply curves was simply assumed away. The impulse behind this approach was the desire to produce results comparable to Newtonian physics. It deflected attention from markets as an institution (which, in accordance with radical fallibility, are liable to be flawed to a lesser or greater extent) and perpetuated the illusion of perfect markets.

The assumption that demand and supply curves are indepen-

*Lionel Robbins, *An Essay on the Nature and Significance of Economic Science* (London: Macmillan, 1969).

dently given is needed to determine market prices. Without it, prices would cease to be uniquely determined. Economists would be deprived of their ability to provide generalizations comparable to those of natural science. The idea that the conditions of supply and demand may be in some ways interdependent or dependent on the behavior of the market may seem incongruous to those who have been reared on economic theory; yet that is exactly what the concept of reflexivity implies and what the behavior of financial markets demonstrates.

The assumption of independently given conditions of supply and demand eliminates the possibility of any reflexive interaction. How significant is the omission? How important is reflexivity in the behavior of markets and economies? In microeconomic analysis, reflexivity can be safely disregarded; when it comes to macroeconomics, the omission is more serious. This corresponds to the distinction we have drawn between humdrum and historic events. I shall test this proposition in the next chapter, using the financial markets as my laboratory.

The Question of Values

I want to complete my critique of economic theory by examining the question of values. Economic theory takes the market participants' preferences as givens. Under the guise of this methodological convention, it tacitly introduces certain assumptions about values. The most important of these is that only market values should be taken into account—that is, only those considerations that enter into a market participant's mind when she decides what she is willing to pay another participant in free exchange. This assertion is justified when the objective is to determine the market price, but it ignores many individual and social values that do not find expression in market behavior. These ought not to be ignored in deciding

issues other than the market price. How society should be organized, how people ought to live their lives—these questions ought
not to be answered on the basis of market values.

Still, that is precisely what is happening. The scope and influence
of economic theory have expanded beyond the confines that the
postulates of an axiomatic system ought to impose. Market fundamentalists have transformed an axiomatic, value-neutral theory into
an ideology that has influenced political and business behavior in
powerful and dangerous ways. That is one of the key issues I want to
address in this book: How market values penetrate into areas of
society where they do not properly belong.

The values taken as given by economic theory always involve a
choice between alternatives: So much of one thing can be equated
to so much of another. The idea that some values may not be nego-
tiable is not recognized, or, more exactly, such values are excluded
from consideration. Generally speaking, only individual preferences are studied; collective needs are disregarded. This means that
the entire social and political realm is left out of account. If the
argument of market fundamentalists—that the common interest is
best served by the untrammeled pursuit of self-interest—were valid,
then no great harm would be done; but the fact that the conclusion
was reached by disregarding collective needs does beg the question.

Empirical studies in decisionmaking have shown that, even
in matters of individual preference, peoples' behavior does not
conform to the requirements of economic theory. The evidence
indicates that instead of being consistent and constant, peoples'
preferences vary depending on how they frame their decision problems. For example, economic theory has assumed ever since Daniel
Bernoulli (circa 1738) that economic agents evaluate the outcomes
of their choices in terms of final states of wealth. In fact, agents generally frame outcomes as gains and losses relative to some reference
point. Furthermore, these variations in framing can have a profound effect on decisions: Agents who frame their outcomes in

terms of wealth will tend to be less averse to risk than agents who think in terms of losses.*

I go further than the behavioral economists. I contend that people behave differently depending on the frame of reference they employ. While there is some consistency in the choice of frames, it is far from dependable, and there is often a noticeable discontinuity between different frames. I can speak from personal experience. I have often felt as if I had multiple personalities: one for business, one for social responsibility, and one (or more) for private use. Often the roles get confused, causing me no end of embarrassment. I have made a conscious effort to integrate the various aspects of my existence, and I am happy to report that I have been successful. I really mean that: Integrating the various facets of my personality has been a major accomplishment and a source of great satisfaction.

I must confess, however, that I could not have achieved this if I had remained an active participant in the financial markets. Managing money requires a single-minded devotion to the cause of making money; all other considerations must be subordinated to it. In contrast to other forms of employment, managing a hedge fund is liable to produce losses as well as profits, and you can never take your eye off the ball. It is noteworthy that the values that guided me in my moneymaking activities did resemble the values postulated by economic theory: They involved a careful weighing of alternatives, they were cardinal rather than ordinal in character,† they were continuous and gradual, and they were single-mindedly directed at optimizing the ratio between risk and reward—including accepting higher risks at times when the ratio was favorable.

I am ready to generalize from my personal experience and admit

---

*Daniel Kahneman and Amos Tversky, "Prospect Theory: An Analysis of Decision Under Risk," *Econometrica* 47 (1979): 263–91.
†This is an important point. In contrast to most fund managers, who are concerned with relative performance, I was guided by and rewarded according to absolute performance. The pursuit of relative performance is a source of instability in financial markets that may not be sufficiently well recognized. I shall revert to this point in Chapter 7.

that the profit-seeking behavior postulated by economic theory is in fact relevant to economic activities in general and financial markets in particular. The generalization is justified because market participants who do not put profits above practically all other considerations are liable to be eliminated or reduced to insignificance by the pressures of competition. But there are other aspects of existence to be considered.

I remember vividly an occasion when I was rushing from one bank to another in the City of London, arranging a line of credit without which my hedge fund could have been wiped out. The pressure was so great that, walking along Leadenhall Street, I thought I was about to have a heart attack. It dawned on me that if I died, I would end up the loser in the game that I was playing with such alacrity.

Economic behavior is only one kind of behavior, and the values that economic theory takes as given are not the only kind of values that are relevant to humanity. The trouble is that economic and especially financial values have come to dominate our lives. Currency traders sitting at their desks buy and sell currencies of Third World countries in large quantities. The effect of the currency fluctuations on the people who live in those countries is a matter that does not enter their minds. Nor should it; they have a job to do. Yet if we pause to think, we must ask ourselves whether currency traders (not to use the more incendiary word, speculators) should regulate the lives of millions.

How do economic values relate to other kinds of values? That is not a question that can be answered in a timeless, universally valid manner, except to say that economic values, on their own, cannot be sufficient to sustain either the individual or society. Economic values express only what an individual market participant is willing to pay another in free exchange for something else. These values presuppose that each participant is a profit center bent on maximizing profits to the exclusion of all other considerations. Although the description may be appropriate to market behavior, there must be some other values at work to sustain society—indeed, to sustain human life. It is difficult to see how the values pertaining to these other spheres could be subjected to differential calculus as if they were indifference curves.

What are these other values, and how can they be reconciled with market values? That question preoccupies me, and it baffles my mind. Studying economics is not a good preparation for dealing with it—we must go beyond economic theory. Instead of taking values as given, we must treat them as reflexive. That means that different values prevail in different conditions, and there exists a two-way feedback mechanism that connects them with actual conditions, thereby creating a unique historical path. We must also treat values as fallible. That means that the prevailing values at any moment in history are liable to prove inadequate and inappropriate at some other point. I contend that at the present moment market values have assumed an importance that is way beyond anything that is appropriate and sustainable.

I must point out that if we want to apply the concept of reflexivity to values as well as expectations we must use the concept somewhat differently than described in Chapter 1. In the case of expectations, the outcome serves as a reality check; in the case of values, it does not. The Christian martyrs did not abandon their faith even when they were thrown to the lions. This renders a discussion of values much more difficult than a discussion of expectations. In the case of expectations, we can speak of a divergence between outcomes and expectations; in the case of values, the divergence is difficult to formulate.

I return to this dilemma in Chapter 4.

CHAPTER 3

Reflexivity in Financial Markets

I have made a very bold claim to the effect that economic theory has fundamentally misrepresented how markets operate. Like every fertile fallacy, this claim is exaggerated. There are many instances where the assumption that the conditions of supply and demand are independently given does not do any violence to reality; in these cases, classical economic theory provides valuable insights. But there is at least one important area where economic analysis has produced profoundly misleading results. I have in mind the financial markets.

Financial markets differ from other markets in that the participants do not deal with known quantities; they are trying to discount a future which is contingent on how the market discounts it at present. This makes the conditions of supply and demand not only unknown but also unknowable. In the absence of knowledge, participants are obliged to rely on an element of judgment or bias in reaching their decisions, which in turn introduces an element of uncertainty into the subject to which their decisions relate. This is an area that cannot be properly understood without taking reflexivity into account; yet economists have made every effort to avoid doing so. The theory that has enabled them to accomplish this heroic feat is the theory of rational expectations.

Rational Expectations

I find myself in a weak position to criticize the theory of rational expectations, because I never studied it closely. As I understand it, the prices of financial instruments are supposed to reflect the "fundamentals": a stream of future earnings and dividends and the prospect of future capital transactions in the case of stocks, a stream of future interest payments in the case of bonds, and (I infer) the future availability of supply combined with anticipated demand in the case of commodities. I don't quite know what rational expectations are supposed to relate to in the case of currencies. The point is that an efficient market already reflects all the information about the fundamentals that is currently known, and it is rational for participants to recognize this fact. Therefore, in the absence of inside information it is irrational for investors to assume that they can outperform the market. The market is in permanent equilibrium and any temporary deviation is in the nature of a random walk.

I am not sure that I have given an accurate account of the theory because, as I said before, I never studied it. I dismiss it out of hand because it is so blatantly in conflict with the concept of reflexivity. It treats markets as a passive reflection of the fundamentals, and it treats decisions as if they could be based on information.

I contend that participants in financial markets, instead of basing their decisions on rational expectations, cannot avoid introducing a bias into their decisionmaking. I use the word *bias* to describe an unavoidable element of judgment that will influence the outcome. Each market participant is faced with the task of putting a current value on a future course of events, but that course is contingent upon prevailing valuations in financial markets. That is why market participants are obliged to exercise an element of judgment. The important feature of biased judgments is that they are not purely passive: They affect the course of events that they are supposed to reflect. They are reflexive.

The fact that as a market participant I could get by without paying any attention to the theory of rational expectations is in itself a powerful indictment, but it falls well short of a reasoned rebuttal. Rather than immersing myself in a theory that I consider worse than useless, I shall put forward a radically different interpretation. Readers can then decide for themselves.

An Alternative View

I envision a two-way connection between thinking and reality. The fundamentals influence the values that participants attribute to financial instruments, and the valuations can also influence the fundamentals. The two-way interaction engenders a never-ending process that does not necessarily lead to equilibrium. Price fluctuations lead toward a theoretical equilibrium part of the time and away from it at other times, but the actual equilibrium remains indeterminate because it is itself at least partially affected by the price fluctuations.

The relationship between fundamentals and valuations is problematic. Apart from the point I have already made, namely that the fundamentals may be influenced by the prices prevailing in financial markets, there is another complication: In buying and selling financial instruments, market participants are not trying to discount fundamentals; they seek to anticipate the future prices of the selfsame financial instruments. The connection between fundamentals and market prices is more tenuous than the prevailing wisdom would suggest, and the role of the participants' bias greater. My scheme focuses on the participants' bias rather than the fundamentals. It needs to be emphasized, however, that it would be just as misleading to neglect the fundamentals as it is to ignore the participants' bias. What makes the bias important is that it can affect the fundamentals. When it does *not* do so it can be safely disregarded without doing any great violence to reality. That is what the theory of rational expectations sought to do.

The Participants' Bias

Bias is a difficult concept to work with. It cannot be properly measured, because we cannot know what an unbiased world looks like. Different people work with different biases, and it is impossible to work without some biases. This holds true even in the limiting case when a participant anticipates the future accurately.

Fortunately, there is a standard in the outside world by which the participants' bias can be judged: namely, the actual course of events. But that standard only provides an indication and not a measurement of the bias. That is because there is no reality independent of the participants' thinking, only a reality that is dependent on it. In other words, there is a sequence of events that actually occurs, and that sequence incorporates the impact of the participants' bias.

Markets often seem to anticipate the future correctly. This is not because events conform to rational expectations, however, but because expectations can influence the so-called fundamentals that they are supposed to discount. Rational expectations theory claims that, by definition, markets are always right. I contend that financial markets are almost always wrong but have the capacity to validate themselves—up to a point. Rational expectations theory concludes that in the long run it is impossible to beat the market averages and that any deviation in individual performance is in the nature of a random walk. This conclusion is patently false, and I am happy to have demonstrated it in practice.

Most of the time the actual course of events is likely to differ from the participants' expectations. This holds true even in those cases where the participants' bias is initially self-validating. The divergence between outcomes and expectations can be taken as an indication of the bias at play. Unfortunately, it can be taken only as an indication—not the full measure of the bias—because the actual course of events already contains the effects of the participants' bias. Nevertheless, we can at least distinguish between a bullish and a bearish bias.

The participants' bias is a phenomenon that is partially observable and partially submerged in the course of events, and as such it is of limited value as an object of scientific investigation. This may explain why economists were so anxious to eliminate it from their universe. Nevertheless, I consider it the key to understanding financial markets, even if it does not lend itself to the formulation of scientific theories. Not every phenomenon can be explained and predicted by universally valid generalizations—otherwise we would not need to rely on hunches in making our decisions.

For the sake of simplicity, let's focus on the stock market. Under the old-fashioned interpretation, stock prices supposedly reflect the fundamentals of the companies in which they provide an ownership participation. As I said before, this view is false. Market prices do not discount a future stream of earnings and dividends, they try to anticipate future market prices. Nevertheless, the fundamentals have an important role to play. Market prices are readily observable, but they do not by themselves reveal anything about the participants' biases. To identify the bias, we need some variable other than the bias. The fundamentals provide such a variable, even if they are contaminated by the bias.

For purposes of this discussion, I shall define "equilibrium" as a correspondence between the participants' views and the fundamentals. This is different from the way the word is used in financial economics, but I believe it accords with the concept of long-term equilibrium. Economists distinguish between short-term equilibrium, which is reached before any reallocation of productive resources has occurred, and long-term equilibrium, which reflects such readjustments. For short-term equilibrium, it is sufficient that the prevailing price should clear the market; that is to say, no buyer or seller should remain unsatisfied. Using this minimalist definition of equilibrium, it can be argued that financial markets are in constant equilibrium—although I have my doubts on this point, which I shall raise later in this chapter. But that does not say much about the role of financial markets in allocating resources. The really interesting question is whether there is such a thing as long-term equilibrium, and that is the question I am addressing here.

The fundamentals that matter are in the future. It is not last year's earnings, balance sheets, and dividends that stock prices are supposed to reflect but the future stream of earnings, dividends, and asset values. That stream is not given; therefore it is not an object of knowledge but of guessing. The guessing is based on a combination of information and bias. Therefore the bias finds expression in stock prices, and stock prices have ways of affecting the fundamentals. For instance, a company can raise capital by selling stock, and the price at which it sells stock will influence the earnings per share. The price of the stock also has an influence on the terms at which the company can borrow. The company can also motivate its management by issuing options. There are other ways in which the image of the company as represented by its stock price can affect the fundamentals. For instance, it can attract customers.

Whenever that happens, the possibility of a two-way, reflexive interaction arises, and equilibrium becomes a deceptive concept because the fundamentals cease to provide an independent variable to which the stock price could correspond. Equilibrium becomes a moving target, and the reflexive interaction may render it altogether elusive because the movement in stock prices may push the fundamentals in the same direction in which the stocks are moving. The recent craze for Internet stocks is a case in point.

Boom-Bust Sequences

The two-way connection between stock prices and fundamentals can set in motion a self-reinforcing process that can carry both the fundamentals and stock prices quite far from where they would be under a conventional equilibrium. This would justify trend-following behavior that could carry financial markets into what I call "far-from-equilibrium territory." Eventually the divergence between image and reality, between expectations and outcomes, is bound to become unsustainable, and the process is bound to be reversed. The important point is that trend-following behavior is not necessarily irrational. Just as certain animals have good reasons to move in herds, so do investors. Only at inflection points where the prevailing trend is reversed will the mindless trend-follower get hurt. By the same token, lone investors who hitch their fortune to the fundamentals are liable to get trampled by the herd. I have always been on the lookout for inflection points.

It is only occasionally that the price of an individual company's stock can affect that company's fundamentals in a self-reinforcing manner, like a dog chasing its own tail. But when we look at the larger, macroeconomic picture, we find that reflexive interactions are the rule, not the exception. For instance, currency movements tend to be self-validating; credit expansion and contraction tend to follow a boom-bust sequence. Self-reinforcing but eventually self-defeating processes are endemic in financial markets.

In *The Alchemy of Finance*, I identified and analyzed several cases of reflexivity that cannot be properly accounted for by equilibrium theory. In the case of the stock market, I focused on the phenomenon of equity leveraging. When a company or industry is overvalued, it can issue stock and use the proceeds to justify inflated expectations—up to a point. Conversely, when a fast-growing company is undervalued it may not be able to exploit the opportunities confronting it, thereby justifying the undervaluation—again, only up to a point.

Looking at currency markets, I discerned the prevalence of vicious and virtuous circles in which exchange rates and the so-called fundamentals they supposedly reflect are interconnected in a self-reinforcing fashion, creating trends that sustain themselves for prolonged periods until they are eventually reversed. I identified a vicious circle for the dollar that culminated in 1980, and I analyzed a virtuous circle that unfolded in the 1980–1985 period. I called it "Reagan's imperial circle." Had I written the book later, I could have analyzed a similar imperial circle in Germany, touched off by German reunification in 1990. It unfolded differently because of its effect on the European exchange-rate mechanism: It led to the devaluation of sterling in 1992. The crisis of 1997–1999 set up a similar vicious circle for periphery countries and a virtuous one for the United States. The presence of such long-lasting, well-identifiable trends encourages trend-following speculation, and the instability tends to be cumulative. This is demonstrated, once again, by the self-reinforcing decline of the euro since its introduction. The authorities are reluctant to intervene; I am convinced that the markets will eventually force them to do so unless the U.S. economy shows signs of slowing down. The authorities could save themselves a lot of grief if they had a better understanding of financial markets. Far from reflecting the fundamentals, markets create their own reality, and the authorities can prevent excesses from going too far by intervening at the right time. This goes against the prevailing orthodoxy.

Studying the banking system and credit markets in general, I observed a reflexive connection between the act of lending and the value of the collateral. The value of the collateral depends on how much the banks are willing to lend. This gives rise to an asymmetrical boom-bust sequence in which credit expansion and economic activity gather speed gradually and eventually come to an abrupt end. The reflexive connection and the asymmetrical pattern were clearly visible in the great international lending boom of the 1970s that culminated in the Mexico crisis of 1982. A similar process was unfolding in 1998 while I was writing *The Crisis of Global Capitalism*.

I want to use for illustration one particular case from *The Alchemy of Finance*: the so-called conglomerate boom, which reached its apogee in the late 1960s. At the time, investors were willing to pay a high multiple of earnings for companies that could produce fast per-share earnings growth. This consideration—earnings growth—loomed larger in investors' minds than the other so-called fundamentals, such as dividends and balance sheets, and investors were not terribly discriminating about the way per-share earnings growth was achieved. Certain companies managed to exploit this bias by using their stock for acquisitions. Typically, conglomerates were high-tech defense companies that had enjoyed fast earnings growth in the recent past and a correspondingly high multiple of earnings. They could use their high-priced stock to acquire other companies whose stock was selling at a lower multiple of earnings, producing higher earnings per share as a result. Investors appreciated the earnings growth and accorded higher multiples to the shares, which enabled the companies to continue the process. Soon there were many imitators. Even companies whose stock started with a low multiple of earnings could attain a higher multiple simply by announcing their intention to become a conglomerate. The boom was launched.

At first, the record of each conglomerate was judged on its own merit, but gradually conglomerates became recognized as a group. A new breed of investors emerged, the so-called go-go fund managers, or gunslingers, who developed a special relationship with the managements of conglomerates. Direct lines of communication were opened between them, and conglomerates learned to manage their investors as well as their earnings. The stocks climbed, but eventually reality could not sustain expectations. Acquisitions had to get larger and larger to maintain the momentum, and in the end they ran into the limits of size. The turning point came when Saul Steinberg tried to acquire Chemical Bank: This was too much for the establishment, and the attempt was defeated. Instead of anticipating a turning point, as could be expected of rational expectations, investors got carried away by the trend. So when the climax came, the market was caught unprepared.

The decline fed on itself. The conglomerates' internal problems that had been swept under the carpet during the period of rapid external growth began to surface. Earnings reports revealed unpleasant surprises. Investors became disillusioned, and after the heady days of acquisitions-based success few managers were willing to buckle down to the arduous work of running their companies. Those who did had to clean house, which meant reporting earnings that shocked investors. As one of these managers told me, "I have no audience to play to." The situation was aggravated by a recession. By then, investors were prepared to believe the worst, and in some cases the worst actually occurred: Some conglomerates literally disintegrated. In some cases, reality turned out to be better than expectations, and eventually the situation stabilized, with surviving companies, often under new management, slowly working themselves out from under the debris.*

Using the conglomerate boom as my paradigm, I devised an archetype of the boom-bust sequence. It starts with a prevailing bias and a prevailing trend. In the case of the conglomerate boom, the prevailing bias was a preference for rapid earnings growth per share

*George Soros, *The Alchemy of Finance: Reading the Mind of the Market* (New York: John Wiley and Sons, 1987), p. 57.

without much attention to how it was brought about; the prevailing trend was the ability of companies to generate high earnings growth per share by using their stock to acquire other companies selling at a lower multiple of earnings. This is illustrated in Graph 3.1: In the initial stage (1), the trend is not yet recognized. Then comes the period of acceleration (2), when the trend is recognized and reinforced by the prevailing bias. A period of testing (3) may intervene when prices suffer a setback. If the bias and trend are maintained, both emerge stronger than ever (4). Then comes the moment of truth (5) when reality can no longer sustain the exaggerated expectations, followed by a twilight period (6) when people continue to play the game, although they no longer believe in it, in the hope that they will be bailed out by greater fools. Eventually a crossover point (7) is reached when the trend turns down and even the greatest fools give up hope. This leads to a catastrophic acceleration in the opposite direction (8), commonly known as a "crash."

As illustrated in Graph 3.1, the boom-bust sequence has an

Graph 3.1

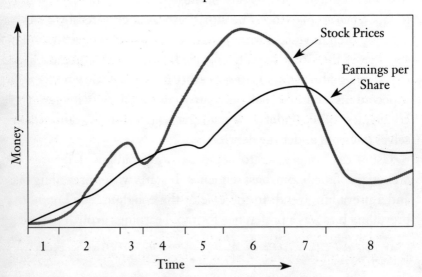

asymmetric shape, with the boom more drawn out and the bust more condensed. This graph presents an archetypal case, but the charts of various actual conglomerates conformed to it quite closely. Not every boom-bust process follows the same pattern. In *The Alchemy of Finance*, I described another archetypal case in which the upside and the downside are more symmetrical. Such is typical of currency markets, where upside and downside are more or less reversible. In reality, various reflexive processes interact, creating weird and unique patterns. Every case is different, and the charts have as many shapes as there are cases. The sudden collapse of confidence in Far East financial markets in 1997—which transformed the fundamentals throughout Asia and much of the world—is an obvious case in point (which will be analyzed in Chapter 7).

There is nothing determinate about the archetypal case I described above. The various stages may be of various amplitudes and durations. However, the sequence of stages seems to have some underlying logic. It would be strange to encounter a period of acceleration after the moment of truth or a crossover point before the moment of truth. But it is impossible to tell where we are in the process except in retrospect; for instance, the twilight period (6) turns into a period of testing (3) unless it is followed by a crossover point (7). Indeed, the process may never get started. In more cases than not, the reflexive feedback mechanism is self-correcting rather than self-reinforcing to start with. A full-fledged boom-bust sequence is the exception rather than the rule, but reflexivity—whether self-reinforcing or self-correcting—*is* the rule in financial markets.

The Internet Boom

We have recently experienced a full-fledged boom-bust sequence in Internet stocks. It started almost imperceptibly when a few companies engaged in Internet commerce went public. These companies offered valuable services greatly appreciated by the public. The stocks were also appreciated by the public, and the popularity of the stocks helped to promote the popularity of the services being provided. The prevailing trend and the prevailing bias became mutually self-reinforcing, and the boom accelerated. As the Internet spread, the number of potential investors increased exponentially, and the supply of stock could not keep pace. The demand for stock was boosted by brokers offering online trading, while the supply was limited by the various legal restrictions on the sale of stock by insiders who bought them before a public offering. Valuations reached outlandish levels. Few of the companies were profitable, but investors did not mind. They were looking at the number of customers or subscribers as the basis for valuing the stocks. Companies started giving away services, realizing that if they increased the number of customers they could raise capital on more advantageous terms. The name of the game became raising capital, not making profits. That is an unsustainable business model, and it did not take a financial genius to realize that the boom was bound to be followed by a bust, but it was much harder to guess when it would occur. The Internet boom refused to follow the pattern of the conglomerate boom illustrated in Graph 3.1. The moment of truth ought to have arrived on July 28, 1999, when the *Wall Street Journal* published a page-one article* explaining the flaw in the business model. This happened to coincide with a flood of new issues and the expiration of the holding period for original investors in some of the industry leaders such as America Online. The insiders could hardly wait to unload their holdings. Internet stocks fell by more than 50 percent. I was convinced that the crossover point had been reached and that a crash was imminent. Yet Internet stocks recovered, and some rose to new highs. Institutions that live and die by relative performance

*George Anders, "Internet Firms Offer Goods in a Bid to Increase Traffic," *Wall Street Journal*, July 28, 1999.

felt obliged to increase their holdings as the year-end approached. When Yahoo! was included in the Standard and Poor's (S&P) index, it jumped 30 percent in a single day. Christmas was coming, and Internet companies pulled out all the stops to boost sales. The wealth effect of the stock market bubble favored a strong Christmas. Giveaways, advertising, and the excitement generated by Internet stocks combined to ensure that so-called e-commerce sales would exceed all expectations. Since Internet stocks are valued on the basis of revenue growth, the boom gained another leg. What should have been the twilight period (6) turned into a successful test (3). People like me who sold Internet stocks short were forced to cover them at whopping losses. I remained convinced that a bust was bound to come, but I could not afford to stand by my convictions. As the Wall Street adage goes, he who runs away lives to fight another day. The bust came at the end of the first quarter, just as I expected, but by that time I did not dare to bet on it anymore. The bubble has now burst. Most Internet stocks sell below their offering price. The Internet is here to stay, but many companies that can no longer finance their growth by selling stock at ever-increasing prices are likely to fail. Eventually only companies capable of operating profitably will survive (see Chart 3.1).

It remains to be seen how the bursting of the Internet bubble will affect the rest of the market. So far it has had remarkably little effect. The Nasdaq index is showing considerable resilience, reminiscent of the behavior of Internet stocks a year ago, and the broader S&P index is hovering not far from its all-time high (see Chart 3.2). People have learned that it pays to buy the dips, and they will not be weaned from the habit until it ceases to pay. I believe that is about to happen because the economy is overheating, and the Federal Reserve is raising interest rates more aggressively than hitherto. At first, investors may switch to high-growth companies in the mistaken belief that they are immune to rising interest rates, but eventually those stocks are also going to be caught up in a

Chart 3.1: Interactive Internet Index

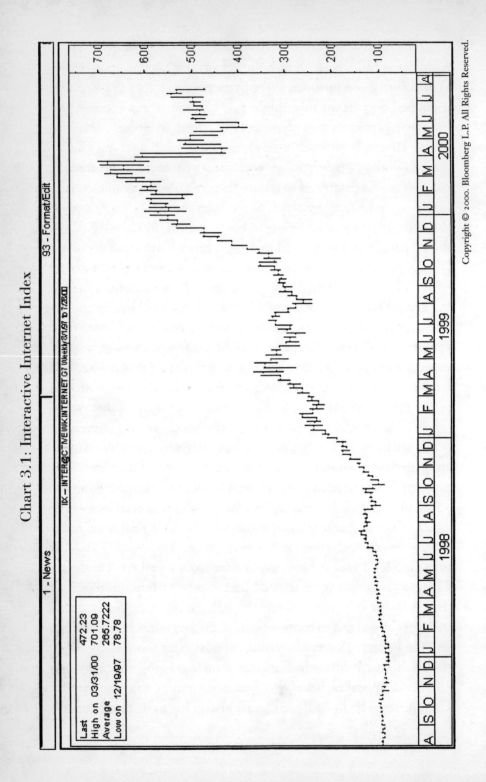

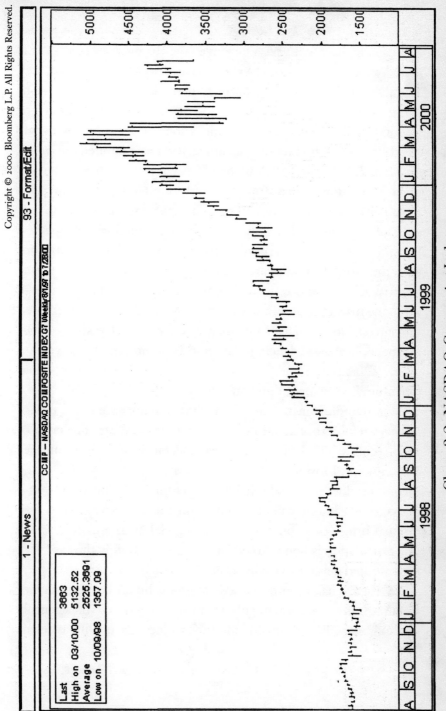

1 - News   93 - Format/Edit

CCMP — NASDAQ COMPOSITE INDEX G7 Weekly 8/1/97 to 7/28/00

Last   3663
High on 03/10/00 5132.52
Average   2525.3691
Low on 10/09/98   1357.09

5000
4500
4000
3500
3000
2500
2000
1500

A S O N D J F M A M J J A S O N D J F M A M J J A S O N D J F M A M J J A
1998   1999   2000

Chart 3.2: NASDAQ Composite Index

bear market. Just as the boom had a positive effect on the fundamentals, the bust will have a negative one. Rising stock prices stimulated consumption through the so-called wealth effect, and they stimulated capital spending on technology even more. The boom had the effect of speeding up time. Companies could not afford to wait in getting aboard the latest innovations for fear of being penalized by the stock market. For instance, John Kay pointed out in the *Financial Times** that Vodafone had to pay top dollar for the largest third-generation wireless franchise in the United Kingdom in order to validate its current stock price. The speeding up tilted the balance of demand and supply in favor of technology companies, boosting their profit margins; it also allowed fledgling companies with the latest technologies to capture market share to an extent unimaginable in more normal times. All this is liable to reverse when the market cools off, but this reflexive feedback is not factored into current stock prices. In my opinion, the music has stopped, but most people are still dancing. I am not. I announced the conversion of my Quantum Fund into a more conservative vehicle called Quantum Endowment Fund on April 30, 2000.

This example is instructive in showing that my boom-bust theory is far from foolproof in predicting the course of events. The crisis of 1997–1999, which I discuss in greater detail in Part II, is another case in point. I lost a lot of money on both. So what is the use of a theory if it does not yield reliable predictions? The answer is that if markets are genuinely unpredictable, then it is better to have a theory that brings this point home; one that claims to provide a scientific explanation is bound to be false. That is certainly the case with the so-called random-walk hypothesis.

My theory has been dismissed as useless by economists such as Robert Solow because it fails to meet the criteria of scientific method.† I readily admit that my theory does not qualify as scien-

*May 1, 2000.
†Robert Solow, "The False Economies of George Soros," *New Republic*, February 8, 1999.

tific, but I would argue that the concept of reflexivity is more conducive to an understanding of financial markets than the concept of equilibrium. Certainly it has produced better results over the years than what could be expected from the random-walk hypothesis. The Quantum Fund provided its shareholders a better than 30 percent annual return (excluding management fees) over more than thirty-one years, even after the 20 percent drawdown in the first half of 2000; $100,000 invested in 1969 would now be worth $420 million.

Reflexivity in Financial Markets

Not every stock market development can be interpreted in terms of an initially self-reinforcing but eventually self-defeating process, yet financial markets cannot be properly understood without taking that possibility into account. As the preceding examples indicate, boom-bust sequences cannot be predicted with any degree of certainty. Indeed, it would be internally inconsistent if that were possible, because the discovery of a correct predictive theory would alter the course of events. That does not mean that some participants cannot be better at guessing than others. On balance, I have done quite well because I am prepared to recognize my mistakes. My working hypothesis of radical fallibility has stood me in good stead.

A theory of reflexivity cannot possibly provide deterministic explanations and predictions; a theory of equilibrium is expected to do so. But when we look at the evidence, we must conclude that the latter has little relevance to reality. Nevertheless, the concept of equilibrium has some utility. Indeed, it would be difficult to shed much light on the reflexive feedback mechanism without invoking the concept. We could not say whether a process is leading away from or toward equilibrium. Neither could we say much about the participants' bias without introducing the concept of fundamentals, even though I contend that the so-called fundamentals do not determine the valuation of stocks. The chart of a conglomerate stock would not make much sense without a line denoting earnings per share (that is, the "fundamentals"), even if the earnings are themselves influenced reflexively by market valuations.

So what is "equilibrium"? I define it as the state in which there is a correspondence between expectations and outcomes. (This is just a more general restatement of my earlier definition). This sort of equilibrium is unattainable in financial markets, but it should be possible to establish whether a prevailing trend is leading toward it or away from it. Knowing that much would already be a major advance in our understanding.

If we can identify a prevailing trend and a divergence between reality and expectations, it may enable us to form a hypothesis about the future course of events. This is not easy to do, and it cannot be done scientifically, yet it provides a suitable basis for making investment decisions.

I have adapted Popper's theory of scientific method for this purpose. I establish a hypothesis (or thesis for short) as the basis of my expectations, then I test it against the future course of events. If the thesis fails, I sell. For instance, I bought Mortgage Guarantee Insurance Corporation ("Magic") at the time of a California real estate crisis on the thesis that the company would survive it and, having passed a severe test, it would be accorded a much higher valuation. It worked like magic. In my days of actively managing money, I used to get particularly excited when I picked up the scent of an initially self-reinforcing but eventually self-defeating thesis. My mouth would water as if I were one of Pavlov's dogs. Often I picked up a false scent. Just as economists are said to have predicted ten out of the last three recessions, I did the same with boom-bust sequences. I was wrong most of the time, because while every situation is reflexive most are self-correcting rather than self-reinforcing. But the few occasions when I was right made the effort worthwhile, because the profit potential was so much greater than it was in near-equilibrium situations. This had much to do with my success as a fund manager. It required imagination, intuition, and a relentlessly critical attitude. Unfortunately, the glory days are over: Too many people have read my books, and I lost my edge.

I documented one particular instance in *The Alchemy of Finance*: real estate investment trusts (REITs) in the early 1970s. The case was remarkable in many ways. I published a brokerage report that forecast a boom-bust process, and afterward the scenario played out, like a Greek drama, exactly as I had predicted. The shape of the charts did not look like Graph 3.1 because my brokerage report caused an initial bubble that was punctured when it attracted the launching of many new REITs. The real boom-bust sequence started thereafter. I was a major player myself, benefiting fully from the scenario on both the upside and the downside. Persuaded by my own analysis that most REITs would end in bankruptcy, I continued to sell the stocks short as they declined, ending up making more than 100 percent on my short positions—a seemingly impossible feat.

Even on those occasions when my thesis turned out to be false, I could often exit with a profit because my self-critical attitude helped me to uncover the flaws in my thesis before others did so. I follow the precept "Invest first and investigate later." When the thesis was plausible, this usually gave me a chance to turn around with a profit, because there were other people ready to believe in the story even after I had discarded it. Even in those cases where I was wrong— and I have mentioned two, the crisis of 1997–1999 and the Internet boom—I would benefit from having a thesis because it would help me to recognize my mistakes. Finding a flaw always gave me comfort; not knowing the potential weaknesses made me nervous, since I firmly believed that every thesis is flawed.

Based on my own experience, I established a rather interesting thesis about the stock market: I postulated that the stock market acts out an adaptation of Popper's theory of scientific method very much along the same lines that I do, with the difference that it does not know that it is doing so. In other words, it adopts a thesis and tests it; when it fails—as it usually does—it tries out another thesis.

That is what produces market fluctuations. It occurs at various levels of significance, and the patterns produced are recursive, very much like Mandelbrot's fractals (that is, recursive structures in which irregular configurations are repeated at all scales).

This has led me to the working hypothesis that markets are in constant disequilibrium. I do not rule out equilibrium, but I regard it as a limiting case. I go even further: I believe that prices do not clear the market. There are always unsatisfied buyers and sellers in the wings, either because they cannot execute the entire order at the last sale or because they cannot make up their minds. Either way, they are bound to be influenced by market action. Economic theory tells us that a rise in prices tends to reduce demand and increase supply. Not so in the stock market. A rise in prices may increase the anxiety of buyers, and vice versa, giving rise to the phenomenon of trend-following behavior. This was systematically exploited by the professional jobbers in the old London stock market, where brokers were obliged to deal through jobbers. When the jobbers wanted to cover their short positions they did not bid up for stocks; on the contrary, they lowered their prices. "Shaking the tree," they called it.

This has important theoretical implications, for it justifies technical analysis.* For instance, upticks and downticks become important predictors of price trends. Needless to say, this view is in direct contradiction to the prevailing view, which maintains that the market is in permanent short-term equilibrium.

The thesis adopted by the market is often trivial; it may not amount to much more than saying that the prices of certain companies, groups, even entire markets are going to move up or down. In these cases, by the time a participant figures out why the market adopted a certain thesis it may be too late—the thesis has already been discarded. It is much better to anticipate the fluctuations by

---

*The two main approaches to security analysis are the "fundamental" and the "technical." Fundamental analysis follows the precepts of economic theory and treats share prices as a reflection of the fundamental value of the company. Technical analysis ignores economic theory and studies the dynamics of price movements and patterns of market behavior.

studying market patterns. That is what technical analysts do. I was never particularly interested in technical analysis, but I recognized its relevance. I preferred to await a nontrivial—that is, historical—boom-bust thesis. Of course, the market had already begun to act it out before I could identify such a thesis, but I could still be ahead of most investors in exploiting it. These historical, reflexive theses would present themselves only intermittently, and there would be long fallow periods in between when I might be better off doing nothing.

I doubt that I would still have a competitive edge in recognizing the larger, historic theses, because market participants have now become aware of the potential held by reflexivity. There has been a noticeable change, for instance, away from fundamentals and toward trading on technical considerations. As the participants' belief in the importance of fundamentals declines, technical analysis becomes even more important. This has some implications for the stability of markets, but before I consider them I must introduce a distinction that plays a key role in my conceptual framework.

Dynamic Disequilibrium

I want to distinguish between near-equilibrium and far-from-equilibrium conditions. I have borrowed these terms from chaos theory, with which my approach has certain affinities. In near-equilibrium conditions, the market operates with trivial theses, which do not have the capacity to affect the fundamentals, so that a move away from equilibrium is likely to provoke a countermove that takes prices back toward the position from which they started. These fluctuations resemble a random walk or ripples in a swimming pool.

By contrast, if a reflexive thesis manages to establish itself, it will affect not only prices but also the fundamentals, and a reversal will not result in a return to the status quo. It will be more like a tidal wave or an avalanche. Full-fledged boom-bust sequences penetrate into far-from-equilibrium territory. That is what sets them apart from a random walk and gives them historic significance. I used to tell myself that I was good at recognizing tidal waves but I could not play the ripples.

Where is the demarcation line? The threshold of dynamic disequilibrium is crossed when a trend prevailing in the real world becomes dependent on a bias prevailing in the participants' minds, and vice versa. Both trend and bias then develop further than would have been possible in the absence of a reflexive, double-feedback connection. For example, in the 1990s the enthusiasm of international investors and bankers for Asian assets produced domestic booms spurred by high valuations and easy credits. These booms accelerated the growth of the economies and increased valuations, which in turn validated and encouraged further capital inflows from abroad. But there was a fly in the ointment: The boom could not have developed as far as it did without the dollar peg that allowed the countries to sustain a trade deficit longer than they should have. When the peg broke, it caused a collapse in the currency, in asset prices, and in the economy.

A prevailing bias is not enough by itself to create a dynamic disequilibrium; it must find a way to become validated by establishing or reinforcing a trend in the real world. I realize this point is tautological: When a double-feedback mechanism is in operation, we can speak of dynamic disequilibrium. But the point is worth making: The participants' thinking is always biased, but it does not always translate into a boom-bust sequence. For instance, the conglomerate boom could have been forestalled if investors had anticipated that their concept of per-share earnings growth was flawed as soon as the conglomerate companies started to exploit it. The Asian boom could have been cut short if investors and lenders had realized that the currency peg was likely to break.

I explore the demarcation between near-equilibrium and far-from-equilibrium conditions in Chapter 4. It will be the main thrust of my theory of history. For the moment, I should like to make an additional point about the repercussions of my interpretation of financial markets on the financial markets themselves.

What happens when the reflexive connection between fundamentals and valuations is recognized by market participants? It can also become a source of instability. It tends to lead to an emphasis on so-called technical factors to the neglect of the fundamentals and tends to generate trend-following speculation. This has a destabilizing effect. How can stability be preserved? One way is to continue relying on the fundamentals, in spite of the fact that they can be affected by our valuations. This can be achieved by exercising ignorance. If market participants are unaware of reflexivity, the belief in fundamentals will tend to keep markets stable; but ignorance renders markets vulnerable to reversals as the flaws in the prevailing interpretation are revealed (as in the conglomerate boom). How can stability be preserved when the market participants become aware of reflexivity? The answer is that it cannot be done by market participants on their own: Preserving stability must become an objective of public policy.

It can be seen that the concept of reflexivity is itself reflexive in the sense that the extent to which it is recognized will alter behavior. Classical economic theory has actually promoted the tendency toward equilibrium by ignoring reflexivity and emphasizing the importance of fundamentals. Similarly, efficient market theory could have a stabilizing effect by encouraging arbitrage activities aimed at evening out pricing anomalies, provided it is not overdone as in the case of Long Term Capital Management (LTCM, a highly leveraged hedge fund that had to be rescued). By contrast, my argument leads to the conclusion that markets cannot be left to their own devices. Awareness of reflexivity only serves to increase instability unless the authorities are equally aware of it and intervene when instability threatens to get out of hand.

The problem of instability is becoming more acute. The belief in fundamentals is eroding, and trend-following behavior is on the rise. It is fostered by the increasing influence of institutional investors whose performance is measured by relative rather than absolute performance and by the large money center banks that act as market makers in currencies and derivatives: They benefit from increased volatility both as market makers and as providers of hedging mechanisms. The role of hedge funds is more ambivalent: As users of leverage, they contribute to volatility, but to the extent that they are motivated by absolute rather than relative performance, they often go against the trend. Because reflexivity is a historical process, it is quite possible that markets have become much more unstable than in recent memory (although I would rule out a replay of 1929). I address this issue in Part II, where I examine the crisis of 1997–1999.

The Two Approaches Compared

I contend that the concept of reflexivity provides a better interpretation of how financial markets work than the concept of equilibrium. Financial markets are always in disequilibrium, sometimes moving away from, and at other times toward, what could be considered equilibrium—that is, a correspondence between expectations and outcomes. Equilibrium itself appears only as a limiting case.

I believe I have provided enough examples to demonstrate the validity of my approach. After all, a single sunspot experiment was sufficient to demonstrate the deficiency of Newtonian physics and to establish the credentials of Einstein's theory of relativity. But there is a big difference between Einstein's theory and mine. Einstein could predict specific phenomena: the Michelson-Morley experiment proved the invariance of the speed of light and the perihelion of Mercury confirmed general relativity. I cannot predict anything except unpredictability—and that is not enough to cloak my theory in scientific respectability.

Economists such as Robert Solow reject my interpretation because it does not provide any determinate explanation or prediction of market behavior. They are right, of course. My contention is that reflexivity injects an element of uncertainty that renders financial markets inherently unpredictable. I claim that recognizing this fact puts us in a better position to anticipate and react to market moves than does a supposedly scientific theory; but I have not produced a scientific theory.

Economists are likely to find this argument unacceptable. They might cite Heisenberg's uncertainty principle in counterargument. It deals with uncertainty, yet it produces testable predictions based on statistical probabilities. That is what one would expect from a scientific theory, they say, and they have a point. My interpretation does not produce statistical probabilities; it treats each instance as a unique, historic event. Moreover I believe that, in contrast to quantum physics, it is impossible to reduce boom-bust sequences to statistical probabilities. The reason is that financial markets are not self-contained. They can affect the fundamentals that they are supposed to reflect. The impact is different every time, making each instance unique.

If we disregard the impact on the underlying fundamentals, we can come up with statistical generalizations. That is what technical analysis does. It treats the stock market as a closed system where only what happens within the market is relevant. That removes the element that renders each instance unique. We are then left with a number of instances that can be made to yield statistical probabilities. For instance, if the market makes a low, rallies, and then retests the low—but the volume and the number of stocks making a new low is lower than on the previous occasion—there is a good chance the market has made a good bottom, from which it is likely to rally. There are many sophisticated technical indicators, and there are many people who make a living by studying them. But there is a flaw in this approach. The market is not a closed system. It affects reality, so that the probabilities that prevail today are not the same as they were on previous occasions. Sometimes this matters, other times not. The reason that boom-bust sequences cannot be reduced to statistical probabilities is that the financial markets interact with different fundamentals each time. Even if the markets followed the same rules of behavior, reality does not, because different sectors of reality are involved at different times. Internet companies at the turn of the twenty-first century are different from the conglomerates of the late 1960s. One of the reasons I misjudged the strength and duration of the Internet boom is that I was too much influenced by previous instances. Every bubble has a basis in reality, and the changes in reality connected with the Internet boom are much more significant than, for instance, those in the conglomerate boom or the bowling boom or the gambling boom. If scientific theories must provide deterministic or statistically probable explanations and predictions, then financial markets may not be amenable to scientific treatment.

Again, my critics disagree. They point out that, during the period since I wrote *The Alchemy of Finance*, a lot of progress has been made in economic theory toward the scientific analysis of reflexive phenomena.

Stung by the criticism, I felt obliged to check into the matter. I have to acknowledge that some of their objections are justified. I am not the only one who is aware of the shortcomings of financial markets. Many of the points I seek to make have been already elaborated by others within the mainstream of modern economic thought. For instance, the idea of multiple equilibria has gained widespread acceptance, and the so-called second-generation theories of currency crises give full play to reflexive feedbacks.* A whole new discipline—behavioral economics—has grown up to study the divergences between actual and rational behavior.

I may be flogging a dead horse when I am attacking rational expectations, much as I did when I tried to set logical positivism on its head. The point has been reached when the theories of perfect

---

*See Robert Flood and Nancy Marion, "Perspectives on the Recent Currency Crisis Literature," National Bureau of Economic Research Working Paper No. W6380, January 1998.

competition, rational expectations, and efficient markets have more holes in them than substance. The situation is ripe for a paradigm shift; yet the shift has not occurred. Arguments that pick holes in efficient markets are still couched in terms of equilibrium rather than dynamic disequilibrium. In my view, the concept of multiple equilibria is a misnomer; "dynamic disequilibrium" would be more appropriate. The main deficiency I find is that most of the discussion is couched in terms of information, not judgment. This leads to arguments about asymmetrical information, not about changes in the prevailing bias. Where shifts in bias are acknowledged, they have an arbitrary quality about them, whereas I emphasize the reflexive feedback mechanism. That is the difference between multiple equilibria and genuine disequilibrium.

I must admit, however, that the boom-bust theory outlined in this book has even less predictive power than some of the recent literature: It can fit any boom-bust process after it has occurred, and it explicitly disclaims any capacity to predict the future course of events. Still, I believe that is the best we can do: formulate hypotheses and test them against events as they unfold. The trouble with these hypotheses is not that they cannot be falsified; it is that they are proven false all too often. But that is still better than the random-walk hypothesis, provided we have some intuition and stand ready to correct our mistakes. The fact is that my boom-bust theory has produced better results than a random walk. The same is true of competent technical analysis, the difference being that it relies on statistical generalizations while my approach treats financial markets as a historical, unique course of events.

I do not think I can be held responsible for failing to provide a scientific theory capable of predicting a historical, unique course of events when my claim is that no such theory is possible. Even so, there must be a better way to study such inherently unpredictable phenomena. I believe I am right in claiming that the time has come to develop a new paradigm. I lack the capacity to do so because I do not have the necessary mathematical skills. Still, the shape of the new paradigm is fairly clear in my mind, and I shall try to describe it in words.

A New Paradigm

We must abandon two of the cherished preconceptions of economic theory with regard to financial markets. One is rational behavior; the other is equilibrium, including the contention that prices clear the market.

Rational expectations are appropriate to a world where the participants' expectations have no impact on the events to which they relate. The participant is then in the position of an observer who can gather all the available information and reach her decision on the basis of that information. Her decisions have something definitive to correspond to—namely, the prospective equilibrium. Naturally, no participant is in possession of all the available information, but by definition some other participant is—otherwise the information would not be available. So the market knows more than any individual participant; it knows everything there is to be known; therefore the market is always right. Participants are assumed to be rational enough to recognize this fact and act accordingly. That is the justification, for instance, for investing in index funds. If reality deviates from the equilibrium there must be a reason for it; the reason is usually to be found in asymmetric information. For instance, the multiple equilibria associated with credit crises can be attributed to the asymmetric information available to different classes of creditors.

That is not how the world works. Participants are not merely observers; their decisions influence the future. They base their decisions on hunches, not on information, and the information about the hunches becomes available only after they have made their effects felt. In these circumstances, it is not rational to act on the basis of rational expectations. Some people may do so, but others may not. Different people follow different decision rules, and they modify them in the light of experience. Instead of rational behavior, it would be more appropriate and illuminating to speak of "adaptive behavior."

This provides the new paradigm we need. Adaptive behavior can be studied either over time, tracing its evolution, or across space, comparing different instances of similar manifestations. Both approaches have accumulated considerable literature. The evolutionary approach is well established in other fields of study, notably evolutionary biology and other forms of evolutionary systems theory. It has also begun to encroach on economics through the application of game theory. Game theory started out with the assumption of rational behavior but it has produced much more interesting results since it has abandoned that assumption. Take the explorations of the prisoner's dilemma through computer contests, a subject I shall discuss in greater detail in chapter 4. The general idea is to identify strategies that participants employ rather than to identify a particular strategy as the rational one. One can then study how these strategies evolve through computer simulation or observation. There is a well-developed methodology for doing so: It consists of establishing the growth or decline of populations employing particular strategies. It is especially suited to studying the interaction between predators and prey, but it can be used more generally. I became familiar with this approach through the work of Peter Allen, who made a study of Canadian fisheries.* He assumed that fishermen divided into two groups: Cartesians, who concentrated on the territories where fish have already been found, and pragmatists, who cast their nets more widely. Jeffrey Frankel and Kenneth Froot[†] used a similar approach when they distinguished between chartists

---

*Peter M. Allen, "Evolving Complexity in Social Science," in *Systems: New Paradigms for the Human Sciences*, edited by Gabriel Altman and Walter A. Koch (Berlin: Walter de Gruyter, 1998), pp. 3–38.
†Jeffrey A. Frankel and Kenneth A. Froot, "Chartists, Fundamentalists, and the Demand for Dollars," in *Private Behavior and Government Policy in Interdependent Economies*, edited by Anthony Courakis and Mark Taylor (Oxford, U.K.: Clarendon Press, 1990).

and fundamentalist investors. This approach reflects the dynamic nature of the reflexive interaction between thinking and reality, expectations and outcomes. It does not rule out an eventual equilibrium, but it does not necessarily produce one. All the conclusions based on the presumption of equilibrium fall by the wayside.

To use this approach in financial markets, it is important to realize that prevailing prices do not necessarily clear the market. This goes against one of the most cherished preconceptions about markets and needs a word of explanation. Economic theory has treated financial markets as if they were in continuous equilibrium; it would be much better to recognize that they are in continuous *dis*equilibrium. At any moment, there are potential buyers and sellers who could be pushed over the edge by market movements. Some are actually unsatisfied: They would like to buy or sell more than they can at that price. Others are wavering, and a market move may be sufficient to trigger a decision either in the same or in the opposite direction. There is no a priori rule to determine which group is stronger. Certainly there is no reason to assume that a decline in price will increase the demand and reduce the supply and vice versa. Trend-followers may outweigh so-called value investors. The increasing use of options and derivatives also creates pent-up demand and supply, which usually goes to reinforce the prevailing trend. In certain circumstances, the impetus coming from derivatives can be strong enough to cause a discontinuity.

One of the advantages of looking at markets in this way is that it justifies technical analysis. If market prices were a passive reflection of the fundamentals, then technical analysis would make no sense; but if markets are in continuous disequilibrium, upticks and downticks provide valuable information about the strength of demand and supply, and technical analysis has a role to play—how big a role depends on the strategies that participants adopt. The important point is that there is room for different strategies, and it makes sense to study adaptive behavior. Evolutionary game theory, such as the iteration of the prisoner's dilemma, seems to me particularly promising. While I am not in a position to fully develop the new paradigm, I can at least see the shape it would take. It would replace the equations of equilibrium theory with the nonlinear programming of evolutionary systems theory.

The new paradigm would deprive market fundamentalism of its scientific underpinning. It could no longer be taken for granted that markets tend toward equilibrium; indeed, the nonlinear models would clearly demonstrate that often they do not.

There is a strong case for free markets, but the case does not rest on the tendency toward equilibrium. It derives from the liberating effect of letting people pursue their goals. Free markets unleash the creative energies of the human intellect. In this respect, they are like the other freedoms, of speech and thought and of political association. Freedom is valuable in its own right, and it is also a source of wealth creation. Wealth creation is a dynamic process, whereas equilibrium theory is static; it therefore misses the main merit of the capitalist system. The market mechanism is an essential part of an open society. This is not because markets tend toward equilibrium but because they offer participants freedom of choice.

Technical analysis, as it is currently practiced, uses the other approach I have mentioned, comparing different instances of similar patterns of behavior and trying to estimate the probabilities on the basis of past experience. Technical analysis is not encumbered by the assumption of rationality but its scope is limited by the fact that financial markets do not constitute a closed system. They constantly receive new impulses from the outside world which ensure that the future will not be a mechanical repetition of the past. Technical analysis itself is such an impulse; that is why it is more like alchemy than science. Since the methods of natural science are ill-suited to the study of social phenomena, technical analysis cannot be dismissed on account of it not being scientific; one must, however, beware of its alchemical nature.

Economists have started to apply comparative analysis to various phenomena other than financial markets. For instance, economists at the World Bank are trying to analyze phenomena like corruption* and armed insurrection† by treating them as economic activities. Their approach is subject to the same limitations as technical analysis: In trying to calculate probabilities, they lose the context in which each particular instance occurs. They suffer from an additional disadvantage: They have to find a way to quantify their data while the students of financial markets have ready-made quantified data at their disposal. Nevertheless, I find these pioneering efforts fascinating. I consider them as fertile fallacies: They offer insights which help to understand the problems but they fall short of providing a comprehensive framework for dealing with them. Generalizations need to be combined with local knowledge‡ and the combination of the two holds out promise for improving the performance of policymakers. Even so, social engineering will never be able to attain the reliability of mechanical engineering. There is a parallel here with the radical uncertainty confronting participants in financial markets.

To sum up: Within the new paradigm of adaptive as distinct from rational behavior, there is room for a longitudinal approach studying the evolution of systems over time and a latitudinal approach comparing similar situations. The first approach tends to use non-linear programming, the second, regression analysis. Both disciplines need to be complemented by local knowledge.

*Daniel Kaufmann, Aart Kraay and Pablo Zoido-Lobaton, "Governance Matters" (Washington DC: World Bank Policy Research Working Paper No. 2196, August 1999). *See also* Daniel Kaufmann, "Corruption: The Facts" (Washington DC: Foreign Policy, Summer 1997).
†Paul Collier, "Economic Causes of Civil Conflict and their Implications for Policy" (Washington DC: World Bank, June 15, 2000).
‡A point well made by Ivan Krustev in "The Strange (Re)Discovery of Corruption" in *The Paradoxes of Unintended Consequences* (Budapest: CEU Press, 2000).

CHAPTER 4

Reflexivity in History

I have interpreted financial markets as an irreversible, historical process; hence my interpretation must also have some relevance to history at large. I have classified events into two categories: humdrum, everyday events that do not provoke a change in perceptions, and unique, historic events that affect the participants' bias and, in turn, lead to changes in the fundamentals. The distinction is tautological but useful. The first kind of event is susceptible to equilibrium analysis, the second is not: It can be understood only as part of a historical process.

Dialectics

In everyday events, neither the participating function nor the cognitive function undergo any significant change. In the case of unique, irreversible developments, both functions operate simultaneously in such a way that neither the participants' views nor the situation remains the same. That is what justifies describing such developments as historic.

The historical process is, as I see it, open-ended. When a situation has thinking participants, the sequence of events does not lead directly from one set of facts to the next; rather, it connects facts to perceptions and perceptions to facts in a shoelace pattern. But history is a very peculiar kind of shoelace. The two sides of the shoe are not made of the same material; indeed, only one side is material—the other consists of the ideas of the participants. The two sides do not match, and the divergences between them determine the shape of the events that tie them together. The knots that have already been tied have a determinate shape, but the future is open-ended.

This is rather different from a mechanism whose functioning can be explained and predicted by universally valid laws. In historical developments, past and future are not reversible, as they are in Karl Popper's model of scientific method. What makes the future different from the past is the choice that the participants are obliged (and privileged) to exercise on the basis of their imperfect understanding. That choice introduces an element of uncertainty into the course of events. Attempts to eliminate it by establishing scientific laws of human behavior are doomed to failure.

This shoelace theory of history is a kind of dialectic between our thoughts and reality. As such, it can be interpreted as a synthesis of Hegel's dialectic of ideas and Marx's dialectical materialism. Georg Wilhelm Friedrich Hegel propounded the thesis that ideas develop in a dialectical fashion and lead eventually to the end of history—freedom. Karl Marx, or more exactly Friedrich Engels, provided the antithesis by claiming that the development of ideas is determined by the conditions and relations of production; the ideological superstructure is merely a reflection of the material base. The shoelace theory could then be regarded as a synthesis. Instead of either thoughts or material conditions evolving in a dialectic fashion on their own, it is the interplay between the two that produces a dialectic process. I call this interplay reflexivity, and the only reason I do not use the word "dialectic" more prominently is that I do not want to be burdened by the excess baggage that comes with it. After all, Marx propounded a deterministic theory of history that is diametrically opposed to my own interpretation. The interplay between the material and the ideal is interesting exactly because they do *not* correspond to or determine each other. The lack of correspondence renders the participants' bias a causal force in history. Fallibility—which finds expression in the mistakes, misinterpretations, and misconceptions of the participants—plays the same role in historical events as genetic mutations in biological events: It makes history.

The Selfish Gene

Evolutionary biology has become an exciting field of study. The method employed is to establish dynamic models that depict the evolution of a species in interaction with its environment. Every species belongs to the environment of other species. Historical developments of all kinds—financial markets, families, institutions—could in theory be studied by the same method. In certain circumstances, we could expect the process to come to rest at an equilibrium point where no further changes would occur without an external disturbance. But that would be a special case. In other cases, the process would continue indefinitely without ever coming to rest. Economic theory is preoccupied with finding the equilibrium point; the study of history has to focus on the ongoing process. There is no evidence that history will ever come to an end as long as humanity exists.

In studying history, it would be a mistake to treat human beings the same as other species. There is some quality—not easy to locate and define—that sets humans apart. More than the ability to make choices—rats in a maze do that—it is the ability to choose one's motivations that distinguishes humans from other animals. There is no uncertainty about the motivation of a rat when it chooses one path rather than another: It wants the cheese. There is no corresponding certainty about human motivations, and it is a common error to ignore the difference.

Modern evolutionary biology has given new life to Darwin's idea of natural selection. Strategies pursued at the level of the species can be seen to be effective at the level of the gene: Successful strategies lead to the propagation of the genes in which those strategies are embedded. This has given rise to the postulate of the "selfish gene." The name is, of course, a figure of speech, because it would be apocryphal to impute a motivation to the gene, and modern Darwinists are careful to point this out. The multiplication of the genes is not intentional; it is the natural consequence of the survival of the fittest—that is, of a successful strategy. This rule seems to be universal, applying to humans as well as other species.

Still, there is a fundamental difference: Humans engage in intentional behavior. The connection between successful strategies and the propagation of genes is less direct than in other species. It is not entirely absent; humans have not shed their animal origins. There is no abrupt dividing line; rather, humans have superimposed another layer of behavior on the animal base, and that layer is not governed by their genetic makeup to the same extent as their more instinctual behavior. It is the intentional layer that accounts for most of the influence that humans have been able to exert over their environment. The intentional layer also introduces an element of uncertainty—namely, uncertainty about intentions—that is missing from the behavior of other animate creatures.

Genetic engineering is now making rapid strides. We can increasingly influence how the human brain functions. But, short of turning humans into robots, we shall not be able to eliminate the uncertainty inherent in human behavior. I believe the concept of reflexivity and the shoelace theory of history give a better expression of this uncertainty than does the selfish-gene theory.

There is a divergence between intentions and outcomes; the outcomes modify the intentions, which in turn modify the outcomes in a never-ending process that is in some ways akin to biological evolution but in some ways different. This is what I mean when I say that biological change consists in the mutation of genes and can be measured by the propagation of genes while historical change consists in misconceptions and can be measured by the gap between intentions and outcomes.

When it comes to human behavior, it is questionable to what extent history can be explained by the rules of the selfish gene. Sometimes people harbor intentions that correspond to the interests of the selfish gene, but not always. The selfish gene plays an obviously important role in dynastic succession, but even there Shakespeare offers some interesting observations—such as Hamlet's "to be or not to be"—that go well beyond the confines of the selfish-gene theory.

A Boom-Bust Model

The interesting question is how historical change could be modeled. As I mentioned in Chapter 3, I believe evolutionary game theory points the way: Studying adaptive behavior seems to make more sense than assuming rational behavior.

As I readily confessed in that chapter, I am unable to develop a new paradigm. Both evolutionary biology and evolutionary game theory follow the evolution of populations pursuing certain strategies: Cartesian and pragmatic fishermen in the case of Canadian fisheries, value investors and momentum traders in the case of the stock market. I consider this approach more promising than rational expectations theory, but I lack the skills to develop it. I have proposed a boom-bust model for financial markets, although it is more an illustration of the workings of reflexivity than it is a scientific theory. I have found it useful as a prop in my investment decisions, but it can easily collapse if one puts too much weight on it. I shall now extend that model to history at large by offering a boom-bust interpretation of the rise and fall of the Soviet system. This will be more a flight of fancy than an illustration, but it has the advantage of allowing me to introduce my conceptual framework by using a concrete example that may come as welcome relief from abstract discussions. In doing this I am merely living up to the postulate of radical fallibility by pushing a fertile fallacy to its limits.

The Rise and Fall of the Soviet System

I was actively involved in the disintegration of the Soviet system. As an opponent of closed societies, I was eager to further its demise. I developed a boom-bust interpretation of the situation, which guided my actions. I published it in a 1990 book entitled *Opening the Soviet System.* The following is how I analyzed the situation at that time.

The initial bias (communist ideology) and the initial trend (repression) led to a closed society. There was a mutually self-reinforcing relationship between the rigidity of the communist dogma and the rigidity of prevailing social conditions. The system reached its zenith in the last few years of Stalin's rule. It was all-embracing: a form of government, an economic system, a territorial empire, and an ideology. The system was comprehensive, isolated from the outside world, and unbending. There was a chasm between the actual state of affairs and its official interpretation that was much wider than could have been sustained in an open society. I regard this as a case of static disequilibrium.

After Stalin's death, there was a brief moment—the moment of truth—when Nikita Khrushchev revealed some of the secrets of Stalin's rule, but eventually the hierarchy reasserted itself. A twilight period began, when dogma was preserved by administrative methods but was no longer reinforced by a belief in its validity. Interestingly, the rigidity of the system increased. As long as there had been a live totalitarian at the helm, the Communist Party line could be changed at his whim. But now that the regime was run by bureaucrats, that flexibility was lost. At the same time, the terror that forced people to accept the communist dogma also abated, and a subtle process of decay set in. Institutions jockeyed for position. Since none enjoyed any real autonomy, each had to engage in a form of barter with other institutions. Gradually an elaborate system of institutional bargaining replaced what was supposed to be central planning. Simultaneously, an informal economy developed that supplemented and filled in the gaps left by the formal system. The planned economy would have broken down without it. This twilight period was what is now called the "period of stagnation." The inadequacy of the system became increasingly evident, and pressure for reform mounted.

Reform accelerated the process of disintegration, because it introduced or legitimized alternatives (whereas the system depended on the lack of alternatives for its survival). Economic reform enjoyed an initial period of success in every communist country, with the notable exception of the Soviet Union itself. The Chinese reformers called this phase the "golden period," when the existing capital stock was redirected to meet consumer needs. The Soviet Union failed to accomplish even this relatively easy task.

Attempts at reforming the communist system are based on a misconception: The system cannot be reformed, because it does not permit the economic allocation of capital. More radical change is needed. When existing capacity has been reoriented, the reform process starts running out of resources. It is understandable why this should be so. Communism was meant to be an antidote to capitalism, which had alienated the worker from the means of production. All property was taken over by the state, and the state was an embodiment of the collective interest as defined by the party. Therefore the party was put in charge of the allocation of capital. This meant that capital was allocated not on economic grounds but on the grounds of a political, quasireligious dogma. The best analogy is with the pyramid-building of the pharaohs: The portion of resources devoted to investment was maximized, while the economic benefit derived from it remained at a minimum. Another point of similarity was that investments took the form of monumental projects. We may view the gigantic hydroelectric dams, the steel mills, the marble halls of the Moscow subway, and the skyscrapers of Stalinist architecture as so many pyramids built by a modern pharaoh. Hydroelectric plants do produce energy, and steel mills do turn out steel, but if the steel and energy are used to produce more dams and steel mills, the effect on the economy is not very different from that of building pyramids.

Our theoretical framework tells us that in the far-from-equilibrium conditions of a closed society there must be distortions that would be inconceivable in an open society. What better demonstration could one ask for than the Soviet economy? The communist system attributes no value to capital; more exactly, it does not recognize the concept of property. As a result, economic activity under the Soviet system is simply not economic. To make it so, the party must be removed from its role as the guardian and allocator of capital. It was on this point that all reform attempts were bound to come to grief.

Interestingly, the failure of economic reforms served to accelerate the process of disintegration because it demonstrated the need for political reforms. With the advent of perestroika in the Soviet Union, the process of disintegration entered its terminal phase because the reform was primarily political and, as I have mentioned previously, the golden period was missing so that the reform produced little or no economic benefit. As living standards started to decline, public opinion turned against the regime, leading to a catastrophic disintegration that culminated in the total collapse of the Soviet Union.

The pattern is almost identical with the one we can observe in financial markets—with one major difference: In financial markets, the boom-bust process seems to manifest itself as a process of acceleration, whereas in the case of the Soviet system the complete cycle comprised two phases, one a process of slowdown culminating in the static disequilibrium of the Stalin regime, the other a process of acceleration leading to a catastrophic collapse.*

I then went on to point out that it is possible to find a similar two-phase boom-bust process in financial markets. That is where the illustration turned into a flight of fancy. I cited the case of the U.S. banking system, which became rigidly regulated after it collapsed in 1933. It remained in hibernation for about thirty-five years. In 1972 I wrote an investment memorandum entitled "The Case for Growth Banks" contending that a moribund industry was about to come to life. The industry was highly regulated, managements were stodgy and risk-averse, and stock prices did not reflect earnings, but all that was about to change. A new breed of bankers was incubating at Citibank, and they were slowly fanning out into the country. Under their management, banks started using their capital more aggressively, and soon they would need to stimulate their stock prices in order to raise additional capital and pursue acquisitions. The signal was given when Citibank hosted a meeting for security analysts—an unheard-of event. My bouquet of recommended stocks rose by 50 percent within a year. Soon thereafter came the oil crisis of 1973, and international banks recycled the surplus of the oil-producing countries, which led to the international lending boom of the 1970s. The banking system swung over into

*Condensed from Chapter 4 of George Soros, *Opening the Soviet System* (London: Weidenfeld and Nicolson, 1990; reprinted by CEU Press, Budapest).

dynamic disequilibrium, culminating in the international banking crisis of 1982.

The point of this far-fetched comparison between the rise and fall of the Soviet system and the fall and rise of the U.S. banking system is to show that far-from-equilibrium conditions can prevail at either extreme of change and changelessness. Closed society is the obverse of revolution and chaos; a reflexive process is at work at both extremes, the difference being in the time scale. In a closed society, little happens over a long period; in a revolution, much happens over a short period. In either case, perceptions are far removed from reality.

This was a significant insight. Discussing boom-bust processes in the context of financial markets, one is normally led to think in terms of acceleration. But the trend may also find expression in the form of deceleration, or lack of change. Once I became aware of this possibility, I could even find an actual example in the stock market: the case of bank stocks from the Great Depression to 1972.* In history, the cases of changelessness, or static disequilibrium, are much more common.

A Conceptual Framework

The foregoing discussion is helpful in establishing a conceptual framework that divides historical situations into three categories: static disequilibrium, near-equilibrium, and dynamic disequilibrium. The possibility of static equilibrium is ruled out by the fact

---

*I ran into a similar case in Sweden in the 1960s. The Swedish stock market was totally isolated from the rest of the world; one had to sell Swedish shares held abroad to buy Swedish shares in Sweden. Companies were allowed to retain their earnings without paying taxes by setting up various reserves, but they could not use those reserves to increase dividends. Shares were valued on the basis of dividend yields. As a result, there were tremendous divergences in price-earnings ratios, and the best companies were tremendously undervalued (until I came along and pointed out the undervaluation in several reports). Swedish shares held abroad rose to hefty premiums, but due to the restrictions on trading, the interest I awakened could not be satisfied, and eventually the market went back to sleep until regulations were changed.

that participants always base their decisions on a biased interpretation of reality. Correspondence between outcomes and expectations is hard to come by, and even if it occurs it may be due to the prevailing bias influencing the prevailing state of affairs rather than participants acting on the basis of perfect knowledge. This leaves three possibilities.

One is that the reflexive interplay between the cognitive and participating functions prevents thinking and reality from drifting too far apart. People learn from experience; they act on the basis of biased views, but there is a critical process at work that tends to correct the bias. Perfect knowledge remains unattainable, but there is at least a tendency for thinking and reality to come closer together. The participating function ensures that the real world, as experienced by the participants, is constantly changing, yet people are sufficiently well grounded in a set of fundamental values that the participants' bias cannot get too far out of line with real events—in other words, near-equilibrium. This state of affairs characterizes open society, as in the West. This kind of society is closely associated with a critical mode of thinking. We may call this the "normal" relationship between thinking and reality, because we are familiar with it from our own experience.

We can encounter a second set of conditions in which the participants' views are quite far removed from the way things really are and the two show no tendency to come closer together—in some circumstances they may be driven even farther apart. At one extreme, there are regimes that operate with an ideological bias, and they are unwilling to adjust to changing circumstances. They try to force reality into their conceptual framework even though they cannot possibly succeed. Under the pressure of the prevailing dogma, social conditions may also become quite rigid, but reality is liable to remain quite far removed from its authorized interpretation. Indeed, in the absence of a corrective mechanism the two are liable to drift even further apart, because no amount of coercion can prevent changes in the real world, while the dogma is liable to remain unbending. This state of affairs is characteristic of closed societies, such as the Soviet Union or the religious dictatorship in Iran. This is static disequilibrium.

At the other extreme, events may unfold so rapidly that the participants' understanding cannot keep up with them and the situation spins out of control. The divergence between prevailing views and actual conditions may become unsustainable, precipitating a revolution or some other kind of breakdown. Again, there is a wide divergence between thinking and reality, but it is bound to be transitory. The ancien régime that has been swept away will eventually be replaced by a new regime. This is the case of regime change, or dynamic disequilibrium. The French Revolution is the classic example, but the Industrial Revolution and the current communications revolution also qualify.

The tripartite division I have just introduced can be compared to the three states of water found in nature: liquid, solid, and gaseous. The analogy may be far-fetched, but it is intriguing. To make it meaningful, we need to identify the two demarcation lines that separate near-equilibrium from far-from-equilibrium conditions. In the case of water, the demarcation lines are expressed in degrees of temperature. In the case of history, the demarcation lines cannot be so precise and quantitative, but they must provide an observable distinction; otherwise the whole framework remains a mere flight of fancy.

To establish what Popper would have called the "criterion of demarcation," I should like to invoke the concepts of closed and open society. These are ideal types, corresponding to static disequilibrium and near-equilibrium conditions.* I constructed them some

---

*Open society and closed society constitute ideal types. Modeling ideal types is a legitimate method for the study of society. It was legitimated by Max Weber and employed by such latter-day practitioners as Ernest Gellner. It has the advantage—or drawback—that it can play not only an informative but also a normative role. Perfect competition as postulated by economic theory is such an ideal type.

forty years ago, in the early 1960s, under the influence of Karl Popper's *Open Society and Its Enemies.* *

Open Versus Closed Society

The models were based on different attitudes toward historical change. I distinguished between a traditional mode of thinking, which ignores the possibility of change and accepts the prevailing state of affairs as the only one possible (that is, organic society); a critical mode, which explores the possibilities of change to the fullest (open society); and a dogmatic mode, which cannot tolerate uncertainty (closed society). I argued that the three forms of social organization correspond to the three modes of thinking (organic/ traditional; open/critical; closed/dogmatic). I felt a need to distinguish between organic and closed society because there is all the difference in the world between the traditional mode of thinking, which ignores the possibility of an alternative, and a dogmatic mode, which forcibly seeks to eliminate the alternatives. Organic society, like the Garden of Eden, is located in the mythical past: Innocence, once lost, cannot be regained. For practical purposes, the choice is between open and closed society.

Needless to say, the correspondence between modes of thinking and social structures is less than perfect. Both open and closed society leave something to be desired that, by definition, could only be

---

*Istvan Rev claims that my preoccupation with ideal types and criteria of demarcation is misguided. History is a process, reflexivity is a process, and I seek to interpret history as a reflexive process. Why should I try to reduce processes conceptually to states? It's a valid question. My aim is to show that the historical process can produce *qualitatively* different states of affairs, as different as water, ice, and steam. The models should be construed as aids to the understanding of reality, not as representations of reality. In other words, they should not be taken too literally. Still, I do take the concept of open society seriously, both as a representation of reality and as a goal worth pursuing. This has caused me enormous conceptual difficulties that I will recount as we go along here and in Chapter 5. I do *not* take the distinction between humdrum and historic events very seriously, and I trust the reader will not do so either.

found in the other. Closed society offers the certainty and permanence that is lacking in open society, and open society offers the freedom that is denied to the individual in closed society. As a consequence, the two principles of social organization stand in opposition to each other. Open society recognizes our fallibility; closed society denies it.

When I established this conceptual framework, in the early 1960s,* I did not dare to assert the superiority of open society, because I could not prove it and it was not supported by the evidence: Communism was still gaining ground. I asserted that a genuine choice is involved (which is true), and I came down firmly on the side of open society. I believed in open society strongly enough that, when the opportunity presented itself, I translated my conviction into action. I shall summarize my philanthropic activities because they are relevant.

I established the Open Society Fund in 1979. Its mission, as I formulated it at the time, was to help open up closed societies, to help make open societies more viable, and to foster a critical mode of thinking. After an abortive start in South Africa, I concentrated on the countries under communist rule—especially my native country, Hungary. The formula was simple: Any activity or association that was not under the supervision or control of the authorities created alternatives and thereby weakened the monopoly of dogma. My foundation in Hungary, established in 1985 as a joint venture with the Hungarian Academy of Science, acted as the sponsor of civil society. Not only did it support civil society, but civil society supported it; as a result, it was exempt from many of the unintended adverse consequences from which foundations usually suffer. Charity tends to turn the recipients into objects of charity; applicants tell the foundation what it wants to hear, and if they receive a grant they

*Reproduced almost verbatim in *Opening the Soviet System*.

proceed to do what they wanted to do in the first place. In Hungary, none of this applied. The foundation empowered civil society to do what it wanted to do in any case, and there was no need for controls: Civil society protected the foundation by alerting us when our funds were misused. I remember one occasion when we were warned that the association for the blind, which received a grant for talking books, misused the grant. Who could ask for better monitoring with no effort on our part?

Encouraged by the success of the Hungarian foundation, I became a philanthropist in spite of my critical attitude toward philanthropy. As the Soviet empire started to crumble, I threw myself into the fray. I realized that in a revolutionary period many things become possible that would be inconceivable at other times. I felt that with the help of my boom-bust model I understood the situation better than most others; I had a strong commitment to open society; and I had the financial means to back it up. This put me in a unique position, and I spared no effort. I increased the size of my foundations a hundredfold—from $3 million to $300 million annually—in the space of a couple of years.

Only in the course of the Soviet collapse did I discover a flaw in my conceptual framework: It treated open and closed society as alternatives. The dichotomy might have been appropriate during the Cold War, when two diametrically opposed principles of social organization were confronting each other in deadly conflict, but it does not fit the conditions that have prevailed since the Cold War ended.

I was forced to realize that the collapse of a closed society does not automatically lead to the establishment of an open society; on the contrary, it may lead to the breakdown of authority and the disintegration of society. A weak state may be as much a threat to open society as an authoritarian state.*

I made another discovery: People living in open societies do not

---

*Stephen Holmes, "What Russia Teaches Us Now: How Weak States Threaten Freedom," *The American Prospect* (July-August 1997): 30–39.

really believe in open society as a universal idea. They may be willing to defend democratic institutions in their own country, but they are not necessarily willing to make any great sacrifices to establish democratic institutions in other countries. This was a bitter pill to swallow. When I rushed in to establish Open Society Foundations in one country after another, I thought I was blazing a trail that others would follow; when I looked back, nobody was behind me. This was not only a disappointment but also a flaw in my conceptual framework, indeed the worst error in my analysis. I was forced to painstakingly reexamine the concept of open society; the framework I present here is the result of that reexamination.

Instead of a dichotomy between open and closed society, I now envisage open society occupying a precarious middle ground, where it is threatened by dogmatic beliefs of all kinds—some that would impose a closed society, others that would lead to the disintegration of society. Open society represents near-equilibrium conditions; alternatives include not only the static disequilibrium of closed society but also the dynamic disequilibrium of chaos and disorientation.

I had been aware of certain deficiencies in open societies that could lead to their breakdown, but I assumed that the breakdown would lead to the formation of a closed society. This was consequent to the dichotomy I had established—that open and closed society were the only alternatives; what one system lacked could only be found in the other. I did not realize that the conditions of dynamic disequilibrium could persist indefinitely, or, more exactly, that a society could hover on the edge of chaos without actually going over the edge. This was a curious oversight on my part, since I was aware of the contention of evolutionary systems theory that life occurs at the edge of chaos.

The actual path followed by history cannot be defined, but we can try to introduce some distinctions into the space within which it occurs. That is what I did when, under the influence of Karl Popper, I distinguished between open and closed society. Today, in the light of experience, I need to redefine the space in which history unfolds and recognize an additional category: dynamic disequilibrium. This leads to a tripartite division similar to water, ice, and steam: open society (near-equilibrium), closed society (static disequilibrium), and chaos or revolution (dynamic disequilibrium). Therefore, in occupying that precarious middle ground, open society is threatened from two sides: by dynamic disequilibrium as well as by static disequilibrium. This is a rather different framework from the simple dichotomy between open and closed society with which I had started. The analogy with water, ice, and steam is apt, because open society is fluid, closed society rigid, and revolution chaotic.

These three cases constitute ideal types—or "strange attractors," to borrow another term from chaos theory. Events take on a different character within their orbit. If we can learn nothing else about history but this, we have learned something valuable. Financial markets behave one way near equilibrium and another way far from equilibrium, and the same is true of history in general. For instance, many things are possible in revolutionary situations that would be inconceivable in normal times. Recognizing the opportunities when they arise is the height of statesmanship, as well as the key to success in financial markets.

I have been fortunate to have a pointed understanding of the difference between near-equilibrium and far-from-equilibrium conditions, something I learned from my father. He had been a prisoner of war during World War I, and he escaped from a camp in Siberia during the Russian Revolution. He went through incredible adventures that taught him the difference between normal and revolutionary conditions. He regaled me with his stories when I was a child. When I was fourteen, in 1944, the Germans occupied Hungary and engaged in genocide against the Jews; I might not have survived had it not been for my father. He realized that this was a far-from-equilibrium situation in which the normal rules did not apply. He made arrangements—not only for his family but for many others around him—to assume false identities.* Most of us survived. At the same time, I saw what happened to those who were less well prepared to cope with these exceptional conditions: They were put in labor camps, deported to Auschwitz, or shot on the banks of the Danube. This was the formative experience of my life, the reason why I take the concept of open society so seriously.

I learned that the same rules do not apply at all times. It is not simply that different rules apply in revolutionary conditions than in normal times; it is the distinguishing feature of dynamic disequilibrium that the rules are also subject to change, and what is the right decision at one moment may be wrong the next. It is difficult to appreciate the full import of this statement, and it is even more difficult to arrive at the right decisions at the right moments. Bureaucratic institutions, in particular, are constitutionally ill-suited for the task. That is why they tend to break down and collapse if the dynamic disequilibrium becomes too severe and events slip out of control.

I am acutely aware that the view of history that I have presented here is highly personal and idiosyncratic. The fact that I had to revise a dichotomy and replace it with a tripartite division should warn us how precarious these divisions are. That does not detract from the value of the insights they provide, but it reminds us forcefully that the categories have been introduced by us and are not found in reality.

This raises the question whether the categories I have introduced, especially the concept of open society, has any relevance to today's conditions. I have no doubt that the distinction between open and closed society was relevant to the Cold War; indeed, it

---

*Tivadar Soros, *Maskerado: Dancing around Death in Nazi Hungary* (Edinburgh: Cannongate Books, October 2000).

provides a better insight into what was at stake than the distinction between capitalism and communism. I also know that the concept of open society is meaningful to me personally. The crucial question is whether it does or should have a meaning for society at large. The purpose of this book is to show that it should.

Demarcation Lines

Let me now return to the question I posed earlier: What separates near-equilibrium from far-from-equilibrium conditions? When does a boom-bust sequence or some other disequilibrium process destroy the near-equilibrium conditions of open society? We have seen that the two-way interaction between thinking and reality can easily lead to excesses that can push the situation in the direction of either rigidity or chaos. For open society to prevail, there must be some anchor that prevents the participants' thinking from being dragged too far away from reality. What is that anchor?

In answering the question, we first must distinguish between expectations and values. After all, decisions are based not only on people's perceptions of reality but also on the values they bring to bear. In the case of expectations, the anchor is easy to identify: It is reality itself. As long as people realize that there is a difference between thinking and reality, the facts provide a criterion by which the validity of peoples' expectations can be judged. Reflexivity may render events unpredictable, but once they come to pass they become uniquely determined, so they can be used to decide whether our predictions were correct. As we have seen, predictions can influence the outcome, so the outcome is not a fully independent criterion for judging the validity of the theories on which the expectations were based. That is why our understanding is fallible and we can speak only of near-equilibrium conditions. Nevertheless, reality constitutes a useful criterion.

In conditions of static disequilibrium, thinking and reality are far removed from each other and exhibit no tendency to come closer together. In an organic society, the distinction between thinking and reality is simply not made: The world is ruled by spirits. In a closed society, expectations are anchored in dogma, not reality, and expectations that deviate from the official dogma cannot even be voiced. There is a built-in gap between the official version of reality and the facts; its removal brings immense relief and a sense of liberation.

In conditions of dynamic disequilibrium, we have the opposite state of affairs: The situation is changing too rapidly for peoples' understanding, causing a chasm between thinking and reality. The interpretation of events cannot keep up with the pace of events; people become disoriented and events run out of control. Therefore reality can no longer act as an anchor for expectations. That is what happened during the disintegration of the Soviet system. As I shall contend, our own society may also be on the verge of dynamic disequilibrium, partly because of the rapid pace of change and partly because of a deficiency of shared values.

The Question of Values

What are the values that are necessary to sustain the near-equilibrium conditions of open society? Here I am on more uncertain ground than in the case of expectations, for both subjective and objective reasons, and my argument is more tentative. I have already mentioned the subjective consideration: I have been trained as an economist and have always struggled to figure out how market values relate to the values that guide decisions in other spheres of existence—social, political, or personal. Often I am genuinely baffled, and I suspect I am not alone in that regard. Contemporary Western society seems confused about values in general and about the relationship between market values and social values in particular. So the subjective difficulty merges into an objective one. Let me state the problem as I see it, first on the theoretical and then on the practical level.

On the theoretical level, cognition has an objective criterion—namely, reality—by which it can be judged. As we have seen, the criterion is not totally independent, but it is independent enough to be called objective: No participant is in a position to impose his or her will on the course of events. By contrast, values cannot be judged by any objective criterion because they are not supposed to correspond to reality: The criteria by which things are to be judged are selected by the person or group that adopts them. In other words, values are valid because we believe in them. This makes them much more reflexive than expectations. Not all expectations can validate themselves because they relate to reality, and the facts—as they evolve—impose an iron constraint on the validity of expectations. But values are not constrained by reality. Compared to cognitive notions, they can vary over a much wider range. They do not even need to be consistent, as long as people can persuade themselves of their validity at the time they act upon them. They do not even need to relate to this world. Many religions attribute greater importance to the other world than to this one. This is what makes any discussion of values so difficult. Economic theory did well to take them as given. With the help of that methodological device, economic theory established the concept of equilibrium. Although I have been critical of the concept, it has been indispensable for my analysis. I could show how far-from-equilibrium conditions could arise in financial markets only because the concept of equilibrium (from which reality could diverge) was well developed. No similar concept is available for the nonmarket sector of society.

I have defined "equilibrium" as the correspondence between expectations and outcomes. How can I apply that definition to the values that are supposed to hold together open society? I shall try to establish a belief in open society as a necessary condition for the existence of an open society, but it will not be an easy argument: Open society is a difficult concept to grasp; it is even more difficult to treat as an ideal. Open society is based on the recognition of our fallibility. Perfection eludes us; we must therefore be satisfied with second-best: an imperfect society that holds itself open to improvement. Is that an ideal that can fire people's imagination?

Surely it has fired mine. But if I am the only one, I am no better than a fanatic. This book is an attempt to convince others to place their faith in open society as a desirable form of social organization.

On a practical level, contemporary society seems to be suffering from an acute deficiency of shared social values. Values do not exist in a vacuum; they are reflexive. They are shaped—but not determined—by experience. Shared values are the result of shared experiences. People have bemoaned the decline of shared social values throughout history, but there is one factor at play that makes the present different from earlier times: the spread of market values that give precedence to self-interest over the common interest. Not only is the pursuit of self-interest identified with the common interest through the intercession of the invisible hand; the pursuit of the common interest is condemned as the source of all kinds of corruption, conflict, and inefficiency—and not without justification. With morality in decline, market values have penetrated into areas of society that were previously governed by nonmarket considerations. These heretofore off-limits areas include personal relations, politics, and professions such as law and medicine. Moreover, there has been a subtle and gradual but nevertheless profound transformation in the way the market mechanism operates. First, lasting relationships have been replaced by individual transactions. The general store—where owner and customer are on familiar terms—has yielded to the supermarket and more recently to the Internet.

Second, national economies have been superseded by an international economy, but the international community, insofar as it exists, shares few social values.

Transactional Society

The replacement of relationships by transactions is an ongoing, historical process that will never be carried to its logical conclusion, but it is well advanced—far more advanced than in the early 1960s, when I arrived in this country and first observed it. I came from England and was struck by the difference: Relations in the United States were much easier to establish and abandon. The trend has progressed even farther since then. There are still marriages and families, but in investment banking, for instance, transactions have almost completely superseded relationships. This offers a clear example of the changes occurring in many other spheres of activity.

When I started work in the City of London in the 1950s, it was almost impossible to transact any business without having a prior relationship. It was not a question of what you knew but of whom you knew. That was the main reason why I left London: Since I was not well connected there, my chances were much better in New York. In a short time, I established regular trading contacts with leading firms even though I was working in a relatively unknown brokerage house; I could not have done that in London. But even in New York the underwriting of securities was still entirely governed by relationships: Firms participated in syndicates in a certain pecking order, and it was a major event when a firm moved up or down a bracket. All this has changed. Each transaction now stands on its own, and investment bankers compete for every piece of business.

The difference between transactions and relationships has been well analyzed by game theory in the form of the prisoners' dilemma: Two suspected crooks have been caught and are interrogated. If one suspect provides evidence against the other she can earn a reduced sentence, but the accomplice is more certain to be convicted. Taken together they will do better if they remain loyal to each other, but separately each can profit at the other's expense. The analysis shows that in the case of an individual transaction it may be rational to betray but in a lasting relationship it pays to be loyal. This can be taken as a demonstration of how cooperative behavior can develop with the passage of time, but it can also be used to show how cooperation and loyalty can be undermined by replacing relationships with transactions.* Globalization works in the same direction by increasing the scope for transactions and diminishing the dependence on relationships.

All of this relates to the deficiency of shared values in contemporary society. We are inclined to take social or moral values for granted. We refer to them as "intrinsic" or "fundamental," implying that their validity is somehow independent of prevailing conditions. Nothing could be farther from the truth. If we could take social values as given—as economic theory does with market values—we would have no difficulty in establishing something approaching equilibrium conditions. But that is not the case. Social values are reflexive. They are influenced by social conditions and, in turn, play a role in making social conditions what they are. People may believe that God handed down the Ten Commandments and, doing so, may make society more just and stable. Conversely, the absence of moral constraints is liable to generate injustice and instability.

A transactional society undermines social values and loosens moral constraints. Social values express a concern for others. They imply that the individual belongs to a community—be it family, tribe, nation, or humankind—whose common interest takes prece-

---

*Robert Axelrod, *The Complexity of Cooperation: Agent-Based Models of Competition and Collaboration* (Princeton: Princeton Studies in Complexity, Princeton University Press, 1997) and *The Evolution of Cooperation* (New York: Basic Books, 1984); Anatol Rapoport and Albert M. Chammah, with Carol J. Orwant, *Prisoner's Dilemma: A Study in Conflict and Cooperation* (Ann Arbor: University of Michigan Press, 1965).

dence over individual self-interests. Yet a global economy is anything but a community. It contains people of different traditions for whom most other people represent the other, not the community to which one belongs. In a tough competitive environment, it is hard enough to have consideration for others; to extend that consideration to all humanity is asking for the impossible. The situation is aggravated by the prevailing creed of market fundamentalism. It maintains that the common interest is best served by everyone pursuing her own self-interest. This gives the pursuit of self-interest a moral blessing. Those who adopt the creed tend to come out ahead because they are not encumbered by moral scruples in a dog-eat-dog world—and such success can be self-reinforcing.

We should not exaggerate. The external constraints imposed by the community may have been undermined by the development of a global, transactional economy, and the pursuit of self-interest may have been endowed with moral justification, yet some internal constraints are bound to remain. Even if people have been transformed into single-minded competitors, they were not born that way. The transformation has occurred quite recently, and it remains incomplete. Although we are closer to a transactional society than at any time in history, a purely transactional society could never exist. People seem to have an innate need for social values. As sentient beings, they cannot avoid being aware of their own ephemeral nature, their mortality. They tend to reach out for values that extend beyond their narrow selves. Even when they pursue their self-interest, they seem to have a need to justify their behavior by appealing to principles that go beyond themselves. As Henri Bergson pointed out, morality can have two sources: tribal belonging and the universal human condition. It is in the latter that open society must be anchored. I shall try to develop this argument in the next chapter.

CHAPTER 5

Open Society as an Ideal

If my contention that we suffer from a deficiency of shared
social values is correct, then the supreme challenge of our time
is to establish a set of fundamental values that applies to a
largely transactional, global society. I should like to take up
that challenge. I propose the concept of open society as an ideal to
which our global society should aspire. My contention is that it is
in the interest of open societies to help foster the development of
open societies throughout the world and to establish the international institutions appropriate to a global open society. I should like
to gather sufficient support for this idea to be able to translate it
into reality.

This sounds like a utopian endeavor. People are not even aware
of the concept of open society; they are very far from regarding it as
a goal worth striving for. Yet the project is not as utopian as it

sounds. It should be remembered that open society is a very peculiar ideal. It is based on the recognition that our understanding is imperfect and that a perfect society is beyond our reach; we must content ourselves with the second best: an imperfect society that holds itself open to, and strives for, improvement. Using this definition, the United States, the European Union, and many other parts of the world come very close to qualifying as open societies. They certainly qualify with regard to being imperfect. What is missing is an understanding of the concept of open society and its acceptance as an ideal. But even in this respect, reality is not too far removed from the desired goal. Representative democracy is an essential ingredient of the open society; so is a market economy. Representative democracy prevails in many countries, and the promotion of democracy in other parts of the world has become an acknowledged policy objective for the Western democracies. The market economy has gone truly global in the past ten years, and its principles are being promoted with truly missionary zeal.

So what is wrong? I believe the promotion of market principles has gone too far and became too one-sided. Market fundamentalists believe that the common interest is best served by the untrammeled pursuit of self-interest. This belief is false, yet it has become very influential. It stands in the way of a global open society. We are very close to that goal, but we cannot get there unless we recognize the errors of market fundamentalism and correct the disparity between the economic and political organization of the world.

It should be emphasized that market fundamentalism is not diametrically opposed to open society the way communism or religious fundamentalism are. It is merely a distortion. Friedrich Hayek, whose ideas have been vulgarized by latter-day market fundamentalists, was a firm believer in the open society. Both he and Karl Popper wanted to protect the freedom of the individual against the threat emanating from collectivist creeds such as communism and national socialism; they only differed about the means by which it could be accomplished. Popper advocated "piecemeal social engineering"; Hayek put his faith in the market mechanism because he was preoccupied with the unintended adverse consequences of state controls. His preoccupation was carried to extremes by his followers in the "Chicago school." The pursuit of self-interest has been promoted into a universal principle that permeates all aspects of existence: not just individual choice as expressed in markets but also social choice as expressed in politics. It even extends its reach to the law of contracts; it governs not just individual behavior but also the behavior of states, not to mention the selfish gene. There is an uncomfortable similarity between market fundamentalism and communism: Both have a foundation in social science—market economics in the one case, Marxism (which is a more comprehensive theory of social systems, including economics) in the other.

I regard market fundamentalism as a greater threat to open society today than communism. Communism and even socialism are discredited, but market fundamentalism is ascendant. If there are any shared values in the world today, they are based on the belief that people should be allowed to pursue their self-interests and that it is both futile and counterproductive to expect them to be motivated by the common interest. Of course, there is no general agreement on this point, but it is certainly more popular than the belief in open society. Moreover, market fundamentalism is receiving powerful reinforcement from the positive results that market-oriented policies are producing, particularly among those who are the beneficiaries of those policies. To the extent that politics is influenced by money, these people tend to be the most influential.

So my task in this chapter is twofold: to demonstrate the errors of market fundamentalism, and to establish the principles of open society. The first part is relatively easy. I have already shown that financial markets do not necessarily tend toward equilibrium. All I need to point out now is that social values do not find expression in markets. Markets reflect the existing distribution of assets; they are not designed to redistribute those assets according to the principles of social justice. It follows that social justice is outside the competence of the market economy. Economics theory takes the distribution of wealth as given, and it claims that any policy that would allow the winners to compensate the losers and still have something left over would enhance welfare. It remains silent on the question of whether the winners should compensate the losers, because that is a question of social values and economics seeks to remain value-free. Based on this argument, fundamentalists argue that the best policy is to give markets free rein.

If markets produced general equilibrium, and if the issues of social justice were taken care of, they would have a valid argument; but neither condition is met. This raises the need for some kind of political intervention in the economy to maintain stability and reduce inequality. The trouble is that political decisions are even more imperfect than markets. This is a powerful argument in favor of free markets, the most powerful in the armory of market fundamentalists, but they tend to abuse it. It does not follow from the fact that political decisions interfere with the efficiency of markets that politics should be kept out of the economy. Politics may be corrupt and inefficient, but we cannot do without it. The fundamentalist argument may apply to a perfect world, but it does not apply to the second best. Open society is the quest for the second best.

The second part of my task is more difficult. Open society is not an easy concept, and I have not done a very good job in clarifying it. On the contrary, I seem to have done my best to confuse the reader. I have used the term in at least three different ways. I equated open society with near-equilibrium conditions; I also said that open society is an ideal type that can be approximated but not attained in reality. There seems to be a contradiction between these two statements, because near-equilibrium can be attained in reality. Now I want to establish open society as a goal worth striving for. All of this is very confusing. Is open society an ideal, or is it a description of actual conditions? More specifically, are Western democracies open societies or not? The answer is that open society is both an ideal and a description of reality, because open society is a very unusual ideal: an imperfect society that holds itself open to improvement. And the Western democracies qualify in most respects except one: They do not recognize open society as a desirable goal. Even if they accept it for their own country, they do not recognize it as a universal principle that ought to serve as an objective of national policy. International relations are still based on the principle of national sovereignty. Could open society serve as a universal principle? Could it be reconciled with the principle of national sovereignty? That is the crucial problem facing us today.

I shall address that problem in the second part of this book, where I deal with the present moment in history. In this chapter I want to examine some of the conceptual difficulties that open society as a universal principle encounters. This chapter has the character of a philosophical exploration in preparation for settling down to a more practical consideration of the crucial issue I have identified.

The Relevance of Universal Ideas

Open society stands for freedom, democracy, rule of law, human rights, social justice, and social responsibility as a universal idea. One of the obstacles to the adoption of open society as a common goal is a fairly widespread rejection of universal ideas. I discovered this after I set up my network of foundations and, frankly speaking, I was surprised by it. In establishing my foundation network, I had no difficulty finding people who were inspired by the principles of open society even if they did not use the same word. I did not need to explain what I meant by open society: Everybody understood that it stood for the opposite of the closed society in which they lived. The attitude of the West was more disconcerting. At first I thought that people in the West were just slow to recognize a historic opportunity; eventually I was forced to come to the conclusion that they genuinely did not care enough about open society as a universal idea to make much of an effort to help the formerly communist countries make the transition. I had been misled by the propaganda of the Cold War. All the talk about freedom and democracy had been just that: propaganda.

After the collapse of the Soviet system, the appeal of open society as an ideal started to fade even in the formerly communist countries. People got caught up in the struggle for survival, and those who continued to be preoccupied with the common good while others were lining their pockets had to ask themselves whether they were clinging to the values of a bygone age—and often they were. People grew suspicious of universal ideas. Communism had been a universal idea and look where it had led!

This forced me to submit the concept of open society to a thorough reconsideration. I had to recognize that the aversion to universal ideas is well founded. They can be very dangerous, especially if they are carried to their logical conclusion. It is a feature of our fallibility that ideas can take on a life of their own, becoming far removed from reality and yet exerting an influence on it. By the same token, we cannot do without universal ideas. (The pursuit of self-interest is also a universal idea, even if it is not recognized as such.) The world in which we live is just too complicated to make any sense of it without some guiding principles. This line of thought led me to the concept of fallibility as a universal idea, and I tried to base the concept of open society on the recognition of our fallibility.

The Enlightenment

Here I ran into insuperable difficulties. The recognition of our fallibility is what makes a society open; but it is not sufficient, by itself, to keep society together. Something else is needed—some concern for others, some shared values. These values have to be infused by the recognition of our fallibility, but they cannot be derived from it by logic. If that were possible, the very idea of our fallibility would be brought into question. This means that open society as a universal idea cannot be properly defined; every society must form its own definition, yet the definition must incorporate some general principles, including fallibility and a concern for others.

Karl Popper was opposed to defining concepts from left to right: *Open society is,* and then follows a definition. He preferred to proceed from right to left: Describe something, and then put a label on it. This cluttered his writings with "isms." Nevertheless, I try to follow Popper's advice. In my foundation network, we have never defined open society. Had we done so, the organization would have become more rigid; as it is, flexibility has been our hallmark. But if I want the concept of open society to be generally accepted, I must say what it is. I must show how the recognition of our fallibility leads to the principles of open society.

As I have been at pains to point out, this will not be an easy task. Every philosophical argument is liable to raise endless new questions. If I tried to start from scratch, I could not make much progress because I would get caught in a web of my own weaving. I speak from experience: It has happened to me. Once I spent three years of my life trying to work out my philosophy, and I ended up where I began.

Fortunately, I do not have to start from ground zero. The philosophers of the Enlightenment, Kant foremost among them, tried to deduce universally valid imperatives from the dictates of reason. Their imperfect success corroborates the postulate of fallibility and provides a basis for my argument.

The Enlightenment constituted a giant step forward from the moral and political principles that prevailed previously. Until then, moral and political authority were derived from external sources, both divine and temporal. Allowing reason to decide what is true and false, what is right and wrong, was a tremendous innovation. It marked the beginning of the modern age. Whether we recognize it or not, the Enlightenment has provided the foundations for our ideas about politics and economics—indeed, for our entire outlook on the world. The philosophers of the Enlightenment are no longer read—I personally find them hard to read—but their ideas have become ingrained in our way of thinking. The rule of reason, the idea of a social contract as the basis of society and state, the supremacy of science, the universal brotherhood of humanity— these were some of their main themes. The political, social, and moral values of the Enlightenment were admirably stated in the Declaration of Independence, and that document continues to be an inspiration for people throughout the world.

The Enlightenment did not spring into existence out of nowhere: It had its roots in Greek philosophy and to a lesser extent in Christianity, which in turn built on the monotheistic tradition of the Old Testament. It should be noted that all of these ideas were couched in universal terms, with the exception of the Old Testament, in which a great deal of tribal history is mixed in with monotheism. Instead of accepting tradition as the ultimate authority, the Enlightenment subjected tradition to critical examination. Traditional relations could be replaced by contractual ones: hence the social contract. The results were exhilarating. The creative energies of the human intellect were unleashed. No wonder that the new approach was carried to excess! In the French Revolution, traditional authority was overturned and reason anointed as the ultimate arbiter. Reason proved unequal to the task, and the fervor of 1789 deteriorated into the terror of 1793. But the basic tenets of the Enlightenment were not repudiated; on the contrary, Napoleon's armies carried the ideas of modernity to the rest of Europe.

Modernity's achievements are beyond compare. Scientific

method produced amazing discoveries, and technology allowed their conversion to productive use. Humankind has come to dominate nature. Economic enterprises took advantage of the opportunities, markets served to match supply and demand, and both production and living standards rose to heights that would have been unimaginable in any previous age.

In spite of these impressive achievements, reason could not quite live up to the expectations attached to it, especially in the social and political arena. The gap between intentions and outcomes could not be closed; indeed, the more radical the intentions, the more disappointing the outcomes. This applies, in my opinion, both to communism and to market fundamentalism, both of which claim to be grounded in science. I want to highlight one particular case of unintended consequences because it is particularly relevant to the current situation. When the original political ideas of the Enlightenment were translated into practice, they served to reinforce the idea of the nation-state. In trying to establish the rule of reason, people rose up against their rulers, and the power they captured was the power of the sovereign. That is how the nation-state, in which sovereignty belongs to the people, was born. Whatever its merits, it is a far cry from its universalist inspiration.

In culture, the debunking of traditional authority gave rise to an intellectual ferment that produced great art and literature, but after a long period of exciting experimentation, by the second half of the twentieth century all authority had been challenged and much of the inspiration seemed to dissipate. The range of possibilities has become too broad to provide the discipline that is required for artistic creation. Some artists and writers manage to establish their own private language, but the common ground seems to have disintegrated.

The same kind of malaise seems to affect society at large. The philosophers of the Enlightenment, Kant foremost among them, sought to establish universally valid principles of morality based on the universal attributes of reason. The task Kant set himself was to show that reason provides a better basis for morality than traditional, external authority. But in our modern, transactional society, the reason for having any kind of morality has been brought into question. The need for some kind of moral guidance lingers; indeed, it is perhaps more intensely felt than in the past because it goes unsatisfied. But the principles and precepts that could provide that guidance are in doubt. Why bother about the truth when a proposition does not need to be true to be effective? Why be honest when it is success, not honesty or virtue, that gains people's respect? Although social values and moral precepts are in doubt, there can be no doubt about the value of money. That is how money has come to usurp the role of intrinsic values. The ideas of the Enlightenment permeate our view of the world, and its noble aspirations continue to shape our expectations, but the prevailing mood is one of money-grubbing.

It is high time to subject reason, as construed by the Enlightenment, to the same kind of critical examination that the Enlightenment inflicted on the dominant external authorities, both divine and temporal. We have now lived in the Age of Reason for the past two hundred years—long enough to discover that reason has its limitations. We are ready to enter the Age of Fallibility. The results may be equally exhilarating and, having learned from past experience, we may be able to avoid some of the excesses characteristic of the dawning of a new age.

Moral Philosophy

We need to begin the reconstruction of morality and social values by accepting their reflexive character. This is self-consistent and leaves ample scope for trial and error. It will be a sound foundation for the kind of global society we need.

Kant could derive his categorical imperatives from the existence of a moral agent who is guided by the dictates of reason to the exclusion of self-interest and desire. Such an agent enjoys transcendental freedom and autonomy of the will, in contrast to the "heteronomy" of the agent whose will is subject to external causes.* This autonomous, rational agent is able to recognize unconditional moral imperatives, which are objective in the sense that they apply universally to all rational beings. Treat all humans as ends, not means; always act as if legislating universal law; and do to others as you would be done to—these are the categorical imperatives. The unconditional authority of the imperatives is derived from the idea of people being autonomous and rational agents.

The trouble is that the rational agent described by Kant does not exist. It is an illusion created by a process of abstraction. Enlightenment philosophers liked to think of themselves as detached and unencumbered, but in reality they were deeply rooted in their society with its Christian morality and ingrained sense of social obligations. They could not even imagine a transactional society where relations are guided by calculations of self-interest. To argue, as the market-fundamentalist students of law and society do, that it may pay to break a contract was outside their frame of reference.

Enlightenment philosophers wanted to change their society. For this purpose, they invented the unattached individual endowed with reason who obeyed the dictates of his own conscience, not the dictates of external authority. They failed to realize that a truly unattached individual may not have a conscience; she may be totally selfish or totally disoriented. A sense of duty is grounded in society, not in the unattached individual. Social values may be internalized, but they are rooted in the family, community, background, and tradition to which the individual belongs, and they evolve in a reflexive fashion.

*Roger Scruton, *Kant* (Oxford, U.K.: Oxford University Press, 1989).

A market economy does not constitute a community, especially when it operates on a global scale; being employed by a corporation is not the same as belonging to a community, especially when management gives precedence to the profit motive over all other considerations and the individual may be fired at the drop of a hat. People in today's transactional society do not behave as if they were governed by categorical imperatives; the calculations exemplified by the prisoner's dilemma seem to throw more light on their behavior. Kant's metaphysic of morals was appropriate to an age when reason had to contend with external authority, but it seems strangely irrelevant today when the external authority is lacking. The very need to distinguish between right and wrong is brought into question. Why bother, as long as a course of action achieves the desired result? Why pursue the truth? Why be honest? Why care about others? Who are the "we" who constitute global society, and what are the values that ought to hold us together? These are the questions that need to be answered today.

It would be a mistake, however, to dismiss the moral and political philosophy of the Enlightenment just because it failed to live up to its grandiose ambitions. In the spirit of fallibility, we ought to correct its excesses, not swing to the opposite extreme. A society without social values cannot survive, and a global society needs universal values to hold it together. The Enlightenment offered a set of universal values, and its memory is still alive even if it seems somewhat faded. Instead of discarding it, we should update it.

The Encumbered Individual*

Enlightenment values can be made relevant to the present day by replacing reason with fallibility and substituting the "encumbered

---

*In writing this section I was influenced by Michael Sandel, *Democracy's Discontent* (Cambridge: Harvard University Press, 1996).

individual" for the unencumbered individual of the Enlightenment philosophers. By "encumbered individuals," I mean individuals in need of society, individuals who cannot exist in splendid isolation yet are deprived of the sense of belonging that was so much a part of peoples' lives at the time of the Enlightenment that they were not even aware of it. The thinking of encumbered individuals is influenced but not determined by their social setting, their family and other ties, the culture in which they are reared. They do not occupy a timeless, perspectiveless position. They are not endowed with perfect knowledge and they are not devoid of self-interest. They are ready to fight for survival, but they are not self-contained; however well they compete, they will not survive because they are not immortal. They need to belong to something bigger and more enduring, although, being fallible, they may not recognize that need. In other words, they are real people, thinking agents whose thinking is fallible, not personifications of abstract reason.

In putting forward the idea of the encumbered individual, I am, of course, engaging in the same kind of abstract thinking as the Enlightenment philosophers. I am proposing another abstraction based on our experience with their theories. Reality is always more complicated than our interpretation. The range of people living in the world varies from individuals who are not far removed from the Enlightenment ideal to those who barely act as individuals, with the distribution curve heavily skewed toward the latter. The concept of the encumbered individual encompasses the entire range.

The point is that a globalized society could never satisfy the encumbered individuals' need to belong. It could never become a community. It is just too big and variegated for that, with too many different cultures and traditions. Those who want to belong to a community must look for it elsewhere. A global society must always remain something abstract, a universal idea. It must respect the needs of the encumbered individual, it must recognize that those needs are not met, but it must not seek to meet them in full, because no form of social organization could possibly satisfy them once and for all.

A global society must be aware of its own limitations. It is a universal idea, and universal ideas can be dangerous if they are carried too far. Specifically, a global state would carry the idea of a global society too far. All that open society as a universal idea could do is to serve as a basis for the rules and institutions that are necessary for the coexistence of the plethora of individuals and the multiplicity of communities that make up a global society. It could not provide the community that would satisfy individuals' need for belonging. Still, the idea of a global open society must represent something more than a mere agglomeration of market forces and economic transactions. There has to be some community of interests, some shared values to hold that society together. The community of interests is created partly by the common problems people face and partly by the community of the people who face those problems.

Common problems are not difficult to find in our interdependent world. Avoidance of devastating armed conflicts, particularly nuclear war; protection of the environment; preservation of a global financial and trading system: Few people would disagree with these objectives. The difficulty lies in establishing the community of people who face these problems.

The Enlightenment based the universal brotherhood of humanity on the rational agent, the unencumbered individual. That base proved unsound because the rational agent is fallible and guided by self-interest rather than universal ideas of brotherhood. We need to find a sounder base. I propose to substitute the fallible agent, the encumbered individual. There is a minimal brotherhood of humanity based on our common fallibility, mortality, and—let's admit it—selfishness. We are incomplete as individuals; we need to belong to society. Now that the economy has become global, we need a global society. We cannot have a society without recognizing that there are some common interests that have to take precedence over individual self-interests; but our fallibility prevents us from *knowing* what those common interests are. Therefore we need rules by which we can agree on what our common interests are and how best we can attain them. This leads us to the need for international law and international institutions. It does *not* lead us to a global state, but it does lead us to the conclusion that national sovereignty has to be subordinated to the international common good. It also leads us to the principle of subsidiarity: Recognizing how difficult it is to decide about the common good, decisions should be made at the lowest possible level. The lower the level, the more likely it is to constitute a community to which the individual is willing to subordinate her self-interest; but belonging to a community should be voluntary—that is a universal principle that ought to be enforced at every level, including the state.

The Principles of Open Society

After all this preparation, I am finally ready to say what I mean by open society. It is liable to be anticlimactic. I shall distinguish between timelessly, universally valid principles and a more time-bound, specific description of what an open society entails at the present moment in history. Of course, different epochs, societies, and individuals may also give different definitions of the universal principles. My own definition would include various freedoms and human rights, the rule of law, and some sense of social responsibility and social justice.

The freedom of thought and expression and the freedom of choice can be directly derived from our fallibility: Since the ultimate truth is beyond our reach, we must allow people to think for themselves and make their own choices. The fact that our understanding is imperfect does not mean that there is no ultimate truth; on the contrary, the lack of adequate knowledge implies the need for an element of faith. Open society has nothing against religion. But the principles of open society would be violated if religion tried to dictate to those who do not subscribe to it.

The freedom of thought allows critical thinking and the freedom of choice allows the market mechanism to operate. Both are inter-personal processes; by assuring the conditions for their proper functioning, we all benefit. The freedom of association has more to do with our being social animals.

Individual human rights can be derived from our being thinking agents conscious of themselves and capable of making autonomous choices. The idea of human rights is also embedded in the Christian idea of the human soul.

We must recognize, however, that different human rights can come in conflict with one another. For instance, the rights of women have been set against the rights of the embryo. Since I derive human rights from being a thinking agent, I have no doubt whose rights ought to take precedence; yet there are those who base their arguments on the human soul and come out on the opposite side. This is a divisive issue in the United States today. Different societies are at different stages of development, and their develop-ment may take different forms. Therefore the realization of human rights is liable to differ among societies. The rulers of less-devel-oped countries claim that they should be held to lesser standards. They have a point as far as living conditions are concerned, but not with regard to the freedom of thought and expression. I would argue that the human rights of those who can think for themselves need to be even more jealously guarded in less-developed countries than in mature democracies because they have scarcity value.

I am altogether leery of so-called social and economic freedoms and the corresponding human rights: freedom from hunger or the right to a square meal. Rights need to be enforced; the enforcement of economic rights would fall to the state and that would give the state too big a role in the economy. This would be less objectionable if the state were in fact the best agency for taking care of economic needs. But that proposition has been tried and turned out a flop. I prefer to recognize the need to alleviate poverty more directly by introducing some sense of social justice as one of the core principles of open society. This approach has the advantage that it cuts across borders. We must recognize that under global capitalism individual states have limited capacity to look after the welfare of their citizens yet it behooves the rich to come to the aid of the poor; therefore social justice is a matter of international concern.

Social justice emphatically does not mean equality, because that would take us right back to communism. I prefer the Rawlsian concept of social justice, which holds that an increase in total wealth must also bring some benefit to the most disadvantaged. What "some" means has to be defined by each society for itself, and the definition is liable to vary over time. But creating a more level playing field must be clearly established as an objective of international institutions. I shall develop this thought in Chapter 12.

What about property rights? Should they be recognized as a core principle similar to human rights? I could answer the question either way. I have no doubt that private property is basic to individual freedom and autonomy and as such an indispensable part of open society; but I also believe that there are no rights without obligations. That is true of human rights as well as property rights; but in the case of property, the rights and obligations fall on the same person, whereas in human rights there is a clear distinction between the individual who enjoys the rights and the authorities that are bound to respect them. We may include property among the freedoms and rights, but we must not forget the flip side: social responsibility as manifested, for instance, in the payment of taxes and death duties.

Generally speaking, there is an ongoing conflict between rights and obligations that requires compromises that need to be worked out and reconsidered all the time. Isaiah Berlin referred to this latent conflict between different social values as "value pluralism." Where the compromises should come out cannot be decided on the basis of first principles, yet the principles must be respected for a society to qualify as a free and open one. Since people are supposed to learn by trial and error, it is only natural that their views should evolve over time, but no society can survive for long without some sense of social justice that most of its members find acceptable.

An open society cannot be satisfied, however, by such a relativistic definition of its basic principles, because a tyranny of the majority (or of a minority, as in the case of South Africa under apartheid) does not constitute an open society. Electoral democracy is not enough; it must be complemented by the constitutional protection of minority rights. Again, what those rights are will vary from case to case. I have rounded out the core principles of open society by including the rule of law. The list is not meant to be exhaustive; it merely indicates the cluster of ideas that go to make up the principles of open society.

How could these principles be translated into the specific conditions of an open society at the present moment in history? The president of my foundation, Aryeh Neier, suggested seven conditions:

- Regular, free, and fair elections;
- Free and pluralistic media;
- The rule of law upheld by an independent judiciary;
- Constitutional protection for minority rights;
- A market economy that respects property rights and provides opportunities and a safety net for the disadvantaged;
- A commitment to the peaceful resolution of conflicts; and
- Laws that are enforced to curb corruption.

Other people may come up with other lists. The interesting point is that we may find individual countries that more or less meet these criteria, but our global society does not. The most glaring deficiency is the absence of the international rule of law; and we are bereft of the most elementary arrangements for the preservation of peace.

Exactly what shape these arrangements should take cannot be derived from first principles. To redesign reality from the top down would violate the principles of open society. That is where fallibility differs from rationality. Fallibility means that we don't *know* what the common interest is. Nevertheless, I believe that fallibility and the encumbered individual provide a better basis for establishing the ground rules for a global open society than reason and the unencumbered individual.

Pure reason and a moral code based on the value of the individual are inventions of Western culture; they have little resonance in other cultures. For instance, Confucian ethics are based on family and relationships and do not sit well with the universal concepts imported from the West. Fallibility allows for a broad range of cultural divergences, and the encumbered individual gives due weight to relationships. The Western intellectual tradition ought not to be imposed indiscriminately on the rest of the world in the name of universal values. The Western form of representative democracy may not be the only form of government compatible with an open society.

Nevertheless, there must be some universal values that are generally accepted. Open society may be pluralistic in conception, but it cannot go so far in the pursuit of pluralism that it should fail to distinguish between right and wrong. Toleration and moderation can also be carried to extremes. Exactly what is right can be discovered only by a process of trial and error. The definition is liable to vary with time and place, but there must be a definition at any one time and place.

Whereas the Enlightenment held out the prospect of eternal verities, open society recognizes that values are reflexive and subject to change in the course of history. Collective decisions cannot be based on the dictates of reason; yet we cannot do without collective decisions. We need laws exactly because we cannot be sure what is right and wrong, so we need to have it spelled out. We need institutions that recognize their own fallibility and provide a mechanism for correcting their own mistakes.

A global open society cannot be formed without people subscribing to its basic principles. People must recognize open society as a desirable form of social organization for open society to prevail. That is the missing ingredient in today's world. Fallibility and reflexivity are universal conditions. If they were combined with the recognition of common interests on a global scale, they would provide common ground for all the people in the world. A global open society would be that common ground—and awareness of our fallibility should help us avoid some of the pitfalls associated with universal concepts.

Of course, open society is not without its shortcomings, but its deficiency consists in offering too little rather than too much. More precisely, the concept is too general to provide a recipe for specific decisions. Rules cannot be established by deductive reasoning. It would contradict the principle of fallibility if all problems had a solution. Those who claim to know all the answers would create a closed society. By the same token, the fact that we do not know what the common interest is does not justify us in denying its existence. Specifically, the idea that the pursuit of self-interest will take care of the common interest is an alluring but false idea.

We need to create institutions for the promotion of the common interest, knowing full well that they are bound to be imperfect. We must also build into these institutions a capacity to change in accordance with the evolving perceptions of the common interest—a very difficult requirement in the light of institutional inertia. These requirements can be met only by a continuous process of trial and error.

Is it possible to forge a consensus around the principles of open society? These are abstract, philosophical principles, and it follows from our fallibility that our beliefs are not dictated by reason: So it is not possible to gain general acceptance for those principles simply by explicating them—quite apart from my own inadequacies in putting them forward. Something else needs to happen. People must be aroused, fired up, and they must coalesce around a common cause for the common interest to override special interests.

It could happen in a closed society, where the yearning for freedom provides a common cause for people with disparate interests. Could it happen in an open society? I have had to ask myself, Would I be so committed to open society as an ideal if I had not learned at an early age how dangerous a closed society can be to your health?

I have seen open society triumph as an idea in my native country, Hungary. Everybody who was opposed to the regime coalesced around my foundation. The foundation supported an opposition of many stripes—and it was supported by them in the sense that the funds were put to the right use without any supervision—but once the regime was overturned the different stripes turned against one another. That is how it should be in a democracy. The trouble is that the various parties that were once united in their opposition to a closed society were no longer guided by the principles of open society in opposing each other. It was an object lesson that forced me to recognize a flaw in the concept of open society of which I had been only dimly aware. I knew, of course, that the concept was flawed because every human construct is flawed, but that was an abstract argument; here I was confronted by a concrete experience.

I have some difficulty in formulating the problem. One way to put it is that open society needs enemies. Karl Popper called his book *Open Society and Its Enemies*. I am, in effect, also inventing a new enemy by attacking market fundamentalism. Enemies build communities: It is they who created walled cities as much as the people who lived in those cities. This is another way of saying that open society is not a community and that it is only communities that can have shared ideas that take precedence over the self-interests of their members.

This brings home the quandary we face in trying to create a global open society. Communities are built on the exclusion of the other, while open society seeks to be inclusive on a global scale. Is it possible to imbue open society with positive content or must it always stand *against* something? Fortunately, there is always something to fight against: poverty, disease, environmental dangers. The enemy need not be a rival state. But unless we identify a common enemy against which we can unite, we are likely to have a divided world in which nation-states will fight against one another. We have managed to unite on the level of the sovereign state: We have democratic states with the rule of law and respect for the other. Now we need to confront the issue on a global scale.

The solution cannot be the same as on the state level: A global state would constitute a greater threat to liberty than the individual state. Nor can we design a solution in the abstract: That would also contradict the principles of open society. We must therefore examine the situation as it is now. That is what I shall do in the second half of this book. Based on that assessment, we can then try to develop a program for creating a global open society. I shall do that in the concluding chapters. For good order's sake, I want to point out in advance that I shall use the term "open society" in yet another sense, an operational sense. Here I have tried to establish it as a universal idea; there I shall try to show how it could be translated into reality at the present moment in history.

CHAPTER 6

The Problem of Social Values

I n this chapter I shall explore the problem of social values in greater depth. This will lay the groundwork for a critical examination of the global capitalist system as it prevails today.

Market Values Versus Social Values

The relationship between market values and social values is not easy to untangle. The problem is not in establishing that there is a difference between the two; it is in deciding when we should be guided by one and when by the other. Market fundamentalists try to disregard social values by arguing that those values—whatever they are—find expression in market behavior. For instance, if people want to care for others or protect the environment, they can express those sentiments by spending money; their altruism becomes just as much part of the gross national product (GNP) as their conspicuous consumption. Of course, there are matters that require collective decisions, but social choice is guided by the same economic principles as individual choice.

To demonstrate that this argument is false I need not resort to abstractions, of which we have had too much already; I can draw on my personal experience.

As an anonymous participant in financial markets, I never had to weigh the social consequences of my actions. I was aware that in some circumstances the consequences might be harmful, but I felt justified in ignoring them on the grounds that I was playing by the rules. The game was competitive, and if I imposed additional constraints on myself I would end up a loser. Moreover, I realized that personal scruples make no difference to the outcome: If I abstained, somebody else would take my place. In deciding which stocks or currencies to buy or sell, I was guided by only one consideration: to optimize my return on capital by weighing risk against reward. Still, my decisions had social consequences: When I bought shares in Lockheed and Northrop after the managements were indicted for bribery, I helped sustain the price of their stocks. When I sold sterling short in 1992, the Bank of England was on the other side of my transactions, and I was in effect taking money out of the pockets of British taxpayers. But if I had tried to take social consequences into account, it would have thrown off my risk-reward calculation, and my profits would have been reduced. Fortunately, I did not need to weigh the social consequences, for they would have occurred anyway: If I had not bought Lockheed and Northrop, then somebody else would have. Britain would have devalued sterling whether I had been born or not. "If I didn't do it, somebody else would" is usually a cop-out; but in this case it is well grounded. Financial markets have so many participants that no single, anonymous participant can have an appreciable effect on the outcome. Bringing my social conscience into the decisionmaking process would make no difference in the real world; but it may adversely affect my own results.

This argument holds true *only* for financial markets. If I had to deal with people instead of markets, I could not have avoided moral choices and, being rather squeamish, could not have been so successful in making money. I blessed the luck that led me to the financial markets and allowed me to keep my hands clean: *Pecunia non olet* (money doesn't smell). Anonymous market participants are largely exempt from moral choices as long as they play by the rules. In this sense, financial markets are not immoral; they are amoral. Perfectly respectable people buying and selling shares or commodities can affect the fortunes of people in faraway places: African copper miners or Indonesian construction workers may lose their livelihood because of a change in commodity prices or exchange rates. But these outcomes are not influenced by the decisions of individual market participants; therefore they need not enter into their calculations. The problems caused by market fluctuations can only be addressed on the policy level.

I realize that this argument no longer applies now that I have become a public figure whose actions and statements *can* influence markets. This raises moral issues from which I was previously exempt and makes my position as a market participant much more complicated.

Here's an example: I have been an active supporter of the treaty to ban land mines, but my funds owned shares in a company that manufactured the devices. I felt obliged to sell those shares even though I considered them an attractive investment, and in fact they appreciated significantly after I sold them. I would not have sold them before I became a public figure. To be sure, my selling the shares had no effect on the manufacture of land mines, but I could no longer justify owning them by claiming to be an anonymous market participant.

No longer anonymous, I must be extremely cautious in what I say. I make a point of not saying anything that could benefit me as an investor. Even so, I often get into trouble. My letter to the *Financial Times* at the time of the Russian crisis (see Chapter 9) is a case in point. The dilemma is even more acute when I have to decide whether to say something that might hurt me as an investor. For instance, advocating the Toobin tax (see Chapter 10), I go directly against my business interests. Usually I plead the Fifth Amendment; that is, I try not to hurt my own interests, but sometimes I cannot avoid saying what I believe. The fact is, being a public figure makes it practically impossible to be an active investor at the same time.* Fortunately, I am no longer active in managing my funds, and I have authorized the active managers to ignore my position as a public figure in making investment decisions. But this is an uneasy compromise, and it makes me appreciate the advantages of anonymity.

It is important to distinguish between amorality and immorality. Treating financial markets as immoral can interfere with their normal functioning and deprive them of one of their most useful attributes—namely, their amorality. Amorality helps to make financial markets more efficient. Morality poses difficult issues that participants in financial markets can conveniently sidestep by relying on the argument I have used.

The argument holds good whether or not investors care about morality. Until rather recently many investors avoided buying shares in distilleries, but their decisions as investors have made very little difference to the consumption of alcohol. The same applies to the environment. Yes, there have been important changes in the attitude of corporations, but these changes have come about as the result of social, political, and legal pressures, not the decisions of

*People taking public office usually have to put their investments into a blind trust.

individual investors. Tobacco shares are out of favor, but their decline has been brought about by court decisions, which are duly reflected in market valuations.

Admittedly, financial markets are not only passively reflecting fundamentals; they can also be an active force in shaping reality. We must distinguish, however, between collective behavior and individual behavior. The collective behavior of markets has far-reaching consequences; the individual behavior of market participants has only a minute effect, because there is always another player ready to step in at a marginally different price. It is the definition of an efficient market that no single participant can affect the price.

Financial markets can be used as an arena for collective action. For instance, the boycott of South African investments turned out to be successful in promoting a change of regime in South Africa. But collective action is the exception rather than the rule, and that is as it should be, because the main merit of markets is their ability to give expression to individual preferences. Collective interests ought to be safeguarded by political and civic action. Using financial markets for civic action is a possibility, but it is not their main use. Accepting the fact that markets are quintessentially amoral ought to lead to the recognition that we cannot do without a nonmarket sector. The amorality of markets makes it all the more important that social values find expression in the rules that govern markets (as well as other aspects of society). The anonymous participant can ignore moral, political, and social considerations, but if we look at the impact that financial markets make we cannot leave such considerations out of account. As we have seen in the crisis of 1997–1999, financial markets can act as a wrecking ball, knocking down economies. Although we are justified in playing by the rules, we ought also to pay attention to the rules by which we play. Rules are made by the authorities, but in democracies the authorities are chosen and influenced by the players.

A Vital Distinction

Market participation and rulemaking are two different functions. It would be a mistake to equate the profit motive that guides individual participants with the social considerations that ought to guide the setting of rules. This is exactly the mistake that some market fundamentalists make when they try to extend the economic calculus to other spheres of activity, such as politics or the law of contracts. How can they get away with it? Their first line of defense is that they are merely modeling how people behave: "People may talk about right and wrong, but when the chips are down they act according to their interests." Unfortunately, there is a large element of truth in this contention. Collective decisionmaking in contemporary democracies is largely a power play between competing interests. People try to bend the rules to their own advantage.

But the market-fundamentalist argument does not hold water. First, they are not modeling actual behavior; rather, they are building models on a peculiar assumption of rationality. Second, values are reflexive, and market fundamentalism tends to reinforce self-serving behavior in politics. The greater the influence of market fundamentalism, the more realistic their model of human behavior becomes. Third, even if their models corresponded to reality, that would not make their argument right. Economic actions have social consequences that cannot be dismissed on the grounds that people are selfish.

That is where the market fundamentalists' second line of defense kicks in: "Markets tend toward equilibrium, so the pursuit of self-interest also serves the public interest." Market fundamentalists claim that they are as concerned with the public welfare as anyone, and general equilibrium theory is a discovery about welfare. It is supposed to be value-free, but it gives free markets a strong moral undertone by arguing that general equilibrium is welfare-maximizing. I believe I have shown some of the deficiencies of equilibrium theory. Here I should like to point out that it is in direct conflict with the concept of open society. General equilibrium theory applies only to a perfect world, and the basic tenet of open society is that perfection is beyond our reach. It follows that this second line of defense does not apply to the real world. In the absence of general equilibrium, the pursuit of self-interest can have adverse social consequences.

Market fundamentalists would overrule my objections on the grounds that the benefits of free markets are there for everyone to see. I would be the first to acknowledge that free markets foster wealth creation; they are also an essential ingredient of open society because they enable people to exercise choice. But market fundamentalists, by appealing to the concept of equilibrium, misinterpret the process. It is not the tendency to equilibrium that creates wealth but the release of creative energies. Wealth creation is a dynamic process. It does not regulate itself, and it does not ensure social justice.

All this is plain enough; the real difficulties begin once the distinction between market values and social values has been made. How do they relate to each other? Clearly market values reflect the interests of the individual market participant, whereas social values touch upon the interests of society as perceived by its members. Market values can be measured in monetary terms, but social values are more problematic: They are difficult to observe and even more difficult to measure. Measuring profits is easy—just look at the bottom line. But how to measure the social consequences of a course of action? Actions have intentional or unintended consequences scattered among all the lines above the bottom line. They cannot be reduced to a single line, because they affect different people in different ways. That makes it much harder to evaluate the results. The common interest is a much more nebulous concept than individual self-interest, and it is easy to fudge. Politicians do it all the time, and because the concept is so nebulous they get away with it.

As a philanthropist, I am trying to serve what I consider the common good, but I am acutely aware of all the unintended consequences that my actions may evoke. I try to weigh them in making my decisions. I make many mistakes, but at least I have the advantage of being my own master so that I can correct them with impunity. Politicians do not enjoy that same luxury: Admitting mistakes is liable to be punished at election time. Therefore they try to justify their actions by whatever argument they can muster, and the common interest gets lost in the process. In the absence of an objective criterion like the bottom line, the debate deteriorates into us-versus-them recriminations until ordinary citizens come to believe that all politics is rotten.

This is the reverse side of the insistence on perfection: We set impossible standards for our leaders and we find them wanting. Any reasonable person would agree that perfection is unattainable. Yet the market-fundamentalist ideology has managed to establish perfection as the standard. It claims that markets are perfect in the sense that they tend toward equilibrium or at least correct their own excesses; we should therefore rely on the market in our political decisions to the greatest possible extent and measure the performance of politics against the performance of markets. The argument is false on all counts, but it has come to dominate public discourse.

The fact is that the decisionmaking process can never work as well in politics and social life as it does in natural science or markets. Science has an independent, objective criterion to work with—namely, the facts—that enables truth to prevail even if it belies common sense. Markets also have an objective criterion: profit. In political and social life, the only available criterion is subjective: what people think. For two reasons, this is not a reliable basis for an interpersonal process of critical thinking. One reason is that it is difficult to establish what people really think. It is only too easy to dissemble. As we have seen, social science works less well than natural science because the question of motives enters into the discussion. Marxists, for instance, used to deflect any criticism of their dogma by accusing their opponents of being guided by class interests. Psychoanalysts used to say that those who resisted analysis were "in denial." So the critical process is less effective when it concerns motives rather than facts. The other reason is that the facts do not serve as an independent criterion by which the truth or validity of beliefs can be judged. This echoes an earlier point: Reflexive processes can be self-validating. The fact that a strategy or policy works does not prove that it is valid; the flaw will become apparent only after it has ceased to work. Take a simple example: running up budget or trade deficits. It feels good while it lasts, but there can be hell to pay later.

A direct comparison between democratic politics and the market mechanism will show that politics tends to work less well than markets. This is not a comparison that is commonly made, so it may offer some interesting insights.

Representative Democracy

Democracy provides a mechanism for making collective decisions. It is meant to achieve the same objective for collective choice as the market mechanism achieves for individual choice. Citizens elect representatives who gather in assemblies to make collective decisions by casting votes. This is the principle of representation.

Representative democracy presupposes a certain kind of relationship between citizens and representatives. Candidates go on the stump and tell citizens what they stand for; citizens then choose the person whom they trust and respect most. That is the sort of representative Thomas Jefferson was in the good old days, except that he stayed at home during the campaign. Therefore democracy is based on an assumption that candidates will be forthright with the electorate, which is of course not realistic. Candidates discovered long ago that their chances for election were better if they instead told the electorate what it wanted to hear. This flaw is not fatal, for the system has allowed for it; if candidates fail to live up to their promises, they can be thrown out of office. In that case, conditions remain near equilibrium. The voters do not always get the representatives they desire, but they can correct their mistakes in the next round of elections.

Conditions may, however, veer rather far from equilibrium through a reflexive process. Candidates develop techniques for exploiting the gap between promises and actions. They conduct public-opinion surveys and focus-group meetings to discover what the electorate wants to hear and then fashion a message to match the electorate's desires. The process produces a correspondence between the candidates' statements and the voters' desires, but it does so by matching candidates' promises to voters' expectations rather than by satisfying those expectations. Instead of providing leadership, politicians follow public opinion, and the country does not get the leadership it really needs. Voters become disappointed and lose faith in the process.

Voters are not blameless. They are supposed to support representatives who have the community's best interests at heart, yet they often put narrow self-interests ahead of the common interests. Candidates in turn appeal to people's self-interest, and because they cannot satisfy everyone, they strike bargains with special interests. The process deteriorates when the voters cease to care whether their candidates cheat and lie as long as they cater to the voters' personal interests. The yardstick is not integrity or intelligence but the ability to garner votes. The distortion is reinforced by money.

Television ads are doubly corrupting: They substitute misleading, negative sound bites for honest statements, and they are paid for by donor (read: special-interest) money. Certainly in the United States candidates cannot get enough money to get elected without striking bargains with special interests. The system is self-perpetuating because it favors the incumbents, and they don't want to change it. These are the conditions that prevail today.

Compare these conditions to the conglomerate boom I described in Chapter 3. Conglomerate managements found a way to exploit the reflexive connection between valuations and fundamentals. They discovered they could increase earnings per share by promising to increase earnings per share through acquisitions. This is similar to finding out what voters think and then telling them what they want to hear. Both are examples of dynamic disequilibrium. But there is a huge difference. The conglomerate boom was corrected by a bust. Markets have a way of correcting their excesses—bull markets are followed by bear markets. But representative democracy is less resilient in this respect. True, legislatures and governments are regularly replaced, but democracy seems incapable of correcting its own deficiencies; on the contrary, electorates seem to become progressively less satisfied with it. This is indicated by the increasing apathy and cynicism among voters and the rise of populist candidates.

A word of caution: I stress that markets can correct their excesses, just at the moment when financial markets may have shed that ability. Investors have lost their faith in the fundamentals, realizing that the game is about making money, not about underlying values. Many of the tired old yardsticks for valuing stocks have fallen by the wayside, and those who continue to abide by them have lost out in comparison with those who believe in the dawning of a "new economy." But the conclusion that we find ourselves in far-from-equilibrium territory would be only strengthened if markets had also lost their anchor.

What is true of politics is equally true of social values. In some ways, social values are inferior to market values. They cannot be quantified—they cannot even be properly identified. They certainly cannot be reduced to the common denominator of money. Nevertheless, a well-defined community would have well-defined values; its members may abide by them or transgress against them, be sustained or oppressed by them, but at least they would know what those values are. We do not live in that kind of community. We have difficulty deciding between right and wrong. Thus the amorality of markets has undermined morality even in those areas where society cannot do without it. There is no consensus on moral values such as the right to life or the right to choose. Monetary values are much less confusing. Not only can they be measured, but we can feel reassured that they are appreciated by the people around us. They offer a certainty that social values have lost. That is how professional values have been superceded by the profit motive and professions such as law and medicine—not to mention politics, academics, and even philanthropic and nongovernmental organizations—have turned into businesses.

Social values may be more nebulous than market values, but society cannot exist without them. Market values have been promoted into the position of social values, but they cannot fill that function. They are designed for individual decisionmaking in a competitive setting and are ill suited for collective decisionmaking in a situation that requires cooperation as well as competition.

A confusion of functions has been allowed to occur that has undermined the collective decisionmaking process. Market values cannot take the place of public spirit or, to use the old-fashioned phrase, civic virtue. Whenever politics and business interests intersect, there is a danger that political influence will be used for business purposes. It is a well-established tradition that elected representatives look out for the interests of their constituencies. But where do we draw the line between what is legitimate and what is not? The prominence given to business interests—and the self-interest of politicians—has pushed the line beyond the point that most voters consider acceptable. Hence their disillusionment and disaffection.

The confusion of functions is particularly pronounced in international affairs. Foreign policy tends to be dictated by domestic policy considerations. The tendency is particularly strong in the United States with its ethnic voting blocs. There is also a tradition of pushing business interests by political means. The president of an Eastern European country told me how shocked he was when in a meeting with President Jacques Chirac, the French president spent most of their time together pushing him to favor a French buyer in the sale of the state-owned cement company. I shall not even mention arms sales.

There has always been corruption in politics, but people are supposed to be ashamed of it and try to hide it. Now that the profit motive has been promoted into a moral principle, politicians in some countries feel positively ashamed when they fail to take advantage of their position. I observe this first-hand in countries where I have foundations. Ukraine, it has been said, has given corruption a bad name. I also made a study of African countries and found that people in resource-rich and resource-poor countries are equally poor; the only difference is that the governments of the resource-rich countries are more corrupt.

And yet to discard collective decisionmaking just because it is inefficient and corrupt is comparable to abandoning the market mechanism just because it is unstable and unjust. The impulse in both cases comes from the same source: a yearning for perfection and an inability to accept that all human constructs are flawed.

Our ideas about both the market mechanism and representative democracy were formed under the influence of the Enlightenment. We are inclined to treat the participants' views and the reality to which they relate as if they were independent of each other. Financial markets are supposed to discount a future that is independent of present valuations; elected representatives are supposed to represent certain values independent of any aspiration to be elected. But that is not how the world works. Values are reflexive. Consequently, neither the market mechanism nor representative democracy are likely to fulfill the expectations attached to them. Still, that is no reason to abandon either one. Both the political process and the market mechanism need to be improved, not abolished.

Market fundamentalists dislike collective decisionmaking in any shape or form because it lacks the automatic error-correcting mechanism of the market. They argue that the public interest is best served indirectly, by giving markets a free hand. There is some merit in their argument, but their faith in markets is misplaced for three reasons. First, markets are not designed to address issues of distributive justice; they take the existing distribution of wealth as given.

Second, the common interest does not find expression in market behavior. Corporations do not aim at creating employment; they employ people (as few and as cheaply as possible) to make profits. Health-care companies are not in business to save lives; they provide health care to make profits. Oil companies do not seek to protect the environment except in order to meet regulations or to protect their public image. The profit motive can be used as an incentive to bring about desirable social outcomes, such as full employment, affordable medicine, or a healthy environment, but if the rules that govern industries such as health care are allowed to be driven by profit, some undesirable social consequences are bound to follow. Indeed, if competition were left to the market mechanism there might be no competition. Firms compete in order to make profits, not to preserve competition, and if they could, they would eliminate all competition. Karl Marx made this point some 150 years ago.

Third, financial markets are inherently unstable. I fully appreciate the merits of financial markets as a feedback mechanism that not only allows but forces participants to correct their mistakes, but I would add that financial markets themselves also make mistakes. The idea that markets are always right is wrong. The market mechanism itself also needs to be corrected by a process of trial and error. Central banks are particularly well-suited for the job because they interact with financial markets and receive feedback that allows them to correct their own mistakes. Market fundamentalists point to the remarkable resilience of financial markets in rejecting the idea of their fundamental instability. Look at how rapidly they recovered from the crisis of 1997–1999, they say. But they leave out of account the equilibrating role played by the monetary authorities; on the contrary, they claim that the crisis arose in the first place because the IMF created a moral hazard that encouraged excessive lending. As I shall argue in Part II of this book, the global financial system would have collapsed without the timely intervention of the Federal Reserve, and it has kept the economy on an even keel ever since; the IMF has been less successful and the emerging economies have paid a heavy price for it. The international monetary authorities are badly in need of reform.

I, too, share the prevailing aversion toward politics. I am a creature of the markets and I enjoy the freedom and opportunities they offer. As a market participant, I make my own decisions and learn from my mistakes. I do not need to convince others to get something done, and the results are not obfuscated by office politics. Strange as it may sound, participating in financial markets gratifies my quest for the truth. So even though I have a personal bias against politics and other forms of collective decisionmaking, I recognize that we cannot do without them.

Social Values in an Open Society

How could the collective decisionmaking process be improved in an open society? I propose a rather simple rule: People should separate their role as market participant from their role as political participant. As market participants, people ought to pursue their individual self-interests; as participants in the political process, they ought to be guided by the public interest.

The justification for this rule is also rather simple. In conditions that approximate perfect competition, no single competitor can affect the outcome; therefore individual market decisions have no effect on social conditions, whether or not one cares about the common good. But political decisions do affect social conditions; therefore it makes all the difference whether or not they serve the public interest.

The observant reader will notice a potential flaw in this argument. If market participants are exempt from considering the social consequences of their actions because their influence on the outcome is only marginal, does not the same consideration apply to the ordinary citizen engaged in the making of rules? Isn't the influence of the individual voter also marginal? Yes, but market participation and political participation are different kinds of activities. The market participants are engaged in the pursuit of individual self-interests through free exchange with others; the voters are expressing their views on the collective interest. Therefore the different activities ought to be judged by different yardsticks: market decisions by the individual consequences, political participation by the social consequences.

There are many instances where political decisions affect the vital interests of certain groups or individuals. It would be asking them too much to be guided by the public interest. It would be sufficient, however, if people observed the separation of roles when their vital interests are *not* involved. The general public would then constitute the umpire to judge the players on either side of an issue. As long as the umpire has the last word, the common interest has a good chance to prevail.

The task of the umpire is greatly complicated by the fact that today's political decisions are mainly about the budget, not about making rules. The budget is a matter of money, and it is difficult to be disinterested about it. Nevertheless, I would argue that the distinction between rulemaking and playing by the rules does apply.

Take the issue of abolishing the estate tax, which arose just at the time of writing. As a citizen I argued against abolition; as a player I take advantage of all the legal loopholes.*

It should be emphasized that I am proposing my rule as a moral precept, not as the rational choice that people are bound to follow as long as they are rational. It would be disastrous if in our rulemaking function we assumed that people are in fact prepared to abide by this moral precept. The founders of the American republic did not make that mistake. They assumed that people are selfish, and established checks and balances designed to blunt the disruptive effects of self-interest.

Nevertheless, the founders could take a modicum of civic virtue for granted. They did not reckon with the rise of highly competitive, transactional markets. The ascendancy of the profit motive over civic virtue undermines the political process. That would not matter if we could rely on the market mechanism to the extent that market fundamentalists claim. But actions do have social consequences. The spread of market fundamentalism and the penetration of the profit motive into areas where it does not properly belong expose the institutions of American democracy to dangers that have been largely absent during its two-hundred-year history.

In practice, the distinction between rulemaking and playing by the rules is widely ignored. Lobbying and influence-peddling are widely practiced and accepted. But we should not simply throw up our hands and join the crowd. There will always be people who put their personal interests ahead of the common interest. This "free-rider" problem bedevils cooperation, but the problem could be overcome if enough people recognized the difference between market values and social values.

*George Soros, ". . . No, Keep It Alive to Help the Needy," *The Wall Street Journal* (New York), July 14, 2000.

Market values are amoral while social values are quintessentially moral. Market values are about winning; moral values are about doing the right thing, win or lose. If we were guided by what others do, we would be acting as participants in a race where winning is what matters. If we really believe in moral values, we ought to do the right thing *even if others do not.* The free-rider problem simply does not apply, because the objective is not gaining competitive advantage but doing the right thing.

I have never forgotten the words of Sergei Kovalev, the Russian dissident and human rights activist, who told me that he takes pride in having fought losing battles all his life. I have not quite lived up to his standards, but I do practice what I preach. I try to be a winner as a market participant and I try to serve the common interest as a citizen and a human being. Sometimes it is difficult to keep the two roles separate, but the principle is clear. At least it is clear to me. If it were clear to enough people, the free-rider problem would disappear. The majority would do the right thing in spite of the free riders and the free riders would cease to dominate the scene. They might even modify their behavior. Encumbered individuals, to use my earlier phrase, care a great deal about what others think of them. They might be single-minded in the pursuit of success, but they could not consider it a success if they suffered general opprobrium. Guided by self-interest, free riders would have to be more clandestine about their behavior. That would be a great improvement over the current state of affairs, where free riding is accepted as legitimate and businesslike.

Morality used to play a more important role in social life, but it was accompanied by a great deal of hypocrisy and pretense. Am I really advocating a return to those conditions? I do not believe it is possible, or wise, to turn back the clock. Every generation must reach its own accommodation between moral principles and expediency. In the Middle Ages, when religion was paramount, there was an accommodation between church and state, represented by the

Pope and the Holy Roman Emperor. Today, when markets have become so influential, a different kind of accommodation is required, one built on the distinction between rulemaking and competing.

People should be able to pursue their self-interest as long as they compete by the rules—and they need not be sanctimonious about it. When it comes to rulemaking, however, the common interest ought to take precedence. True, an element of hypocrisy would creep in as people affected public-spiritedness in arguing their case, but that is preferable to the blatant pursuit of self-interest that prevails in politics today.

The trouble is that people cannot afford to pay attention to the public interest. The global capitalist system is based on competition, and competition has become so intense that even the most successful are reduced to having to fight for survival. Indeed, it is the most successful who are under the most intense pressure, as the case of Microsoft illustrates.* This is a sorry state of affairs. Under previous dispensations, the rich and successful enjoyed a large degree of autonomy and leisure. The landowning aristocracy could devote itself to the finer things in life. Even John D. Rockefeller could take off for an extended European tour at the height of his success. But today's capitalists are slaves of the financial markets: They have to perform every quarter. There used to be a large number of people who were not caught up in competition: professionals, intellectuals, civil servants, rentiers, peasants; their numbers have diminished. Our society is wealthier, but I believe we are all poorer for it. There ought to be more to life than survival, yet survival of the fittest has become the hallmark of our civilization.

I believe all this has distorted what ought to be an open society,

---

*People used to reproach Bill Gates, the chairman of Microsoft, for not giving away more of his wealth. They did not realize that the demands of his business absorbed all of his energies. Now that he is fighting against a Justice Department antitrust judgment, philanthropy is part of his business strategy.

but I must be careful how I present the case. I cannot set myself up as the ultimate arbiter who adjudicates on what constitutes open society. All I can say is that the substitution of the profit motive for social values is an aberration. People are guided by different kinds of values that are often in conflict with one another. As competitors, they try to maximize their profits; as human beings, they also have other concerns. Isaiah Berlin called it "value pluralism." Value pluralism can be seen as a facet of fallibility because there is no way to avoid conflict between different values and aspirations. For instance, friendship or other human concerns may come in conflict with the profit motive when it comes to firing people. Market fundamentalism, by defining rational behavior as the pursuit of self-interest, is in effect subordinating all other considerations to the profit motive. Therefore market fundamentalism violates a core principle of open society by denying value pluralism.

To reiterate: Financial markets are not immoral, they are amoral. By contrast, collective decisionmaking cannot function properly without drawing a distinction between right and wrong. We do not know what is right. If we did, we would have no need for democratic government; we could be governed by a philosopher king. But we must have a basic sense of right and wrong, an inner light that guides our behavior as citizens and politicians. Without it, representative democracy cannot work. The profit motive dims that inner light. Expediency takes precedence over moral principles. In a highly competitive transactional society, concern for the interests of others can turn into a handicap. There is a process of adverse natural selection at work: Those without the baggage of scruples tend to come out on top. If the profit motive is allowed to dominate the political arena, society is deprived of any moral basis. While it is possible for a society to exist without a moral basis, it would not qualify as an open society. In any case, who would want to live there?

A Reconsideration

I have discovered from the reaction to the original version of this book that people have difficulties in accepting that markets are amoral. Many people who care about morality (and some journalists who are looking for a good angle) consider financial markets immoral. The idea that market behavior is amoral is outside their frame of reference. They suspect that my argument is self-serving: I am using it as an excuse to justify my immoral activities as a financial speculator. The fact that I encounter this reaction so often makes me think that I may be saying something novel and important. It should be remembered that the development of morality and religion predates the development of financial markets. As a financial speculator I may have a different perspective from other people who think about these matters.

I have engaged in a running battle on the subject with Frederik van Zyl Slabbert, chairman of the Open Society Initiative for Southern Africa (OSISA). He is a deeply religious man who cannot accept the idea that any activity can be amoral. Indeed, he considers amorality a worse sin than immorality. This raises the question of whether morality is concerned with intentions or outcomes; given the law of unintended consequences, the two are not identical. I am willing to grant him the point that morality has to apply to intentions, because the outcome cannot be known in advance. Even so, I insist that there is no point in applying moral judgments to decisions that have *no* outcome—and that is the case regarding the social effects of individual investment decisions. Those decisions affect only the profits of the individual, not the prices prevailing in the market. That is what I mean when I say that markets are amoral: The anonymous participant need not be concerned with the social consequences of her decisions. By contrast, political actions, such as voting or lobbying or even arguing, do have social consequences. That is why we need to distinguish between our role as market participants and as political participants, between rulemaking and playing by the rules. As players, we ought to be guided by self-interest; as rulemakers, we ought to be guided by our view of the common interest. If we followed this precept, both self-interest and the common interest would be well served.

I arrived at this precept when I was an anonymous market participant. That covers my career in finance up to and including the devaluation of sterling in 1992. I blew my cover when I allowed myself to be identified as the "man who broke the Bank of England." Since then, I have had a different kind of experience. I have lost my anonymity. I became a public person whose utterances *can* influence the outcome. I can no longer escape having to make moral judgments. This has made it practically impossible for me to function as a market participant.

This experience has taught me the limitations of my precept. It does not resolve the dilemmas of those who are *not* anonymous participants, and that includes practically everyone engaged in business and politics. The two roles are in conflict over a wide range of situations: for instance, when a business executive is asked to join a political action committee, or when a politician is asked to take a position on an issue that is of concern to one of her supporters. The precept poses moral dilemmas; it does not resolve them. That has to be done by each individual and each society to their own satisfaction. Moreover, the precept does not offer a reliable guide to the ordinary conduct of business. There are no general rules about how to treat people, how to balance consideration for others with the demands of business performance; everyone must make up her own and live with the consequences.

The criticism I received made me conscious of what an exceptional position I occupied as an anonymous market participant. For most of my career, I did not even have a business organization to contend with. I was a loner. I could focus on the market without distraction. I considered dealing with humans—in the form of investors, partners, employees, brokers—a distraction. To be successful in financial markets one needs to be single-minded about it. I wanted to be successful, but I was unwilling to surrender my own identity to the pursuit of success. That is why I preferred to keep my business life and personal life strictly separate. That is also why I set up a foundation once I had more money than I needed for my personal use. The formula worked. I found it easier to make money and to give it away than to bring moral considerations into my moneymaking activities. As I have said elsewhere, I became like a gigantic digestive tract, taking in money at one end and pushing it out at the other.

It was from this vantage point that I formed my views about the role of financial markets as an efficient but inhuman mechanism, and I believe my insight is valuable. Financial markets *are* amoral, and that is why they are so effective in aggregating the views of the participants. Exactly because of that quality, they cannot be left in charge of deciding the future. I believe the distinction between rulemaking and playing by the rules is valid; but it falls well short of a comprehensive moral guide. Very few people find themselves in a position similar to mine, and my position has also changed.

When I became active as a philanthropist, I was determined to keep my foundations as strictly separate from my business as I had kept my private life. I am sure that this contributed to their success, because it allowed me to be as single-minded about my philanthropy as I had been about my business. But I have not been able to maintain the segregation. The countries where I have foundations need investment as badly as they need philanthropy, and after much soul-searching I decided to invest in Russia. This got me into deep trouble, as I shall recount in Chapter 9. At the same time, the foundations became increasingly involved in business activities, supporting newspapers, publishing, enterprise incubators, Internet, and microlending. These developments have forced me to reconsider my stance. I am still leery of mixing business and philanthropy, but I realize that it cannot be avoided. I was privileged to be able to avoid it as long as I did. Now I am prepared to go even further: It *should* not be avoided. I have argued that we cannot do without politics, even if it is corrupt and inefficient. The same argument applies to social responsibility in business. If we cannot avoid mixing business and morality (as can the anonymous participant in an efficient market), we might as well try to do it well. The results are bound to be unsatisfactory: Business enterprises are liable to subordinate social responsibility to the pursuit of profit. Image takes precedence over substance, and even those who are genuinely motivated are obliged to give due weight to their business interests. But some results are better than none. If social pressures serve to induce companies to act with greater regard to the environment or other social concerns, so much the better—although we cannot ignore that environmental groups often make unreasonable demands.

It would be a mistake, however, to leave social concerns to the care of corporations. Publicly owned companies are single-purpose organizations—their purpose is to make money. The tougher the competition, the less they can afford to deviate. Those in charge may be well-intentioned and upright citizens, but their room for maneuver is strictly circumscribed by the position they occupy. They are duty-bound to uphold the interests of the company. If they think that cigarettes are unhealthy, or that fostering civil war to obtain mining concessions is unconscionable, they ought to quit their jobs. Their place will be taken by people who are willing to carry on. That is the process of adverse natural selection I referred to earlier.

The same applies to nongovernmental organizations (NGOs). They, too, are single-purpose organizations that cannot divorce themselves from the causes for which they stand. In some ways, the leaders of NGOs are more committed to their cause than business executives are to profits because they feel they are on the side of the angels, whereas businesspeople may feel less righteous about their business interests. I know whereof I speak, because I am the founder of probably the largest network of NGOs in the world. I think NGOs can do a lot of good in protecting the interests of neglected sectors of society, but they cannot be entrusted with making the rules any more than the business sector. They can advocate a particular point of view, and so can business, and a democratic government will hold itself open to all perspectives, but the decisions must be ultimately left in the hands of the citizens. To fulfill their role as umpire, citizens must be able to distance themselves from their role as participants whose interests are at stake. This is more easily accomplished than getting publicly owned companies to subordinate the profit motive to the public interest. As I said before, it is not necessary that all citizens should abide by this rule, as long as some citizens do so irrespective of what others do. I shall certainly continue to do so *even if others do not.*

Where I have modified my stance is with regard to social entrepreneurship. I used to be negative toward it because of my innate aversion to mixing business with philanthropy. Experience has taught me, however, that I was wrong: As a philanthropist I saw a number of successful social enterprises, and I became engaged in some of them. Eventually, I discovered an error in my logic. There is no duplicity, no mixing of motives in social enterprise as there is in reconciling social responsibility with the profit motive; in social entrepreneurship, profit is not a motive, it is a means to an end. Not-for-profit enterprises face a more difficult task than for-profit enterprises because they lack a single criterion, the bottom line, by which their success can be judged. But that is no reason to shy away from them; on the contrary, they present a greater challenge. Philanthropy, social work, and all forms of official intervention are mired in bureaucracy. Yet there are imaginative, creative people who really care about social conditions. I have come around to thinking that entrepreneurial creativity could achieve what bureaucratic processes cannot. For instance, I gave a $50 million guarantee for a mortgage-finance institution in South Africa that has financed more than 100,000 low-cost housing units. So far, not a penny of my guarantee was called down, because the institution is well-managed. The difficulty is in establishing the appropriate yardsticks for success. Consider microlending: It is an effective method for alleviating poverty. The Grameen Bank and its peers have changed the social landscape of Bangladesh. The trouble is that microlending requires outside capital for growth. If the proper criteria could be developed, I am sure that a lot more outside capital could be attracted to the field.

In short, I stick by my distinction between rulemaking and playing by the rules, but I revise my previously negative view on social entrepreneurship.

PART II

The Present Moment in History

7

The Global Capitalist System

Now we come to the crux of the matter: How can the abstract theoretical framework I just elaborated shed light on the present moment in history? My contention is that the global capitalist system that prevails today is a distorted form of open society. It gives too much credence to the profit motive and competition and fails to protect common interests through cooperative decisionmaking. At the same time, it leaves too much power in the hands of sovereign states, often beyond civilian control. These excesses need to be corrected in full awareness of human fallibility, recognizing that perfection is unattainable.

We live in a global economy that is characterized not only by free trade in goods and services but even more by the free movement of capital. Interest rates, exchange rates, and stock prices in various countries are intimately interrelated, and global financial markets exert tremendous influence on economic conditions. Given the decisive role that international financial capital plays in the fortunes of individual countries, it is appropriate to speak of a "global capitalist system."

The system favors financial capital, because capital is free to go where most rewarded. This in turn has led to the rapid growth of global financial markets. The result is a gigantic circulatory system, sucking capital into the financial institutions and markets at the center, then pumping it out to the periphery either directly, in the form of credits and portfolio investments, or indirectly through multinational corporations. As long as the circulatory system is vigorous, it overwhelms all local sources of capital. Indeed, most local capital eventually turns international. Capital brings many benefits: an increase in productive capacity as well as improvements in the methods of production and other innovations; an increase in wealth as well as a general sense of progress. This makes countries vie to attract and retain capital, and if they are to succeed they must give precedence to the requirements of international capital over other social objectives.

The system itself is deeply flawed. Economic and political arrangements are out of kilter. The development of a global economy has not been matched by the development of a global society. The basic unit for political and social life remains the nation-state. The nation-state has been able to render certain social services to citizens; its ability to do so is impaired by the difficulties of taxing capital and the pressures of competition in international markets. But the state has not faded away as the ultimate source of power; it merely ceased to be the main source of welfare. In many ways, this is a welcome development: The level of taxation in welfare states has been far too high, and freer trade and capital movements are bringing enormous economic benefits; but many social needs previously covered by the nation-state go unsatisfied.

The relationship between the center of the capitalist system and its periphery is also profoundly unequal. Countries at the center enjoy far too many advantages over the periphery. They are not only wealthier but also more stable because they control their own destiny. Foreign ownership of capital deprives peripheral countries of autonomy and often hinders the development of democratic institutions. The international flow of capital is subject to catastrophic interruptions. As a consequence, it is more difficult to preserve capital at the periphery than at the center, and capitalists in peripheral countries tend to accumulate capital abroad. At times the reverse flow exceeds the outward movement. The disparities are cumulative, and the disadvantages accruing to periphery countries resulting from membership in the global capitalist system may sometimes exceed the benefits.

The troubles go even deeper. International institutions for preserving peace among states and the rule of law within states are not up to the task. This lack of institutional structure is likely to cause the eventual disintegration of the global capitalist system. If and when the global economy falters, political pressures could tear it apart. It has happened before. The previous incarnation of a global capitalist system, a century ago, was destroyed by World War I and the subsequent revolutions. Though I am not predicting world war, I must point out that technological advances since then have increased our capacity for destruction without a corresponding improvement in security arrangements.

My critique of the global capitalist system falls under two main headings. One concerns the defects of the market mechanism, primarily the instabilities built into international financial markets. The other concerns the deficiencies of the nonmarket sector, primarily the failure of politics at the national and international levels. The deficiencies of the nonmarket sector far outweigh the defects of the market mechanism.

The first three chapters in Part II (Chapters 7–9) are devoted to the failings of the global capitalist system, the last three (Chapters 10–12) to the creation of a global open society. This chapter provides a general analysis of the global capitalist system in light of the theoretical framework established earlier. Chapter 8 analyzes the financial crisis of 1997–1999. Chapter 9 examines the way the capitalist system handled the collapse of the Soviet system. Chapter 10 proposes a new financial architecture that would make the global capitalist system more stable and equitable. Chapter 11 discusses one of the toughest tests we face at the present moment in history—namely, stability in the Balkans. If we cannot tackle that problem in accordance with the principles of open society, there is not much point in discussing such principles in the abstract. Chapter 12 moves from the particular to the general and seeks to develop a political architecture appropriate to a global open society.

The trouble with the present moment in history is that it does not stand still. We live in a period of dynamic disequilibrium in which the pace of change is very rapid. In November 1998, when my book first went to print, the global capitalist system looked as if it would soon come apart at the seams. Two years later the crisis of 1997–1999 seems almost like a distant memory. It is not irrelevant, therefore, when the various parts of the text were written. This chapter originated from a February 1997 article published in *The Atlantic Monthly*, so much of it predates the crisis; the latter sections of this chapter and Chapter 8 were written in early 1998 and updated just as the crisis neared its climax in the fall of 1998. I tried to put the crisis in the context of my boom-bust model, and events superseded my predictions, often falsifying them. However, in order to preserve the authenticity of the original analysis I have not revised my predictions, although I allowed myself to make revisions that elucidate and elaborate the original arguments. Where my views have changed I say so explicitly, so the reader can follow the evolution of my ideas. I did not feel similarly constrained in the rest of the book; thus Chapters 9–12 have been thoroughly revised or contain entirely new material.

An Abstract Empire

The first question that needs to be answered is whether there is such a thing as a global capitalist system. My answer is yes, but it is not a thing. We have an innate tendency to reify or personify abstract concepts—it is built into our language—and doing so can have unfortunate consequences. Abstract concepts take on a life of their own, and it is only too easy to go off on the wrong track and become far removed from reality; yet we cannot avoid thinking in abstract terms, because reality is just too complex to be understood in its entirety. That is why ideas play such an important role in history—more important than we realize.

Having warned against reification, I shall now proceed to engage in it. The capitalist system can be compared to an empire that is more global in its coverage than any previous empire. It rules an entire civilization, and those outside its walls are considered barbarians. It is not a territorial empire, for it lacks sovereignty and all its trappings; indeed the sovereignty of the state represents the main limit on its power and influence. Therefore the empire is almost invisible, possessing no formal structure.

The empire analogy is apt because the global capitalist system governs those who belong to it—and it is not easy to opt out. Moreover, it has a center and a periphery like every empire, the center benefiting at the expense of the periphery. Most important, global capitalism exhibits expansionist tendencies. Far from seeking equilibrium, it is hell-bent on conquest. It cannot rest as long as there are markets and resources that remain unincorporated into the system. When I speak of "expansion," I do not mean it only geographically but also in terms of its scope and influence. This is another way of saying that market values are extending their sway over spheres of activity that were previously governed by nonmarket values.

Although the empire analogy is apt, it is also dangerous. The dominance of market values has aroused fierce opposition from various quarters—nationalist, religious, cultural, and intellectual. There is talk of a new kind of imperialism. It may sound subversive to American and European ears, but it is important to understand the emotions behind it. Global capitalism looks and feels very different at the periphery than at the center.

In contrast to the nineteenth century, when imperialism found a literal, territorial expression in the form of colonies, the current global capitalist system is almost completely nonterritorial—even extraterritorial—in character. Territories are governed by states, and states often pose obstacles to the expansion of capitalism. This is true even of the United States, the most capitalist of countries. As a consequence, the ownership of capital has a tendency to go offshore.

The global capitalist system is purely functional in nature, and not surprisingly the function it serves is economic: the production, consumption, and exchange of goods and services. It is important to note that exchange involves not only goods and services but also the factors of production. As Marx and Engels pointed out some 150 years ago, the capitalist system turns land, labor, and capital into commodities.* As the system expands, the economic function comes to dominate the lives of people and societies. It penetrates areas not previously considered economic—culture, politics, medicine, education, and law. Of course, the excessive influence of money is nothing new. Perhaps the first instance was when Moses returned from Mount Sinai and smashed the tablets upon discovering that people had started to worship Moloch in his absence.

Despite its nonterritorial nature, the system does have a center and a periphery. Although the exact location of the center is nebu-

*In writing this section, I was greatly influenced by Karl Polanyi, *The Great Transformation* (Boston: Beacon Press, 1989).

lous, for practical purposes it is identified with the United States and to a lesser extent with Europe, and Japan is poised somewhere between center and periphery. The center is the provider of capital; the periphery is the user of capital. The center is also the trendsetter, innovator, and clearinghouse for information. The center's most important feature is that it controls its own economic policies and holds in its hands the economic destinies of periphery countries. This would be true even if there were no great differences in wealth and development between center and periphery. For instance, in the European Monetary System, Germany was at the center; after German reunification, the Bundesbank raised interest rates for domestic reasons and plunged the periphery countries into recession. But of course within the global capitalist system there are tremendous differences in wealth and development.

The Current Regime

The international capitalist system is not new or even novel. Its antecedents go back to the Italian city-states and the Hanseatic League, in which different political entities were linked together by commercial and financial ties. Capitalism became dominant in the nineteenth century and remained so until it was disrupted by World War I. The regime that prevails today may have some novel features that set it apart from previous incarnations. The speed of communications is one, but it is questionable how novel that is: The advent of railroads, telegraphy, and telephony represented as great an acceleration in the nineteenth century as computer communications does at present. It is true that the information revolution contains unique features, but so did the transportation revolution in the nineteenth century. On the whole, then, the current regime is quite similar to the one that prevailed a hundred years ago, although it is fundamentally different from that which prevailed just fifty years ago.

The distinguishing feature of the global capitalist system is the free movement of capital. International trade in goods and services is not enough to create a global economy; the factors of production must also be interchangeable. Land and other natural resources do not move, and populations move with difficulty; thus the mobility of capital, information, and entrepreneurship is responsible for economic integration.

Because financial capital is even more mobile than physical investment, it occupies a privileged position: It can avoid countries where it is subjected to onerous taxes or regulations. Once a plant has been built, it is difficult to move. To be sure, multinational corporations enjoy flexibility in transfer pricing and can exert pressure at the time they make investment decisions, but their flexibility does not compare to the freedom of choice enjoyed by international portfolio investors. The range of available investment opportunities is also enhanced by being at the center of the global economy rather than at the periphery. All these factors combine to attract capital to the financial centers and to allocate it through the financial markets. That is why financial markets play such a dominant role in the world today and why their influence has increased so rapidly.

In fact, the free movement of capital is a relatively recent phenomenon. At the end of World War II, economies were largely national in character, international trade was at a low ebb, and both direct investments and financial transactions were practically at a standstill. The Bretton Woods institutions—the International Monetary Fund and the World Bank—were designed to make international trade possible in a world devoid of international capital movements. The World Bank was meant to make up for the lack of direct investments, the IMF for the lack of financial credit to offset imbalances in trade. International capital in less-developed countries was engaged mainly in the exploitation of natural resources, and those countries, far from encouraging international investment, were more likely to expropriate it. For instance, Anglo-Iranian Oil was nationalized in 1951 (to be followed by other waves of nationalization and the establishment of the Organization of

Petroleum Exporting Countries [OPEC] in 1973). Nationalization of strategic industries was the order of the day in Europe as well. Most of the investment in less-developed countries was in the form of government-to-government deals, like Britain's ill-fated groundnut scheme in Africa.

After the war, international trade picked up first, followed by direct investment. U.S. firms moved into Europe, then into the rest of the world. Companies originating in other countries caught up later. Many industries—autos, chemicals, computers—came to be dominated by multinational corporations. International financial markets were slower to develop because many currencies were not fully convertible and many countries maintained controls over capital transactions. Capital controls were lifted only gradually; in the United Kingdom they were formally abolished only in 1979.

When I started in the business in London in 1953, financial markets and banks were strictly regulated on a national basis, and a fixed exchange-rate system prevailed with many restrictions on the movement of capital. There was a market in "switch sterling" and "premium dollars"—special exchange rates applicable to capital accounts. After I moved to the United States in 1956, international trade in securities was gradually liberalized. With the formation of the Common Market, U.S. investors began to buy European securities, but the accounting of the companies concerned and the settlement arrangements left much to be desired; conditions were not very different from some of the emerging markets today, except the analysts and traders were less skilled. It was the beginning of my financial career: I was a one-eyed king among the blind. And as late as 1963 U.S. President John F. Kennedy proposed a so-called interest equalization tax on U.S. investors buying foreign stocks; signed into law in 1964, it practically put me out of business.

Global financial markets started to emerge in the 1970s. The oil-producing countries banded together under OPEC and raised the price of oil, first in 1973 from $1.90 to $9.76 per barrel, then in 1979 (in response to political events in Iran and Iraq) from $12.70 to $28.76 per barrel. The oil exporters enjoyed sudden large surpluses, while importing countries had to finance large deficits. It was left to commercial banks, with behind-the-scenes encouragement from Western governments, to recycle the funds. Eurodollars were invented, and large offshore markets developed. Governments started to make tax and other concessions to international financial capital to entice it back onshore. Ironically these measures gave offshore capital even more room to maneuver. The international lending boom ended in a bust in 1982, but by that time the freedom of movement for financial capital was well established.

The development of international financial markets received a big boost around 1980 when Margaret Thatcher and Ronald Reagan came to power with a program of removing the state from the economy and allowing the market mechanism to do its work. This meant imposing strict monetary discipline, which had the initial effect of plunging the world into recession and precipitating the international debt crisis of 1982. It took several years for the world economy to recover—in Latin America they speak of the "lost decade"—but recover it did. From then on the global economy has enjoyed a long period of practically uninterrupted expansion. In spite of periodic crises, the development of international capital markets has accelerated to a point where they can be described as truly global. Movements in exchange rates, interest rates, and stock prices in various countries are intimately interconnected. In this respect, the character of the financial markets has changed beyond all recognition during the forty-five years that I have been involved in them.

When did the current capitalist regime begin? Was it in the 1970s, when the offshore market in Eurodollars was established? Was it around 1980, when Thatcher and Reagan ascended to power? Or was it in 1989, when the Soviet empire disintegrated and capitalism became truly global? I opt for 1980, because that is when market fundamentalism became the dominant creed at the center.

Today the ability of the state to provide for the welfare of its citizens has been severely impaired by the mobility of capital. Countries that have overhauled their social security and employment regimes—the United States and United Kingdom foremost among them—have flourished economically, while others that have sought to preserve them—exemplified by France and Germany—have lagged behind.*

The dismantling of the welfare state is a relatively new phenomenon, and its full effect has not yet been felt. Since the end of World War II, the state's share of GNP in the industrialized countries taken as a group has almost doubled.† Only after 1980 did the tide turn. Interestingly, the state's share of GNP has not declined perceptibly. What has happened instead is that the taxes on capital and employment have come down while other forms of taxation (particularly on consumption) have continued to ratchet upward. In other words, the burden of taxation has shifted from the owners of capital to the consumers, from the rich to the poor and the middle classes. That is not exactly what had been promised, but one cannot say they are unintended consequences because that was exactly what the market fundamentalists intended.

An Incomplete Regime

Although we can describe global capitalism as a regime, it is an incomplete regime: It governs only the economic function, even if the latter has come to take precedence over others; political and social functions remain grounded in the sovereign state.

The balance of advantage has swung so far in favor of financial

---

*The same is not true for health care. France ranks first, the United Kingdom eighteenth, and the United States thirty-seventh.
†Dani Rodrik, *Has Globalization Gone Too Far?* (Washington, D.C.: Institute for International Economics, 1997).

capital that it is often said that multinational corporations and international financial markets have somehow supplanted the sovereignty of the state. That is not the case. States retain their sovereignty and wield legal and enforcement authority that no individual or corporation can hope to possess. The days of the East India Company and the Hudson's Bay Company are gone forever. There is an encroachment upon sovereignty, however, that is more subtle.

Although governments retain the power to interfere in the economy, they have become increasingly subject to the forces of global competition. If a government imposes conditions that are unfavorable to capital, then capital will go elsewhere. Conversely if a government keeps down wages and provides incentives for favored businesses it can foster the accumulation of capital. So the global capitalist system consists of many sovereign states, each with its own policies, but each subject to international competition not only for trade but also for capital. This is one of the features that makes the system so complicated: Although we can identify a global regime in economic and financial matters, there is no global regime in politics; each state maintains its own regime. In mature democracies, enforcement powers are under civilian control, but in other parts of the world that is not the case.

There is nothing new in the combination of a global economy with political arrangements based on the sovereignty of the state. The same applied a century ago. The difference is that a whole century has passed and both states and markets have changed. For instance, a century ago states provided only rudimentary social services; after World War II the idea of the welfare state took root throughout the West, and some countries find it difficult to abandon it. A century ago colonies proliferated; today colonialism is unacceptable. Moreover, we enjoy a hundred years of hindsight. We can see that the previous global capitalist regime ended in world war, followed by revolutions, dictatorships, and another world war. Can we not do better?

. . .

It is a central thesis of this book that the current version of global capitalism is an incomplete and distorted form of global open society. The deficiencies are more in the political and social arrangements than on the economic side. Indeed, the main failing of global capitalism is that it is too one-sided: It puts too much emphasis on the pursuit of profit and economic success and neglects social and political considerations. This is particularly true in the international arena.

There is a widespread belief that capitalism is somehow associated with democracy in politics. It is a fact that the center countries today are democratic, but the same is not true of all the countries at the periphery. In fact, many claim that some kind of dictatorship is needed to generate economic development. Development requires the accumulation of capital, which in turn requires low wages and high savings rates. An autocratic regime capable of imposing its will upon the people can be more favorable to capital than a democratic one responsive to an electorate.

Take Asia, home to the most successful recent cases of economic development. Under the Asian model, the state has allied itself with local business interests and helped them to accumulate capital. The strategy required government leadership in industrial planning, a high degree of financial leverage, and some degree of protection for the domestic economy, as well as the ability to control wages. This strategy was pioneered by Japan, which had the benefit of democratic institutions, introduced with postwar U.S. occupation. Korea tried to imitate Japan quite slavishly but without democratic institutions. The policy was carried out by a military dictatorship holding sway over a small group of industrial conglomerates (*chaebol*). The checks and balances that prevailed in Japan were therefore missing. In Indonesia, there was a similar alliance between the military and the mainly Chinese business class. In Singapore, the state itself became a capitalist by setting up well-managed and highly successful investment funds. In Malaysia, the ruling party balanced favors to business interests with benefits for the ethnic Malay majority. In Thailand, the political arrangements are too difficult for an outsider to understand: Military meddling in business and financial meddling in the elections were two glaring weaknesses. Hong Kong alone was spared an incestuous relationship between government and business thanks to its colonial status and the strict rule of law. Taiwan also stands out for having successfully completed the transition from an oppressive to a democratic political regime.

It is often argued that successful autocratic regimes eventually lead to the development of democratic institutions. The argument has some merit: An emerging middle class is very helpful in the creation of democratic regimes. But periodic financial crises that afflict periphery countries will often stunt the development of a middle class. That is what happened in Southeast Asia and Russia in the aftermath of the crisis of 1997–1999. Moreover, it is not true that economic prosperity necessarily leads to the evolution of democratic freedoms. Rulers are reluctant to relinquish their power—they usually need to be pushed. For instance, Lee Kwan Yu of Singapore became more strident in propounding the merits of the "Asian way" after decades of prosperity.

There is a more fundamental difficulty with the argument that capitalism leads to democracy. The forces within the global capitalist system that might nudge countries toward democracy are rather feeble. International banks and multinational corporations often feel more comfortable with a strong autocratic regime than a weak democratic one. Foreign capital has often become a source of corruption and the mainstay of dictatorships, particularly where natural resources such as oil or diamonds are involved.

Perhaps the most potent force for democracy is the free flow of information, which makes it difficult for governments to misinform the people. But the freedom of information should not be overestimated. In Malaysia, for instance, the regime holds sufficient sway over the media to allow Prime Minister Mahathir Mohammed to put his own spin on events with impunity. Information is even more restricted in China, where the government controls even the Internet. In any case, the free flow of information will not necessarily impel people toward democracy, especially when people living in democracies do not believe in democracy as a universal principle.

Truth be told, the connection between capitalism and democracy is tenuous at best. Still, capitalism does need democratic institutions in order to contain and correct its own excesses. In nineteenth-century Europe, the dire predictions of the *Communist Manifesto* were in fact frustrated by the broadening of the political franchise. And today both autocratic regimes and disintegrating states constitute potent threats to peace and prosperity, both internally and internationally.

The Role of Money

A global economic system that is not matched by a global political system is difficult to analyze, especially in light of the tortuous relationship between capitalism and democracy. The task is simplified by that fact that there is a unifying principle in the global capitalist system: money. Money is not a principle that is introduced for the sake of simplification; it is truly dominant. Talking about free-market principles can confuse the issue, because money can be amassed in ways other than competition; but in the end it all boils down to profits and wealth measured by money.

Any understanding of the global capitalist system has to start with the role that money plays in it. The textbooks say that money serves three major functions: unit of account, medium of exchange, and store of value. The first two functions are well understood; there are some doubts about the third. In the classical interpretation, money is a means to an end, not an end in itself; it represents exchange value, not intrinsic value. That is to say, the value of money depends on the value of the goods and services for which it can be exchanged. But what are the intrinsic values that economic activities are supposed to serve? Nineteenth-century economists spoke in terms of "utility," but the concept did not survive critical examination. Eventually economists decided that they need not resolve the issue—they took economic agents' values as given. Their preferences can be expressed in the form of "indifference curves," and indifference curves can be used to determine prices.

The trouble is that in the real world values are not given. In a market economy, people are free to choose, but they do not necessarily know what they want. In conditions of rapid change, when traditions have lost their sway and people are assailed with suggestions from all sides, exchange values may well come to replace intrinsic values. Money has certain attributes that intrinsic values lack: It has a common denominator, it can be quantified, and it is almost uniformly appreciated by others. These are the attributes that qualify money as a medium of exchange—but not necessarily as the ultimate goal. Most of the benefits attached to money accrue from spending it; in this respect money serves as a means to an end. But money can also serve as a store of value. To the extent that other people want money and are willing to do almost anything to get it, money is power, and power can be an end in itself. Those who succeed may not know what to do with their money, but at least they can be sure that other people envy their success, and wealth gives them a sense of power. This may be enough to keep them going indefinitely even in the absence of any other motivation. The ones who keep it up wield the most power and influence in the capitalist system.

Far be it for me to belittle the benefits of wealth; but to make the accumulation of wealth the ultimate goal disregards many other aspects of existence that also deserve consideration, especially if the material needs for survival have been satisfied. I cannot specify what those other aspects are; it is in the nature of intrinsic values that they cannot be reduced to a common denominator. Thinking people are entitled to decide for themselves—it is a privilege they enjoy once they have met the requirements of survival. But instead of enjoying the luxury we go out of our way to exacerbate the fight for survival.

The capitalist system emphasizes competition and measures success in monetary terms. Monetary values have usurped the role of intrinsic values, and markets have come to dominate spheres of existence where they do not properly belong. Law and medicine, politics, education, science, the arts, even personal relations— achievements or qualities that ought to be valued for their own sake are converted into monetary terms; they are judged by the money they fetch rather than their intrinsic merit.

Without belaboring the issue further, I shall take it as fact that the dominant value in the global capitalist system is the pursuit of money. I can do so because there are economic agents whose sole purpose is to make money, and they dominate economic life today as never before. I am speaking of publicly owned corporations. These corporations are managed by professionals who apply modern management techniques with the sole objective of maximizing profits. These techniques are applicable universally to all fields and impel corporate managers to buy and sell businesses much as portfolio managers buy and sell stocks. The corporations, in turn, are owned mainly by professional portfolio managers whose sole objective in owning stock is to make money.

In the theory of perfect competition, the firm is a profit-maximizing entity, but in practice business has not always been conducted with that sole purpose in mind. Private owners are often guided by other goals: pride in the goods and services they produce, employment for family and friends, religious, moral, or immoral principles, power and reputation. Even publicly traded corporations used to have managers who felt sufficiently well entrenched to be motivated by other goals: perks, lifestyle, power, perhaps altruistic or nationalistic aspirations. The managers of the large German multinationals have traditionally considered themselves beholden to workers and the general public as well as to shareholders. Japanese managements pursued market share, and relationships used to take precedence over profits. Korea carried the Japanese example to extremes.

Still, in today's global capitalist system there has been a pronounced shift in favor of profit-maximizing behavior and a corresponding heightening of competitive pressures. Owners of private businesses enjoy more latitude than corporate managers; but as markets become global, privately held companies are at a disadvantage in preserving or gaining market share; companies need to raise capital from outside shareholders to exploit the opportunities presented by globalization. As a result, publicly traded companies have come to dominate the scene, and they have become increasingly single-minded in the pursuit of profits.

In the United States, shareholders have become more assertive toward managements. Success is measured by short-term performance, and managers are rewarded by stock options rather than perks. Those who fail are more quickly replaced. In Europe, companies used to deemphasize profits, both in their public image and in their public accounts. Higher profits tended to generate higher wage and tax demands, and it was considered inadvisable to attract attention to one's profitability. But the pressures of global competition have served to moderate wage demands and reduce the ability of the state to impose taxation; by contrast, the need to finance expansion has become more pressing. As a result, management attitudes have undergone a miraculous transformation, and European multinationals have come to resemble their American counterparts.

The creation of the European Union as a single market with a single currency has set off a scramble for market share. The price of one's stock has become much more important, both for raising capital and as a vehicle for acquisitions (or in the case of a low stock price, as an enticement for being acquired). Social goals, such as providing employment, have to take a backseat. Competition has forced consolidation, downsizing, and the transfer of production abroad. These are important factors in the persistently high level of unemployment in Europe.

Therefore the hallmark of the current form of global capitalism—the feature that sets it apart from earlier versions—is its pervasive success: the intensification of the profit motive and its penetration into areas previously governed by other considerations. Nonmonetary values used to play a larger role in peoples' lives; in particular, culture and the professions were supposed to be governed by cultural and professional values and not construed as business enterprises. Family background and breeding counted for more than wealth; patriotism and religion used to loom larger. To understand how the current capitalist regime differs from previous ones we must recognize the growing role of money as the yardstick. It is no exaggeration to say that money rules peoples' lives as never before. The tendency was always present, but lately the pursuit of profit has been carried to its logical conclusion. And any principle becomes more dangerous when it is no longer mitigated by other considerations.

Credit as a Source of Instability

Money is closely connected to credit, but the role of credit is not so well understood. Credit is a reflexive phenomenon in that the availability of credit depends on the value of collateral and the value of collateral is influenced by the availability of credit. This is particularly true for real estate, a favored form of collateral. Banks are usually willing to lend against real estate without recourse to the borrower, and the main variable in the value of real estate is the amount that banks are willing to lend against it. Strange as it may seem, the reflexive connection is not recognized in theory, and it is often forgotten in practice. The construction industry is notorious for its boom-bust character, and after every bust bank managers become very cautious and resolve never to expose themselves again. But when they are awash with liquidity and desperate to put money to work, a new cycle begins.

The same pattern can be observed in international lending: The creditworthiness of sovereign borrowers is measured by certain ratios—debt as a percentage of GNP, debt service as a percentage of exports, and the like. These measures are reflexive because the prosperity of the borrowing country is dependent on its ability to borrow. Again, the reflexive connection is often ignored. That is what happened in the great international lending boom of the 1970s: After the crisis of 1982, one would have thought that excessive lending would never recur. Yet it did, in Mexico in 1994 and again in Korea, Russia, and elsewhere in 1997.

Most economic theoreticians do not recognize reflexivity. They seek to establish the conditions of equilibrium, and reflexivity is a source of disequilibrium. John Maynard Keynes was very much aware of reflexive phenomena—he described financial markets as a beauty contest where people have to guess how other people guess how other people guess and personally made a great deal of money as a speculator—but even he presented his theory in terms of equilibrium in order to make it academically acceptable.

A favorite way to avoid the reflexivity inherent in credit is to concentrate instead on the money supply. It can be measured, and presumably it reflects credit conditions. In this way the reflexive phenomena connected with the expansion and contraction of credit can be left out of account. Still, a stable money supply does not create a stable economy. Excesses can be self-correcting—but at what cost? In the nineteenth century, when the money supply was regulated by the impersonal rules of the international gold standard, devastating panics were followed by economic depressions.

In the Great Depression of the 1930s Keynes discredited monetarism and replaced it with a theory that recognized the importance of credit. His prescription for curing deflation with government spending led to the emergence of bloated state sectors and inflationary tendencies. After his death, his approach fell out of favor. (Had Keynes lived, he would have probably changed his prescription.) The preservation of monetary stability once again became the prime objective. This led to the reinvention of monetarist theory by Milton Friedman. But Friedman's theory is flawed, because it disregards the reflexive element in credit expansion and contraction.

In practice, monetary policy since the mid-1980s has worked quite well, but largely by disregarding monetarist theory. Central banks do not rely exclusively—or even mainly—on measurements of the money supply but take into account a large variety of other factors (including the irrational exuberance of markets) in deciding how to maintain monetary stability. The German central bank went to great lengths to maintain the illusion that it was guided by monetary aggregates, but market participants learned from its behavior that this was largely a myth. By contrast, the Federal Reserve has been more agnostic and openly admits that monetary policy is a matter of judgment. Federal Reserve Chairman Alan Greenspan's statements are exercises in reflexivity and resemble the utterances of the Delphic oracle. When he was thanked by the chairman of a congressional panel for describing the economic situation so clearly, Greenspan replied, "Then I am afraid I must have been misunderstood."

Credit plays an important role in economic growth. The ability to borrow greatly enhances the profitability of investments. The more an investment can be leveraged, the higher the rate of return—provided the cost of money remains the same. The cost and availability of credit thus become important elements in influencing the level of economic activity. Given its reflexive character, credit exhibits no tendency toward equilibrium; indeed it is probably the most important factor in determining the asymmetric shape of the boom-bust cycle. There may be other elements at play, but it is the contraction of credit that renders the bust so much more abrupt than the boom that preceded it. When it comes to forced liquidation of debts, the sale of collateral depresses collateral values, unleashing a self-reinforcing process much more compressed in time than the expansionary phase. This holds true whether the credit was provided by the banks or the financial markets and whether the borrowing was against securities or physical assets.

International credit is particularly unstable because it is not nearly as well regulated as domestic credit in economically advanced countries. Ever since the birth of capitalism, there have been periodic financial crises, often with devastating consequences. To prevent recurrences, banks and financial markets have been subjected to regulation, but regulations usually addressed the last crisis and not the next one, so each new crisis led to a new financial architecture. That is how central banking, banking supervision, and the supervision of financial markets have evolved to their current, highly sophisticated state.

But such developments were not linear in character. The crash of 1929 and the subsequent failure of the U.S. banking system led to a restrictive regulatory environment for American banks as well as the stock market. After World War II, a thawing-out process began, very slowly at first but gradually accelerating. And even though the separation between banks and other financial institutions imposed by the Glass-Steagal Act was not repealed for decades, the regulation of both banks and financial markets was progressively relaxed.*

Deregulation and the globalization of financial markets have gone hand in hand in a reflexive fashion. Most regulations were

---

*The Glass-Steagal Act was finally repealed on November 12, 1999.

national in scope, so the globalization of markets meant less regulation and vice versa. But it was not a one-way street. Even as national regulations were relaxed, new international regulations were introduced. The two Bretton Woods institutions, the IMF and the World Bank, adapted to the changing circumstances and became more active as global watchdogs. The monetary authorities of the leading industrial nations established channels for cooperation, and some genuinely international regulations were introduced. By far the most important are the capital requirements for commercial banks that were established under the aegis of the Bank for International Settlements in Basle in 1988.

In fact, without the intervention of the monetary authorities the international financial system would have collapsed on at least four occasions: 1982, 1987, 1994, and 1997. Nevertheless, international controls remain quite inadequate compared to the regulatory environment that prevails in advanced countries. Moreover, monetary authorities at the center are more likely to respond to crises that affect them directly versus those whose victims are at the periphery. It is noteworthy that the U.S. stock market crash of 1987, which was purely domestic in origin, led to regulatory changes, namely, the introduction of so-called circuit breakers; disturbances in the international financial markets did not provoke a similar response. Although the introduction of capital requirements by the Basle Accord of 1988 was a belated answer to the crisis of 1982, the fact remains that international regulations have not kept pace with the globalization of financial markets.

The inadequacy of international regulations can be attributed partly to the failure to understand the reflexive nature of credit and partly to the prevailing antiregulatory mood, but mainly to the lack of appropriate international institutions. National financial systems are in the charge of central banks and other financial authorities. By and large, they do a good job, and there has been no systemic breakdown in major industrial countries for decades. But who is in charge of the international financial system? The international financial institutions and the national monetary authorities cooperate at times of crisis, but there is no international central bank, no international regulatory authorities akin to those at the national level. The Bretton Woods institutions tried to fill the void and succeeded for a while. But eventually the gap between their resources and the volume of international capital movements grew too large, and in the crisis of 1997–1999 they failed spectacularly. The political response has been to reduce rather than reinforce the power and influence of the IMF. As I shall contend in Chapter 10, this leaves the international financial architecture greatly weakened.

Asymmetry, Instability, and Cohesion

By definition, the center is the provider of capital, the periphery the recipient. Abrupt changes in the willingness of the center to provide capital to the periphery can cause great disruptions in recipient countries. The nature of the disruptions depends on the form of capital provided. Debt instruments or bank credits can cause bankruptcies and a banking crisis; if the investment was in stocks, it can precipitate a stock market crash. Direct investments are the least disruptive; the worst that can happen is the absence of new investment. Usually all forms of capital move in the same direction.

What happens when a country defaults on its debt? The answer is shrouded in mystery, because formal defaults are usually avoided. There is a general impression that the country concerned will suffer irreparable damage, but in reality many countries fail to meet obligations, and ways have been found to accommodate them. Following the international debt crisis of 1982, the Paris Club was set up to deal with official debt, the London Club for commercial debt. When the dust settled, so-called Brady bonds were issued to replace the outstanding bonds.

Until recently, creditors tended to fare much better than debtors in international debt crises. They may have had to roll over loans, extend dates of maturity, or even grant concessional rates, but they did not have to abandon their claims. Although the IMF was not supposed to be partial to lenders, its primary mission was to preserve the international monetary system, and it sought to avoid sudden shocks to the creditworthiness of major banks. Moreover, it did not have sufficient resources to act as lender of last resort; therefore it had to mobilize help from the banks, and the banks knew how to exploit their strategic position. Sometimes they could even persuade debtor countries to assume liability for the debts of domestic banks that would otherwise be wiped out (that is what happened in Chile in 1982, in Mexico in 1994, and, again, to a limited extent, in Korea in 1998). Of course, the lenders had to set up reserves, but they tended to eventually recover a significant part of the bad debts. Moreover, banks could usually rely on the assistance of national monetary authorities to recoup credit losses. The Federal Reserve deliberately kept short-term interest rates low in the United States from 1991 to 1993 in order to allow struggling American banks to rebuild profitability; the Bank of Japan has been doing the same since 1995. But debtor countries enjoy no comparable relief. International assistance is usually designed to enable them to meet debt obligations. Although they may not be able to pay off their obligations in full, they will be obliged to pay to the limit of their ability. The burden usually weighs them down for years.

This is in sharp contrast with domestic debt crises in advanced countries, in which bankruptcy procedures tend to protect debtors. For instance, U.S. banks lost more money in the savings-and-loan crisis of 1985–1989 than in the international debt crisis of 1982. In the case of international lending, the net result of IMF policies has been to bail out the creditors, creating a dangerous moral hazard. All this is now changing (see Chapter 10).

The asymmetry in the treatment of lenders and borrowers is a major source of instability. Every financial crisis is preceded by an unsustainable expansion of credit. If credit is freely available, it is too much to expect the debtors to exercise self-restraint. If the public sector is the borrower, the debt will have to be repaid by future governments—running up debt is a wonderful escape hatch for weak regimes. For instance, the so-called reform communist regime in Hungary tried to buy the allegiance of the people with borrowed money until the crisis of 1982 put an end to the practice. But it is not just the public sector that lacks restraint, and if the debts are incurred by the private sector the financial authorities might not even be aware of it until too late. That was the case in several Asian countries in 1997.

Still, the asymmetry is also a source of cohesion. All sorts of financial and political pressures are brought to bear on debtor countries, making it difficult for them to opt out of the system by reneging on obligations. The pressures serve to hold the system together even if it is painful for countries to belong. For instance, the first democratic elections in Hungary in 1990 would have offered an excellent opportunity to draw a line between past indebtedness and obligations entered into by the new democratic regime. I tried to prepare such a scheme, but the future prime minister, Joseph Antall, reneged on it because he was far too beholden to Germany, Hungary's largest creditor. There are other instances; Chile in 1982 sticks in my memory. Under the influence of the Chicago school of economists, the Chilean banking system had been privatized, and entrepreneurs bought banks using money borrowed from the banks themselves. In 1982, when the banks could not meet their international obligations, the state assumed responsibility for the debts of the privatized banks because the Pinochet regime, lacking legitimacy at home, was eager to maintain its credit standing abroad. As a result, taxpayers had to foot the bill.

Another asymmetry needs to be noted. Issuing money is a national prerogative, and nations whose currency is readily accepted in international financial transactions are much better situated than those that cannot borrow in their own currency. This is one of the main advantages of being at the center versus the periphery. The benefits of earning seignorage (the interest saved by issuing banknotes rather than treasury bills) are relatively insignificant compared to the advantage of being in charge of one's own monetary policy. Countries on the periphery must take their cues from the center—the United States foremost. Because the monetary policies of center countries are guided by domestic considerations, those on the periphery have little control over their destinies.

The fact that the major currencies fluctuate against one another can also be a source of instability. Changes in interest rates and exchange rates hit dependent countries as exogenous shocks, although in reality they are endogenous to the system. The international debt crisis of 1982 was precipitated by a drastic rise in U.S. interest rates; the Asian crisis of 1997 was associated with a rise in the U.S. dollar. In 2000, the weakness of the euro is causing tensions.

The disparity between center and periphery is not confined to the global financial system; it was also present in the European exchange-rate mechanism (ERM). The Bundesbank played a dual role: It was charged by the German constitution to preserve the value of the deutsche mark, and at the same time it was the de facto arbiter of monetary policy for the European monetary system. The two roles came into conflict after German reunification. Domestic considerations dictated a tight monetary policy; economic conditions in the rest of Europe would have demanded the opposite. Not surprisingly domestic considerations won out, and the ERM collapsed in 1992.

These two asymmetries—between lenders and borrowers and between center and periphery—are the primary—but not the only—sources of instability in the international financial system.

Portfolio investments also are notoriously unstable. Historically, crossborder investments used to occur in the advanced stages of bull markets, when domestic stocks were overvalued and overexploited, and investors became more adventuresome. The sudden interest in a foreign market would drive prices there through the roof, only to fall equally fast when the domestic bull market ended and investors became anxious to bring money home. This was my initial area of specialization, and I lived through several such episodes. Conditions have since changed. Crossborder investment is no longer an occasional activity but rather the bread and butter of institutional investors. Although the peculiar rhythm of foreign investing to which I became accustomed may have gone out of style, it would be foolish to think that stock markets are no longer susceptible to dynamic disequilibrium. In times of uncertainty, capital tends to return to its place of origin. That is another reason why disturbances tend to have a disproportionally larger effect at the periphery than at the center. Usually a minor disturbance at the center gets magnified into a crisis at the periphery. The financial crisis of 1997–1999 was unusual, even unique, in this respect because the impulse did not come from the center.

In spite of its asymmetry and instability—or rather because of it—the global capitalist system exhibits considerable cohesion. Being at the periphery has its disadvantages, but opting out is not a viable option. Isolation would deprive poor countries not only of capital but also of technological innovations.

To put matters in perspective, the global capitalist system has brought great material benefits. It is estimated that globalization has added 1 percent per annum to the world economy. Although the cards are stacked in favor of the center, periphery countries that can attract capital have also prospered. The crisis of 1997–1999 hit Asia after a period of explosive growth, and the recovery has been faster than could have been expected. So in addition to its cohesion, the system also shows considerable resilience, counterbalanced on the negative side by its asymmetry and instability.

The Future of the Global Capitalist System

What can we say about the future of the global capitalist system? History offers some clues. This is not the first time that capital has flowed freely. In some ways, the nineteenth-century version of global capitalism was more stable. It had a single currency—gold— whereas today there are three major currencies—dollar, yen, and euro—crushing against one another like tectonic plates. Back then imperial powers, Britain foremost among them, derived enough benefit from the system to justify dispatching gunboats to faraway places to preserve peace and collect debts; today the United States refuses to be the policeman of the world. Most important, people were more firmly rooted in fundamental values than they are today. Reality was still regarded as something external, and thinking was still considered a means of attaining knowledge. Right and wrong, true and false were considered objective criteria upon which people could depend. Science offered deterministic explanations and pre- dictions. Granted, there were conflicts between the precepts of reli- gion and science, but together they offered a dependable guide to the world. They created a civilization that in spite of its internal contradictions dominated the world.

This global capitalist system was brought to an end by World War I. There were a number of financial crises prior to the war, some of them quite severe, causing several years of economic dislo- cation and decline. Still, it was not the financial crises that destroyed the system but war and the subsequent political revolutions.

Another incarnation of international capitalism followed in the 1920s, although it was not quite global in scope. It crashed in 1929, but I doubt a similar episode will recur, for allowing the U.S. bank- ing system to collapse was a policy error we are not likely to repeat. Nevertheless, I do see instability ahead.

Boom-Bust

I am reluctant to apply the boom-bust model to the global capital-ist system because I consider the system too open-ended and incomplete to fit the pattern. Almost against my better judgment—not every-thing should be interpreted as a boom-bust phenomenon—I can identify the makings of a boom-bust pattern: a prevailing trend—namely, international competition for capital; and a prevailing bias—namely, an excessive belief in the market mechanism. In the boom, both bias and trend reinforce each other; in the bust, both of them will fall apart. What would bring about the bust? I believe the answer is to be found in the tension between the global scope of the financial markets and the national scope of politics. Earlier I described the global capitalist system as a gigantic circulatory system sucking capital into the center and pushing it out into the periphery. The sovereign states act like valves within the system. While the global financial markets are expanding, the valves are open, but if and when the flow of funds is reversed they may close, causing the system to break down. To follow up this hypothesis, I shall examine the prevailing ideology first, the prevailing trend second.

Market Fundamentalism

The global capitalist system is supported by an ideology rooted in the theory of perfect competition. According to this theory mar-kets tend toward equilibrium, and the equilibrium position repre-sents the most efficient allocation of resources. Any constraints on free competition interfere with the efficiency of markets; therefore they should be resisted. This ideology was called "laissez-faire" in the nineteenth century, but I have found a better term for it: "mar-ket fundamentalism." Fundamentalism implies a belief that has been carried to the extreme. It is a belief in perfection, a belief that provides a solution to every problem. It posits an authority that is endowed with perfect knowledge, even if such knowledge is not readily accessible to ordinary mortals. Religion can be such an authority, and in modern times science has become a credible substitute. Marxism claimed to have a scientific basis, and so does market fundamentalism. The scientific basis of both ideologies was established in the nineteenth century, when science still promised to deliver the ultimate truth. We have learned a great deal since then about the limitations of scientific method and the imperfections of the market mechanism. Both Marxist and laissez-faire ideologies have been thoroughly discredited. The laissez-faire ideology was the first to be dismissed, as a consequence of the Great Depression and the rise of Keynesian economics. Marxism lingered on despite the excesses of Stalinism, but following the collapse of the Soviet system it is now in near-total eclipse.

In my student days in the early 1950s, laissez-faire was even more unacceptable than is state intervention in the economy today. The idea that it would stage a comeback seemed inconceivable. I believe that the revival of market fundamentalism can be explained only by a faith in magic that is even more potent than the scientific base. President Reagan spoke of the "magic of the marketplace"—the invisible hand is powerful magic indeed.

A key feature of any fundamentalist belief is reliance on black-and-white, either-or judgments. If a proposition or policy is wrong, its opposite must be right. This logical non sequitur lies at the heart of both Marxism and market fundamentalism. Marxism holds that private ownership of capital is unjust and intolerable; therefore it must be replaced by state ownership. Market fundamentalism holds that state intervention is inefficient and harmful; therefore nothing should be allowed to interfere with the market mechanism. In truth, state intervention in the economy has always produced some negative results. This has been true not only of central planning but also of the welfare state and of Keynesian demand management. From this banal observation, market fundamentalists jump to the conclusion that free markets must be perfect.

To be fair, arguments that favor unregulated markets are rarely presented so crudely. On the contrary, people like Milton Friedman have amassed voluminous statistics, and the theoreticians of rational expectations have employed arcane mathematics that we ordinary mortals have difficulty following. Sophisticated models have been developed that ascribe shortfalls from the conditions of perfection—namely, welfare-maximizing equilibrium—to imperfect or asymmetric information. Most but not all of these models serve the purpose of establishing the conditions of equilibrium. I am reminded of theological discussions in the Middle Ages about the number of angels dancing on the head of a pin.

Market fundamentalism plays a crucial role in the global capitalist system. It provides the ideology that motivates many successful participants and drives policy. In its absence, we would not be justified in talking about a global capitalist system. Market fundamentalism came to dominate policy around 1980, with the ascent of Reagan and Thatcher. The prevailing trend—international competition for capital—started earlier, with the two oil crises in the 1970s and the establishment of offshore markets in Eurocurrencies, but it was only after the political changes introduced by Thatcher and Reagan that capital—and entrepreneurship—gained the upper hand. Bias and trend have been reinforcing one another ever since.

The Triumph of Capitalism*

The global competition for capital has given financial capital the upper hand. Individual countries have to compete to attract and

*This section, written in August 1998, has not been updated for the sake of historical accuracy except where specified.

retain it. The trend is reinforced by the United States, which exerts political pressure to open capital markets.

In the United States, publicly traded companies are increasing in number and size, and the interests of shareholders loom ever larger. Managements are as much concerned with the market for their shares as with the market for their products. If it comes to a choice, the signals from financial markets take precedence over those from product markets: They will readily divest divisions or sell the entire company if it will enhance shareholder value. Companies must either acquire or be acquired in an increasingly integrated global market; either way, managements need high prices for their stock. Personal rewards are also increasingly tied to the price of stock. The change is most pronounced in the banking sector, which is undergoing rapid consolidation. Bank shares are selling at several times book value, but managers, mindful of their stock options, continue to repurchase shares, reducing the number of shares outstanding and increasing their market value whenever possible.

Mergers and acquisitions are reaching unprecedented levels as industries consolidate on a global basis. Cross-country transactions are more common. The establishment of a single currency in Europe has given Europewide consolidation a tremendous push. And this realignment of companies is occurring faster than one could have imagined. Global monopolies and oligopolies are emerging (Microsoft and Intel being early examples). There are only four major auditing firms left in the world; similar but less pronounced concentration is taking place in other financial functions.

At the same time, the number of shareholders is growing, and the relative importance of share ownership in household wealth is accelerating. This is happening against a background of a sustained and rapid rise in equity prices. Prior to August 1998 the last major break in the bull market that started in the early 1980s was in 1987, and the Standard and Poor's (S&P) index has risen by more than 350 percent since. In Germany, the market has risen by 300 percent since September 1992.* The growth in economic activity has been more modest but sustained. The focus on profitability has led to reductions in the number of employees and increases in the output per employee, while rapid advances in technology contribute to rising productivity. Globalization and exploitation of cheaper sources of labor have kept the cost of production down, and interest rates have, on balance, shown a declining trend since the early 1980s, contributing to the rise in equity prices.

The spread of stock ownership through mutual funds has introduced two potential sources of instability, particularly in the United States. One is the so-called wealth effect. Thirty-eight percent of household wealth and 56 percent of pension funds is invested in stocks. Stock owners have big paper profits, they feel rich, and their propensity to save has been reduced to the vanishing point. Personal savings of households as a percent of disposable income has now fallen to 0.1 percent from a peak of 13 percent in 1975. Should there be a sustained decline in the stock market, shareholders' sentiments would be reversed, contributing to a recession and reinforcing the market decline.

Another source of potential instability comes from mutual funds. Fund managers are judged on the basis of their performance relative to other fund managers, not on the grounds of absolute performance. This may sound like an arcane point, but it has far-reaching implications, as it practically forces fund managers into trend-following behavior. As long as they keep with the herd, no harm will come to them even if the investors lose money; but if they try to buck the trend and their relative performance suffers even temporarily, they may lose their job. (This is precisely what happened to Jeff Vinik, the manager of Fidelity's largest fund. He has been very successful on his own ever since, earning a performance fee based on absolute performance.) By the fall of 1998, mutual funds,

*Between the fall of 1998 and mid-March 2000, the S&P has risen another 42 percent, Nasdaq 238 percent, and the German DAX 100 percent.

having become accustomed to a constant inflow of new cash, were carrying the lowest cash reserves ever. Should the trend turn, they will be forced to raise cash, again adding to the downward pressure.

However worrisome this may be, the main sources of instability are found in the international arena. The global capitalist system is currently undergoing the most severe test of its existence: the Asian crisis and its aftermath. Testing constitutes the third stage in the boom-bust pattern. As in every boom-bust sequence, it cannot be predicted with certainty whether a trend will be successfully tested or abruptly reversed. It is more productive to lay out possible scenarios for a successful or an unsuccessful test.

If the global capitalist system survives the current period of testing, this period will be followed by one of further acceleration that will carry the system into far-from-equilibrium territory (indeed if it is not there already). One of the features of this new, more extreme form of global capitalism will be the elimination of one plausible alternative to free-market ideology that recently emerged: the so-called Asian, or Confucian, model. As a result of the current crisis, overseas Chinese and Korean capitalists whose wealth has been severely impaired will have to give up family control. Those who are willing to do so will survive economically; the others will likely perish. The crisis has also aggravated the situation of heavily indebted companies in all Asian countries. Those with foreign debts have seen their debt-to-equity ratios deteriorate; those with domestic debt have been hit by the combination of rising interest rates and declining earnings. The only way out is to convert debt to equity or to raise additional equity. This cannot be done by the family; usually it cannot even be done locally. There will be no alternative but to sell out to foreigners.

The net result will be the end of the Asian model and the beginning of a new era in which periphery countries will be more closely integrated into the global capitalist system. International banks and multinational corporations will gain strong footholds. Within local companies, a new generation of family members or professional managers educated abroad will come to the fore. The profit motive will take precedence over Confucian ethics, and the market fundamentalist bias will be reinforced. Some countries, such as Malaysia, may fall by the wayside if they persist with their xenophobic, anti-market policies, but others will make the grade.*

So if the global capitalist system emerges triumphant from the current crisis, it can be anticipated that the world economy will be dominated even more by publicly owned international corporations. Severe competition will not allow them to pay much heed to social concerns. They will, of course, give lip service to worthy causes such as the environment, particularly if they have direct dealings with the general public, but they will not be able to afford to maintain employment to the detriment of profits.

Still, it is quite possible that the global capitalist system will not survive the current test. Storm clouds are gathering on the political horizon, even though the initial impact of the crisis was to reinforce democracy. Corrupt and authoritarian regimes were overturned in several countries. Korea was fortunate to elect a new president, Kim Dae Jung, who has long been an outspoken critic of the incestuous relationship between government and business. The current prime minister in Thailand is generally admired for his honesty, and he is surrounded by a Western-educated, market-oriented cabinet. In Indonesia, Suharto was swept from office by revolution. Only in Malaysia did Mahathir succeed in keeping himself and his cronies in power by imposing capital controls. But the economic decline has not yet run its course, and political tensions are rising. In China, economic reformers are in charge, but there is a real danger that if economic conditions continue to deteriorate the reformers will lose out to hard-liners. Already, anti-American, anti-IMF, anti-foreign

---

*In the event, Malaysia weathered the storm better than Indonesia and Thailand.

resentment is building throughout Asia—including Japan. Elections in Indonesia could well produce a nationalistic, Islamic government inspired by Mahathir's ideas.*

What happens at the center will be decisive. Until recently the trouble at the periphery has benefited the center. It has counteracted incipient inflationary pressures, induced the monetary authorities not to raise interest rates, and allowed stock markets to reach new highs. But the positive effects of the Asian crisis are beginning to wear off, and the negative ones are beginning to surface. Profit margins are coming under increasing pressure. Some companies are directly affected by reduced demand or tougher competition from abroad; service industries that are not directly affected by international competition feel the impact of rising labor costs.

The U.S. stock market boom has also run its course.† Should the market turn down, the wealth effect is liable to translate a market decline into an economic decline. That could arouse resistance to imports, which could in turn fuel resentment at the periphery.

Ever since the outbreak of the Asian crisis capital has been fleeing from the periphery. If the periphery countries give up hope that the flow will resume, they may start using their sovereign authority to prevent outflows. That will induce foreign investors to flee from other countries while they can, and the system will collapse. The United States is also looking increasingly inward. The refusal of Congress to provide additional funds to the IMF may play the same role today as the protectionist Smoot-Hawley tariffs did during the Great Depression.‡

Which of the two scenarios is likely to prevail? As a market par-

---

*Again, events turned out differently. Indonesia elected as president an Islamic cleric, Abdurrahman Wahid, who is a firm believer in open society. In China, the reformers regained their influence after a rocky interlude, although nationalism has become even more firmly entrenched as the ideology that has replaced communism.
†I hardly need point out that this conclusion was premature.
‡While this dire scenario has been contradicted by events, I consider developments at the IMF a source of future trouble (see Chapter 10).

ticipant, I must maintain an open mind. I have no hesitation, however, in asserting that the global capitalist system will succumb to its defects, if not on this occasion then on the next—unless we recognize that it is defective and act in time to correct the deficiencies.

I can already discern the contours of the final crisis. It will be political in character. Indigenous political movements are likely to arise that will seek to expropriate the multinational corporations and recapture national wealth. Some of them may succeed in the manner of the Boxer Rebellion in China or the Zapatista Revolution in Mexico. Their success may then shake the confidence of financial markets, engendering a self-reinforcing process on the downside. Whether it will happen on this occasion or the next is an open question.

As long as a boom-bust process survives testing, it emerges reinforced. The more stringent the test, the greater the reinforcement. After each successful test comes a period of acceleration; after a period of acceleration comes the moment of truth. Exactly where we are in this sequence it is impossible to determine except in retrospect.

A Critical Postscript

This text was written in the fall of 1998. The global economy has weathered the storm much better than I expected. Looking back from the perspective of 2000, we see the financial crisis of 1997–1999 as a glitch in the triumphant march of capitalism. If I want to stick with my boom-bust approach I would have to say that the global capitalist system has survived a severe test, thereby reinforcing the market-fundamentalist bias. But I shall argue in Chapter 10 that the heightened reliance on market discipline has weakened the global financial architecture for the next test.

I feel obliged, however, to point out a flaw in my own analysis. I have focused on the role of capital, especially financial capital, and did not give sufficient weight to the benefits of entrepreneurship. This was a serious omission. I have berated economic theory for being rooted in the past, and I fell into the same trap.

The debate between capitalism and socialism has its origins in the nineteenth century, and so it is influenced by nineteenth-century economic concepts. The very term "capitalism" is derived from a division of the factors of production into labor, land, and capital. Entrepreneurship was a latecomer to this division when it was discovered that the value of output could not be derived from the factors of production that went into producing it; entrepreneurship was introduced to account for the difference. So when we speak of giving capital a "free hand," we are really talking about entrepreneurship: the pursuit of higher returns on capital—profit. Profit is more the product of entrepreneurship than of capital. For instance, as a hedge fund manager my team and I invest other people's money, and we get 20 percent of the profits. So without any money to start with, I could become a capitalist.

Entrepreneurship can increase the productivity of capital. Globalization, removing government restrictions, and giving the profit motive a free hand have led to a veritable explosion in productivity. How could I have ignored that? I might argue that the acceleration in the pace of technological innovations was a mere coincidence, but even then it remains a fact. In any case, as a believer in reflexivity I would not want to hang my hat on that peg. There may be an element of coincidence; after all, the gains in productivity are closely connected with the development of a network economy, and the Internet happened to reach critical mass in the past few years. But the explosive growth of the Internet is itself the triumph of the profit motive. The Internet started off as a government-sponsored research network that people then hooked into, much like squatters siphoning off electricity. Only when it started being used for commerce and advertising did it become a significant factor in fostering productivity, economic growth, and a stock market boom.* Techno-logical innovations, of which the Internet protocol is only one, are also reflexively connected with the abolition of regulated monopolies in the telephone industry. And the penetration of the profit motive into biological research has accelerated the revolution in biotechnology. It has to be acknowledged that removing regulations and giving the profit motive free reign can release creative energies—like letting a genie out of the bottle.

It was a serious error not to give this factor greater weight. It ought to have been an integral part of my boom-bust analysis. I argued that the financial collapse in periphery countries gave center countries breathing space from the onset of inflation. There was an element of truth in that argument, and it carried a lot of weight with the monetary authorities. But the world economy has now recovered and inflation has still not raised its ugly head. The Federal Reserve finds itself in practically the same position as before the onset of the 1997–1999 financial crisis: It feels obliged to raise interest rates, partly to prevent inflationary pressures from developing, but mainly to preempt an eventual bust in the stock market.

As I pointed out earlier, what makes financial markets inherently unpredictable is that the boom-bust process is grounded in something real, and the reality that interacts with the participants' perceptions takes a different shape on each occasion. If financial markets were a closed system they would be more predictable. On this occasion the influence of technological innovations was real and significant, and I made a serious mistake in leaving it out of my analysis. It does not change my view that the stock market boom is liable to be followed by a bust, and the Federal Reserve is right in

*I must confess a bias with regard to the Internet that amounts to blindness. I was aware of the Internet before it was born because I was an investor in Bolt, Beranek, and Newman, which designed its precursor, Arpanet, in the late 1970s. I saw the potential of Internet technology as a means to promote open society, and I spent tens of millions of dollars introducing it to the former Soviet Union; yet I did not invest in it during the early stages when it went commercial.

trying to preempt it. How to keep excesses in asset valuation within tolerable bounds has become part of its mission.

But I must change my prophecy with regard to the ultimate demise of the capitalist system. I predicted that nationalist forces will engage in an orgy of expropriation. This is much less likely when foreign investment brings with it up-to-date technology than it was when investment was directed mainly at the exploitation of natural resources and the technology required for production was well established. Under current conditions it simply does not pay to opt out of the system. That does not mean that some countries will not make the attempt, but it does mean that the tendency is unlikely to spread. There may be some rogue states, but they are unlikely to bring down the capitalist system. The end of the system is not currently in sight. There are more subtle dangers looming, which I shall explore in greater depth in the last three chapters of the book.

CHAPTER 8

The Financial Crisis of 1997–1999

The Asian Crisis[*]

The financial crisis that originated in Thailand in 1997 was particularly unnerving because of its scope and severity. We at Soros Fund Management could see a crisis coming six months in advance as did others, but the extent of the dislocation took everyone by surprise. Several latent and seemingly unrelated imbalances were activated, and their interaction touched off a far-from-equilibrium process whose results are entirely out of proportion with the ingredients that went into creating it.

The financial markets played a role far different from the one assigned to them by economic theory. Financial markets are sup-

[*]Originally written in the summer of 1998; updated as necessary.

posed to swing like a pendulum: They may fluctuate wildly in response to exogenous shocks, but eventually they are supposed to come to rest at an equilibrium point that is supposed to reflect the fundamentals. Instead financial markets behaved more like a wrecking ball, swinging from country to country, knocking over the weakest and transforming the fundamentals.

The most immediate cause of trouble was a misalignment of currencies. The Southeast Asian countries maintained informal arrangements that tied their currencies to the U.S. dollar. The apparent stability of this "dollar peg" encouraged local banks and businesses to borrow in dollars and convert dollars into local currencies without hedging; the banks then loaned to or invested in local projects, particularly real estate. This seemed to be a riskless way of making money as long as the informal peg held. But the arrangement came under pressure, partly from the credit boom it engendered, partly from the slowdown in Japan, partly from the appreciation of the U.S. dollar against the Japanese yen. The balance of trade of the countries concerned deteriorated, although the trade deficits were offset by continuing and substantial inflows on capital accounts.

By the beginning of 1997, it was clear to Soros Fund Management that the discrepancy between the trade account and the capital account was becoming untenable. We sold short the Thai baht and the Malaysian ringgit early in 1997 with maturities ranging from six months to a year.* Subsequently Prime Minister Mahathir of Malaysia accused me of causing the crisis, a wholly unfounded accusation. We were not sellers of the currency during or several months before the crisis; on the contrary, we were buyers when the currencies began to decline—we were purchasing ringgits to realize the profits on our earlier speculation. (Much too soon, as it turned out. We left most of the potential gain on the table because we were

---

*That is, we entered into contracts to deliver at future dates Thai baht and Malaysian ringgit that we did not currently hold.

afraid that Mahathir would impose capital controls. He did so, but much later.)

If it was clear to us in January 1997 that the situation was untenable, it must have been clear to others. Still, the crisis did not break out until July 1997, when the Thai authorities abandoned the peg and floated the currency. The crisis came later than we had expected because the local monetary authorities continued to support their currencies far too long and international banks continued to extend credit, although they must have seen the writing on the wall. The delay undoubtedly contributed to the severity of the crisis. Reserves were depleted, and the break, when it came, was bigger than necessary. From Thailand, the breakdown of the currency pegs quickly spread to Malaysia, Indonesia, the Philippines, South Korea, and other countries. But some other countries that became engulfed in the Asian crisis did not have an informal dollar peg. What, then, did the stricken economies have in common? Some argue that the problem was their common dependence on a distorted or immature form of the capitalist regime now described pejoratively as "crony capitalism" but previously extolled as the "Asian model." There is some truth to that claim, but attributing the crisis to specifically Asian characteristics obviously does not give the full picture, as the crisis then spread to Latin America, Russia, and Eastern Europe. Practically all periphery countries were affected, although those with closed capital markets and those that allowed their currencies to depreciate fared better.

It is hard to escape the conclusion that the international financial system itself constituted the main ingredient in the meltdown. It certainly played an active role in every country, although the other ingredients varied from country to country. This conclusion is difficult to reconcile with the widely held notion that financial markets tend toward equilibrium. If my point is valid, then the attitude toward keeping financial markets under some kind of control ought to be radically reconsidered. To test this thesis, let us take an inventory of the other ingredients involved and then look at the actual course of events.

Demise of the Asian Model

There were many structural weaknesses in the Asian economies. Most businesses were family owned, and in accordance with Confucian tradition families wanted to run the business for their own benefit. If they issued shares to the public, they were inclined to disregard the rights of minority shareholders. To the extent that they could not finance growth out of earnings, they preferred to rely on credit rather than risk losing control. At the same time, government officials used bank credit as a tool of industrial policy; they also used it to reward their family and friends. There was an incestuous relationship between business and government, of which this was only one expression. This combination of factors resulted in very high debt-to-equity ratios and a financial sector that was neither transparent nor sound. The idea that banks would exercise some kind of discipline over the companies to whom they loaned simply did not apply.*

For instance, the South Korean economy was dominated by family-controlled *chaebol* (conglomerates). The *chaebol* were highly leveraged. The average debt-to-equity ratio of the thirty largest *chaebol* (indirectly accounting for about 35 percent of Korea's industrial production) was 388 percent in 1996, with individual *chaebol* going up to 600–700 percent. By the end of March 1998, the average had risen to 593 percent. The owners used their control to cross-guar-

---

*Many have argued that bank lending was a key mechanism to exert political control over business in Asia. See, e.g., Joseph E. Stiglitz, "Credit Markets and the Control of Capital," *Journal of Money, Credit, and Banking* 17(2) (May 1985): 150.

antee the debt of other members of the group, thereby violating the rights of minority shareholders. To make matters worse, Korean companies operated with very low profit margins: The interest coverage of the thirty largest *chaebol* in 1996 was 1.3 times but only .94 by 1997 (meaning that interest charges were not covered by earnings). Korean banks extended easy credit as part of industrial policy. The government decided to encourage certain industries, and the *chaebol* rushed in, fearing they would be left out. This led to headlong expansion without regard to profits. In this respect, Korea was consciously imitating the Japan of earlier days, but it turned out to be a crude imitation of a much more subtle model. As I mentioned before, Japan had the benefit of democratic institutions, whereas South Korea had a military dictatorship during much of its postwar history. The consensus-building tradition of Japan and the checks and balances that characterize a democracy were missing.

When nonperforming loans began to accumulate, Korean banks tried to earn their way out of the hole by borrowing even more money abroad and investing it in high-yield, high-risk instruments in countries like Indonesia, Russia, Ukraine, and Brazil. This was an important contributing factor in the Korean crisis.

Not that Japanese banks performed much better. Japan's troubles go back to the Wall Street crash of 1987. The Japanese financial system was tightly controlled by the Ministry of Finance (MOF). Officials at the MOF constituted an intellectual elite, comparable to the Inspecteurs de Finance in France. They understood reflexivity better than any other group I have encountered, and they conceived the grandiose idea that Japan could translate its industrial might into financial dominance by supplying liquidity to the world. The concept was spelled out to me after the crash of 1987 by an MOF official. He assured me that there would be no repeat of 1929 because Japan would "flood the world with liquidity." Unfortunately the Japanese failed to take into account an important aspect of reflexivity—namely, their own fallibility—which led to unintended consequences. Their decision to dominate international lending helped the world to overcome the effects of the Wall Street crash, but it left Japanese financial institutions with many losses abroad. Japanese policy also engendered a financial and real-estate bubble at home that reached its climax in 1991. Due to its tight control over financial institutions, the MOF was able to deflate the bubble without a crash—the first time in history such a feat was accomplished. But it left a lot of undigested bad assets festering in the balance sheets of the financial institutions. The decline in asset values was more drawn out but no less severe than it would have been in a crash. The Nikkei stock market index declined from a high of 39,000 in January 1991 to a low of 14,000 in August 1992 and a second bottom of 12,800 in October 1998. The decline in real-estate values was even greater and longer lasting. Taxpayer money could not be used to bail out the banks until the need became irresistible; even then, Japanese custom required that the heads of MOF officials should roll, and eventually they did. No wonder that the MOF resisted the idea of radical restructuring as long as it could.

At the outbreak of the Asian crisis, Japan was engaged in a policy of reducing the budget deficit. It was exactly the wrong policy, and the Asian crisis came at exactly the wrong time. The Japanese banks, which had big exposures in Thailand, Indonesia, and Korea, started reducing their balance sheets, causing a credit crunch in the midst of overflowing liquidity. The consumers, frightened by the Asian crisis and by some domestic bankruptcies, increased their propensity to save. The low interest rates encouraged capital to be transferred abroad. The yen declined and the economy slipped into recession. Eventually the government was persuaded to cut taxes and to use public money to recapitalize the banks, but it was too little, too late. The recession in Japan, the second-largest economy in the world and an important trading partner of the other Asian countries, aggravated the severity of the economic downturn throughout Asia.

We can identify many deficiencies in the Asian model of economic development: structural weaknesses in the banking system and in the ownership of enterprises, the incestuous relationship between business and politics, lack of transparency, and the absence of political freedom. Although these deficiencies were present in many of the affected countries, none of them was present in all: Hong Kong was exempt from most of them. Japan and Taiwan enjoyed political freedom; family ownership of major enterprises was not characteristic of Japan; Singapore had a strong banking system.

Moreover, the Asian model as such was an extremely successful economic development strategy and was widely admired in business circles. The Asian model produced dramatic increases in living standards, averaging 5.5 percent annual per capita income growth over an extended period—faster growth than was achieved in any economy over the same period at any time in recorded history. Therefore even as the crisis unfolded, Asian leaders like Lee Kwan Yu of Singapore, Suharto of Indonesia, and Mahathir of Malaysia proudly proclaimed their belief that Asian values were superior to Western values. They went so far as to challenge the UN's Universal Declaration of Human Rights. Lee Kwan Yu considered Western democracies decadent, Mahathir resented the tradition of colonialism, and Suharto extolled the virtues of nepotism. The Association of Southeast Asian Nations (ASEAN) admitted Myanmar (Burma) as a member in June 1997—a direct challenge to Western democracies, which found Myanmar's repressive regime politically and humanely unacceptable. (My public condemnation of ASEAN's move may have prompted Mahathir's attack against me.)

How could such a successful model of economic development

turn so sour so fast? The question cannot be answered without taking into account the deficiencies of the global capitalist system. The fact that the Asian crisis was not confined to Asia but engulfed all emerging markets before it ran its course reinforces the case that the main source of instability is to be found in the international financial system itself.

The Instability of International Finance

Looking at the system, we must distinguish between direct investors, portfolio investors, commercial banks, and financial authorities such as the IMF and central banks. Direct investors, like multinational corporations, did not play a destabilizing role except perhaps by hedging and speculating with their liquidity. In the case of portfolio investors, we can single out institutional investors that handle other people's money, hedge funds that employ leverage, and individual investors.

Institutional investors measure performance relative to one another, creating a herd of trend-followers. They allocate their assets between different national markets; as one market rises in value they feel obliged to increase their allocation and vice versa. In addition, mutual funds are likely to attract investors when they perform well and lose them when they incur losses. Institutional investors did not precipitate the crash, but they aggravated it, first by overstaying their welcome, then by rushing for the exit. Often they were forced sellers in order to meet redemptions.

Hedge fund managers and others who speculate with borrowed money play a similar role. During a winning streak they can increase their bets; when they lose they are forced to sell to reduce leverage. This is also a major source of contagion: Investors and speculators sustaining losses in one market are often forced to sell in other markets. Options, hedges, and other derivative instruments have a similar trend-reinforcing quality about them. Hedge fund managers and other speculators may trade in currencies directly without buying or selling securities. So do banks, both for their own account and for their customers. Banks are far more important in currency markets than hedge funds, but it must be admitted that hedge funds like mine did play a role in the Asian currency turmoil. Because hedge funds tend to be more concerned with absolute rather than relative performance, they are more likely to be actively involved in precipitating a change in trend. Of course, this exposes them to criticism when the change is undesirable, but if a trend is unsustainable it is surely better if it is reversed sooner rather than later. For instance, by selling the Thai baht short in January 1997 the Quantum Funds managed by my investment company sent a market signal that the baht may be overvalued. Had the authorities responded to the depletion of their reserves, the adjustment would have occurred sooner and been less painful. But the authorities allowed their reserves to run down; the break, when it came, was catastrophic.

This raises the question whether or not currency speculation is desirable. Reviewing the evidence, countries with freely convertible currencies have suffered worse dislocations in the current crisis than those that maintained some controls on currency trading. Thailand was more open than Malaysia, and Thailand had a bigger dislocation; mainland China was less affected than Hong Kong, although Hong Kong has a much sounder banking and financial system. The case of China versus Hong Kong is particularly persuasive because a weak banking system tends to aggravate the crisis. If the Chinese renminbi had been freely tradable, the Chinese banking system would have collapsed. Does it follow that currency speculation should be banned? Not necessarily. First, it is far from certain that currency speculation is harmful. As we have seen in the case of Thailand, speculation can provide useful market signals. Second, even if speculation is harmful, currency trading is indispensable for international trade, international investment, and access to the international banking system. Where to draw the line about currency speculation depends on the stage of development of the domestic banking systems and financial markets. There are ways in which speculation can be curbed without unduly interfering with legitimate currency trading. In any event, the correct policy mix can be decided only on a case-by-case basis. In the Asian countries, there was probably too much pressure from the United States and the IMF to open domestic financial markets before they were properly prepared for it; this was an important contributing factor to the crisis.

This brings us to the role of commercial banks. Each country has its own banking system and regulatory authorities; they interact through an intricate web to form the international banking system. Some large banks at the center of the system are so heavily involved in international transactions that they qualify as international banks. Often they own domestic banks or conduct in-country operations such as consumer credit in multiple countries. Most of the countries involved in the 1997–1999 crisis, however, had relatively closed banking systems, that is, few in-country banks were foreign-owned. Hong Kong and Singapore were exceptions: The major banks there qualified as internationals.

International and national banks are linked by credit lines that define the limits for entering into various transactions such as currency trades, interest-rate swaps, and the like. They may also be connected through longer-term credits. Both the credit lines and the loans are fixed in dollars or some other hard currency. In countries such as Korea and Thailand there were implicit or explicit guarantees from the central bank for the obligations of the major commercial banks. Those guarantees account for the reluctance of the international banks to reduce their credit lines even when they could see trouble coming.

In the countries that were pegged either formally or informally to the dollar, in-country banks and borrowers assumed that the peg would hold. Often they failed to hedge against the currency risk. Therefore when the peg finally broke they found themselves with large uncovered currency exposures. Scrambling for cover, they put tremendous pressure on local currencies by buying the currencies in which the loans were denominated. The currencies overshot on the downside, causing a sudden deterioration in the balance sheets of the borrowers. For instance, Siam Cement, the largest and strongest company in Thailand, incurred a loss of 52.6 billion Thai baht in 1997 compared to its beginning equity of 42.3 billion and 1996 profits of 6.8 billion.* Weaker companies fared much worse. Many of the borrowers had used the loans to finance real estate, and real-estate values were already declining when the peg broke. Suddenly there was a credit risk as well as a currency risk, which reduced the willingness of lenders to extend credit. Together with foreign investors fleeing from declining markets, this set up a self-reinforcing process that resulted in a 42 percent decline in the Thai currency and a 59 percent decline in the Thai stock market (expressed in local currency) between June 1997 and the end of August 1998. The combined result was a 76 percent loss in dollar terms over fourteen months. (Compare Wall Street's 86 percent loss over three years between October 1929 and April 1933.)

The panic was spread to the neighboring countries by the financial markets—I used the image of a wrecking ball; others have described financial contagion as a modern version of the bubonic plague. The imbalances in some of the newly stricken economies were less pronounced. The Malaysian economy was overheating, but the monetary expansion had been mainly internal; the trade deficit was quite modest. Nevertheless, Malaysia was hit just as hard as Thailand. The fundamentals in Indonesia seemed quite sound; the main problem was that Indonesia had borrowed heavily from

*The exchange rate was 24.35 Thai baht to the U.S. dollar before the currency peg was abandoned on July 2, 1997; it was at 45.9 at the end of the year.

Korean and Japanese banks that had their own problems and were not in a position to renew their loans. Nevertheless, the devastation in Indonesia was much greater than in Thailand. When the Hong Kong dollar came under attack, the currency-board system caused a rise in local interest rates that in turn depressed the value of real estate and stocks. International banks doing business with Hong Kong banks discovered a heretofore unknown credit risk. When they entered back-to-back interest-rate swaps,* they had assumed that the exposure was the same on both sides, so the credit risks canceled each other out; soon they realized that if the exchange rate changed their Hong Kong counterparty would suddenly owe them more money than they owed to the Hong Kong counterparty. This forced international banks to curtail their credit lines to Hong Kong. The Hong Kong market fell by 62 percent before the authorities intervened to stabilize the market.

Credit risk became an even bigger issue in Korea, where some banks actually defaulted on their guarantees. It was not long before the financial crisis forced Thailand, and then Korea and Indonesia, to seek the assistance of the IMF.

The Role of the International Monetary Fund

The IMF found itself confronting problems it never had to face before. The Asian crisis was a complex crisis, with a currency component and a credit component. The credit component, in turn, had an international aspect and a domestic aspect, and all the various components were interactive. What made the Asian crisis dif-

---

*Such a swap occurs when one bank switches between a fixed-rate and variable-rate loan for its customer against the inverse switch by its correspondent bank abroad.

ferent from any previous one was that it originated in the private sector; the public sector was in relatively good shape.

The IMF prescribed the traditional medicine used when the public sector is in trouble: raise interest rates and reduce government spending in order to stabilize the currency and restore the confidence of international investors. It did recognize the structural defects in individual countries and also imposed tailor-made conditions, such as the closing of unsound financial institutions. But the IMF programs did not restore the confidence of international investors because they addressed only some aspects of the crisis, not all. Since those aspects were interrelated, none could be cured separately. Specifically, currencies could not be stabilized until debt problems were tackled, because debtors rushing to cover their exposure depressed the currency, and currency weakness in turn increased the debtors' exposure in a vicious circle.

Why did the IMF not realize this? Perhaps the answer is that the IMF had not developed a methodology for dealing with imbalances in the private sector; certainly some IMF officials had an inadequate understanding of how financial markets operate. This was demonstrated in Indonesia, where the IMF insisted on closing some banks without making provisions for the protection of depositors, provoking a classic run on practically all banks. (A similar lack of understanding was shown later in Russia.)

In Indonesia, the financial panic weakened President Suharto's resolve to abide by the conditions of the IMF rescue program, which he already found distasteful because it encroached upon the privileges of his family and friends. The squabble between Suharto and the IMF pushed the Indonesian rupiah into a free fall. Soros Fund Management was badly hurt because we had bought Indonesian rupiah at around four thousand to the dollar, thinking that the currency had already overshot when it had fallen from 2,430 as of July 1997. It proceeded to fall to more than 16,000 in short order— a chastening experience. I had been fully aware of the corruption of the Suharto regime, and I had insisted on selling our share in an Indonesian power plant in which Suharto family members had a financial interest purely because I did not want to be associated with them. Yet here we were, losing money in Indonesia just when the chickens came home to roost.

The IMF has been criticized for setting too many conditions and interfering too much in the internal affairs of the countries that turned to it for assistance. What business is it of the IMF, it is asked, if a regime is corrupt or the banking and industrial structure over-leveraged? All that matters is that a country should be able to meet its obligations. The job of the IMF is to help contain a liquidity crisis; the structural problems are best left to the country concerned.

I would argue the opposite. Liquidity crises are inextricably interconnected with structural imbalances. When banks and corporations are overindebted, their condition cannot be corrected just by lending them more money—an infusion of equity is required. The trouble is that during a crisis neither new equity nor further credit is readily available.

The only effective solution would have been to impose a moratorium on debt repayments followed by a debt-to-equity conversion scheme, but that was far beyond the power and competence of the IMF. It would have relieved the pressure on the exchange rates and obviated the need for imposing punitive interest rates; it would have achieved the necessary structural adjustments without plunging the countries into depression. But it could not have been accomplished without mustering the necessary political will both locally and internationally. Kim Dae Jung in Korea might have welcomed it, but it is unlikely that Indonesia's Suharto would have gone along. In any case, it is inconceivable that the international community, particularly the United States Treasury, would have tolerated a temporary moratorium on debt payments. That would have sent shudders through the international banking system and precipitated the dislocations that occurred later in connection with the Russian default.

It would have also represented a complete break with past practices. The entire IMF doctrine had been built around the need to protect the interests of the international banking system. This is now under reconsideration, but only after the crisis has passed. Therefore events unfolded as in a Greek tragedy. And even though the inevitable debt-to-equity reorganizations are taking place, it is only after the countries have passed through a devastating experience.

Obviously there is a systemic problem here, and the IMF is part of the problem rather than the solution. The IMF is now in a crisis of its own. Market confidence has been an essential ingredient in its past successes, and its credibility has been impaired. The international financial institutions also find themselves under political pressure from the U.S. Congress. Most important, the IMF has itself lost confidence in the doctrine that guided its actions in the past, and it is flailing about trying to find a way to "bail in" the private sector. I shall explore this subject more fully in Chapter 10.

The Unfolding of the Crisis

In the fall of 1997 the Indonesian debacle put the Korean and Japanese banks on the defensive and undermined the confidence of international lenders in the Korean banking system. From Korea, the wrecking ball swung to Russia and Brazil, grazing Eastern Europe and demolishing Ukraine on the way. Korean banks had invested in Russia and Brazil, and Brazilians had invested in Russia. The Koreans and the Brazilians had to liquidate their holdings, and Brazil and Russia had to raise interest rates high enough to protect their currencies against the selling. Brazil used the crisis to enact long overdue structural reforms, which helped contain the situation—but only for a few months.

The international crisis reached its first climax at the end of December 1997 when, in spite of an IMF program, foreign banks refused to roll over their loans to Korean banks. The central banks had to intervene and strong-arm the commercial banks under their jurisdiction to renew their loans. A second IMF rescue package was put together. Soon afterward the panic started to abate. Federal Reserve Chairman Alan Greenspan made it clear that the Asian troubles ruled out any possibility of an interest-rate increase, and the bond and stock markets took heart. The wrecking ball stopped swinging without having penetrated Latin America, with the exception of the initial hit on Brazil. Both Korea and Thailand benefited from the election of new governments dedicated to reform. Only Indonesia continued to deteriorate, and eventually Suharto was forced out of power. Bargain-hunters appeared; currencies strengthened; and by the end of March 1998 Asian stock markets, including Indonesia's, recovered between a third and a half of their losses (again, measured in local currencies). This is a typical rebound after a major market break.

It was a false dawn. The financial collapse was followed by economic decline. Domestic demand in the heavily indebted countries came to a standstill and imports shrank, yet exports did not expand in dollar terms because of the fall in currencies. A high proportion of exports was directed toward countries that were also affected. In addition, exports were concentrated in a limited number of commodities where increased selling pressure drove down prices. Semiconductors, in which Korea, Taiwan, and, to a lesser extent, Japan vied for the world market, were particularly hard-hit. The economic decline quickly spread to countries that originally had not been involved. Japan slipped into a recession, and the economic situation in China worsened. Hong Kong also came under renewed pressure. The fall in commodity prices, especially oil, hurt Russia and other commodity-producing countries.

The problem in Japan was almost entirely internal. Given the tremendous currency reserves and a large and growing trade surplus, it was within the power of the Japanese government to recapitalize the banking system and stimulate the economy. Unfortunately its policies were misconceived. Banks had to fail and heads had to roll before public money was made available. Bankers and MOF officials did everything in their power to delay the evil day. The result was a credit crunch that pushed the economy into recession, putting immense pressure on the other Asian countries.

China faced some of the same difficulties as South Korea. It has a banking system that has been guided by political rather than commercial considerations, and the accumulation of bad debts was even worse than in Korea. There had been a tremendous boom in commercial property development (at the outbreak of the Asian crisis it was said that half the cranes in the world were working in Shanghai). The influx of foreign investment—with 70 percent of the total coming from overseas Chinese—came to a halt.

The big difference—China's saving grace in fact—has been that its currency is not convertible; otherwise the wrecking ball would surely have done its work in spite of enormous official currency reserves. China has foreign currency loans outstanding whose magnitude, as in other Asian countries, is not reliably reported, and foreign investors, particularly overseas Chinese, would probably have taken flight, or at least hedged their investments in the forward market, if they had the opportunity. As it is, capital controls bought the government time.

The Chinese government tried to use the interval to stimulate domestic demand. The Chinese Communist Party had lost the "mandate of heaven" in the Tiananmen Square massacre, so it must provide prosperity on earth in order to be tolerated. This means a growth rate of 8 percent. But the engines of growth—exports and foreign investment—were now switched off. Domestic demand had to take their place. The government resorted to good-old Keynesian remedies: fostering large infrastructure projects and trying to stimulate housing construction. China was determined to avoid devaluing its currency for a number of reasons. It wanted to enhance its stature in the world, build a stronger relationship with the United States, and attain membership in the World Trade Organization (WTO); it was also afraid of provoking protectionist countermeasures in the United States if it devalued. Devaluation would have also undermined the Hong Kong currency board, and the Chinese government was passionately committed to the idea of "one country, two economic systems" because it wanted mainland China to become more like Hong Kong. It also wanted to create a favorable precedent for the future reunification with Taiwan.

In the summer of 1998 it was far from clear whether these policies would work. The Chinese government was hoping to achieve the same effect as a devaluation by imposing import restrictions and providing export subsidies, but there was a lively trade in clandestine imports, particularly by enterprises associated with the People's Liberation Army, which undercut the demand for domestic products. The banking system and the balance sheets of China's state-owned enterprises (SOEs) continued to deteriorate. The trade surplus was illusory because of all the smuggling. The official reserves were barely maintained because of the hidden flight of capital. Steps to encourage private ownership of homes had the perverse effect of encouraging savings. The banking system used the savings to preserve moribund SOEs, which merely increased the state's indebtedness to its citizens without stimulating the economy. Radical structural reforms were needed, but they had to be put on hold because they might have provoked social unrest.

The global financial crisis reached its final culmination in the fall of 1998 when Russia defaulted on its internal debt, thereby shaking the international banking system to its core and causing the near-failure of Long Term Capital Management (LTCM), a highly leveraged hedge fund.

I shall analyze the Russian experience in greater detail in Chapter

9. For now, let us focus on the effect of Russia's default on financial markets. The markets at the center had weathered the crisis at the periphery remarkably well. Stock and bond prices actually benefited from the abatement of inflationary pressures. The Federal Reserve had been about to raise interest rates when the Asian crisis erupted; the removal of that threat came as a relief to the markets. The spreads between less risky and more risky financial instruments widened as a result of the crisis, and banks with heavy exposure to periphery countries were inclined to reduce their balance-sheet exposure, but until Russia defaulted these deflationary pressures were well contained.

The Russian default changed all this. Some banks and investment banks had been heavily involved in financing Russian banks, which speculated in Russian domestic treasury bills through currency as well as credit transactions; they also had some direct exposure, both for their own accounts and for clients. They now faced write-offs. But this direct effect paled in significance compared to the indirect effects. After all, the Russian treasury-bill market was tiny in comparison with the various international swap and spread markets: government bonds versus mortgage-backed securities; treasury bills versus Eurodollars; Eurodollars versus Eurosterling; fixed rates versus variable rates, and so on. The proprietary trading desks of large banks and investment banks as well as some hedge funds (not mine) were engaged in arbitraging these spreads: buying those that seemed underpriced in the expectation that the spreads would revert to more normal levels. The spreads were already at or near record levels because of the Asian crisis; now they went through the roof.

By far the largest player in the field was LTCM, the hedge fund formed by John Merriweather and his team when they left Salomon Brothers, a large investment bank that is now part of Citigroup. They had been successful, providing excellent returns to their investors and enjoying the highest reputation. They used sophisticated models based on efficient market theory for trading, and they had two Nobel economists on their board. Their counterparties were willing to trade with them without asking for any margin. In addition, they were able to obtain a large unsecured standby credit. At the beginning of 1998 they dividended out a significant portion of their investors' capital in order to increase the return on their remaining capital. They ran a balance sheet of over $100 billion and off-balance sheet obligations of more than $1 trillion with equity capital of $5 billion. They now suffered major losses, and their equity capital had shrunk to around $600 million by the time the Federal Reserve Bank of New York brought together in a room LTCM's major counterparties, who had the most to lose from its default, and encouraged them to form a large enough pool to prevent a meltdown. Had they not done so, the counterparties would have suffered major losses both on their exposure to LTCM and on their own proprietary accounts. Had it come to a liquidation of the outstanding positions, it would have been difficult to find buyers; moreover, the creditworthiness of counterparties would have been brought into question, precipitating a classic panic. But the Federal Reserve Bank of New York did step in. The stock markets suffered a temporary sinking spell, but the Federal Reserve lowered interest rates three times in quick succession, and markets regained their composure. It was the closest the international financial system has come to a meltdown, and it was the only occasion that the stock markets at the center were adversely affected by the global financial crisis.

I was finishing *The Crisis of Global Capitalism* just after the Russian default and just before the near-failure of LTCM. I saw it coming and was greatly affected by it. It pushed me overboard and made me predict the imminent demise of the global capitalist system. This is exactly what I wrote:

> The global capitalist system was severely tested in the Mexican crisis of 1994–1995, but it survived and came back stronger than ever. That is when the period of acceleration occurred and the boom became increasingly unsound. The fact that the holders of Mexican treasury bills emerged from the crisis unscathed set a

bad example for speculators in Russian treasury bills. The turning point came with the Thai crisis of July 1997. It reversed the direction of the flow of funds. . . .

At first, the reversal benefited the financial markets at the center for the reasons I already explained and the buoyancy of the center also brought hope to the periphery. The Asian stock markets retraced almost exactly half their losses in local currency terms before retreating again. This might be interpreted as the twilight period. Eventually the financial markets at the center also succumbed to the bust. At first the erosion was gradual and the flow of funds into mutual funds remained positive, but the meltdown in Russia precipitated a selling climax that had some, but not all, of the earmarks of a market bottom. I believe that it is a false bottom, just as the bottom made by the Asian stock markets at the beginning of 1998 turned out to be false. I expect a retracement of up to 50 percent but I cannot rule out the possibility of a further decline before the rebound. Eventually the markets should go much lower, leading to a global recession. The disintegration of the global capitalist system will prevent a recovery, turning the recession into a depression.

I have three main reasons why I believe that the bottom has not been reached. One is that the Russian meltdown has revealed previously ignored flaws in the international banking system. Banks engage in swaps, forward transactions, and derivative trades among each other and with their clients. These transactions do not show up in the balance sheets of the banks.

When Russian banks defaulted on their obligations, Western banks remained on the hook both on their own account and on behalf of clients. Hedge funds and other speculative accounts also sustained large losses. Banks are now frantically trying to limit their exposure, deleverage, and reduce risk. Their own stocks have plummeted and a global credit crunch is in the making.*

*Since then, Long Term Capital Management collapsed with disastrous consequences. [Original footnote.]

Second, the pain at the periphery has now become so intense that individual countries have begun to opt out of the global capitalist system or simply fall by the wayside. First Indonesia, then Russia, suffered pretty complete breakdowns. What happened in Malaysia and, to a lesser extent, in Hong Kong is in some ways even more ominous. The collapse in Indonesia and Russia was unintended, but Malaysia shut itself off from international capital markets deliberately. Its action has brought temporary relief to the Malaysian economy and allowed its rulers to maintain themselves in power but, by reinforcing a general flight of capital from the periphery, it has put additional pressure on those countries that are trying to keep their markets open. If the capital flight makes Malaysia look good in comparison with its neighbors, the policy may easily find imitators.

The third major factor working for the disintegration of the global capitalist system is the evident inability of the international monetary authorities to hold it together. IMF programs do not seem to be working and the IMF has run out of money. The response of the G7 governments to the Russian crisis was woefully inadequate, and the loss of control was quite scary. Financial markets are rather peculiar in this respect: They resent any kind of government interference but they hold a belief deep down that if conditions get really rough the authorities will step in. This belief has now been shaken.*

The reflexive interaction among these three factors leads me to conclude that we have passed the crossover point and the trend reversal is reinforced by a reversal of the prevailing bias. How events will unfold depends largely on the response of the banking system, the investing public, and the authorities at the center. The range of probabilities lies between a cascading decline of the stock markets and a more drawn-out process of deterioration. I think the latter alternative more likely. The shock to the

*These points figured in my congressional testimony on September 15, 1998. [Original footnote.]

international financial system is likely to wear off; the forced liquidation of positions will be absorbed. One of the main sources of tension, the strength of the dollar and the weakness of the yen, has already been corrected. Another trouble spot, Hong Kong, seems to have found a way to regain control over its destiny. Russia has been written off. An interest rate cut is in prospect. Stocks have fallen far enough that many of them appear attractive. The public has learned that it pays to buy dips in an everlasting bull market and it will take time before it discovers that the bull market does not last forever. Therefore it will take time for the three main negative forces to make their effect felt.

But the false dawn will be followed by a prolonged bear market, just as in the 1930s and in Asia currently. The public will stop buying dips and start moving out of stocks into money market funds or treasury bills. The wealth effect will take its toll and consumer demand will decline. Investment demand will also decline, for a number of reasons: Profits are under pressure, United States imports are rising and exports falling, and the supply of capital for the less well established enterprises and for real estate deals has dried up. Reductions in interest rates will cushion the market decline and the economy would eventually recover if the global capitalist system held together. But the chances of it falling apart have greatly increased. If and when the U.S. domestic economy slows down, the willingness to tolerate a large trade deficit will decrease and free trade may be endangered.

Earlier I had thought that the Asian crisis would lead to the ultimate triumph of capitalism: Multinational corporations would replace the overseas Chinese families and the Asian model would be assimilated into the global capitalist model. That could still happen, but it is now more likely that countries at the periphery will increasingly opt out of the system as their prospects for attracting capital from the center fade away. Banks and portfolio investors have suffered severe losses and there are more to come.

Russia is likely to default on its dollar obligations. Losses in Indonesia will also have to be recognized. Banks are punished by their shareholders for their exposure to the periphery: They will not want to increase their commitments. Only international governmental action could pump money into the periphery, but there is no sign of international cooperation.

In retrospect, my prediction was clearly wrong. It illustrates how dangerous it is to make unequivocal predictions, especially as my conceptual framework of reflexivity regards the future as open-ended. Of course, one cannot participate in financial markets without adopting some hypothesis about the future. Here, I made my bet and lost. It was a painful experience to endure both personally and professionally.

Although chastened, I do find some value in the experience because it exposed some of the weaknesses in my original analysis. I quote my misguided prognosis in full because it is important to understand where it went wrong. My specific mistake was to think that the Fed would fail to intervene to save LTCM. After all, its job is to protect the U.S. financial system, and the failure of LTCM could have endangered that. I have been arguing that the playing field of global capitalism is skewed in favor of the center. What better demonstration could I ask for than the disparity between the ability of the U.S. monetary authorities to protect the U.S. economy and the inability of the international monetary authorities to protect the global economy?

My mistake went deeper that that, however. Preoccupied with the flaws in international financial arrangements, I failed to give adequate weight to the tremendous improvements in productivity brought about by technological innovations, particularly in communications and information processing. These reached critical mass and began to exert powerful influence on the economy as well as the stock market. The Internet has created its own bubble, one that resembles previous bubbles but exceeds them in scale. Helped by that bubble, the Internet and other innovations are bringing fundamental changes to the way business is transacted. These will have far-reaching effects on the fortunes of individual companies and industries. They have also enhanced the competitive advantage of the United States and altered the relationship between center and periphery. This has made it much harder to opt out of a system that gives access not only to capital but also to improvements in technology. Nationalizing assets could be at least initially rewarding when the technology for using those assets was more or less stable and known; that was the case with oil companies. But when it is entrepreneurship rather than capital that counts, there is no readily available alternative to encouraging entrepreneurship.

Looking back, it is obvious that my analysis was permeated by a bearish bias. I envisaged declines of various shapes and sizes, but the idea that the stock market may go on to new heights did not enter my field of vision. It is difficult to reverse one's bearish bias when many of the underlying considerations remain in force. A global credit crunch has been avoided, and the pressure to opt out of the system did not materialize. Still, the disparity between center and periphery has become more pronounced, and the capacity of international financial institutions to control or influence financial markets has been weakened. The instability of the system is greater than ever; I shall address that issue in Chapter 10.

Soros Fund Management has had great difficulty in shaking off its bearish bias. My boom-bust model calls for a period of acceleration after a successful test, and we managed to participate in it but not wholeheartedly enough. We tried to play Internet stocks on the short side too soon, and we had our head handed to us: By May 1999, Quantum Fund had dropped 20 percent from the beginning of the year. Once again we managed to rectify the situation by correctly identifying the next group of leaders among technology companies, and we ended the year with a gain of 35 percent. That meant a jump of nearly 70 percent from the low point of 1999. This time we overstayed our welcome and got caught in the downdraft that started in March 2000. The roller-coaster ride was too much for the man at the helm: Stan Druckenmiller, the chief investment manager of the fund, decided to quit. I, on my part, felt obliged to call it a day and convert Quantum Fund into a more conservative investment vehicle with a broad diversification of risks.

It is very tempting to stay engaged and play the market on the short side now that the chickens are finally coming home to roost, but that would be a recipe for disaster. I am no longer qualified to take an active role in managing a hedge fund. The job requires single-minded attention to the task, and I have too many other interests and commitments.* Neither do I have any longer the endurance to absorb the tension and pain that the job entails. I would have a lot more to lose than to gain by going back into the ring. There is nothing quite so pathetic as an overage champion trying to slug it out. Even if I managed to cash in on an impending bust, it would not resolve my real problem: how to arrange for the proper management of my estate. I have the rare privilege of being able to act as the executor of my own estate; to discharge my duties properly I must not manage the estate myself.

In reviewing the events of the last few years, I have to question the usefulness of the boom-bust model. It was never meant to be more than an illustration of how near-equilibrium conditions can turn into far-from-equilibrium situations, but I carried an example that worked for the conglomerate boom too far. Already the analogy between the Soviet system and the U.S. banking system was stretching a point, and in the end my attempt to fit this pattern to the course of events in the 1997–1999 crisis became counterproductive. I rode what had been a fertile fallacy into exhaustion.

---

*It is interesting to conjecture that the writing of *The Crisis of Global Capitalism* left me with a bearish bias that hindered us in the subsequent boom. A similar connection occurred in 1987 when I was too busy discussing *The Alchemy of Finance* with economists in Boston to take evasive action just before the crash. In my heydey I used to have a rule against public pronouncements.

. . .

I do not think this exercise in self-flagellation invalidates my approach. On the contrary, it reinforces the importance of recognizing our fallibility. I overused a specific boom-bust model, but the basic idea remains valid: A prevailing bias and a prevailing trend can interact in an initially self-reinforcing but eventually self-defeating way. It is also true that a successful test tends to reinforce a prevailing bias, whereas an unsuccessful one tends to reverse it. The moment of truth and the twilight period are more doubtful concepts: They can be identified only by hindsight, if at all.

Admittedly it was methodologically incorrect to make such an unconditional prediction, since the theory of reflexivity permits only the formation of alternative scenarios. But market participants do not have the luxury of abiding by scientific method; they have to act on the basis of false hypotheses. Having made a false prediction, I have at least demonstrated that the hypotheses I work with are falsifiable. In a peculiar way my erroneous analysis serves to justify an approach that is based on recognizing fallibility and correcting mistakes—as Soros Fund Management was able to do for thirty years.

CHAPTER 9

Who Lost Russia?

The collapse of the Soviet empire in 1989 and then the Soviet Union in 1991 offered a historic opportunity to transform the region into open societies. But Western democracies failed to rise to the occasion; the entire world suffers the consequences. The Soviet Union and then Russia needed outside help because open society is a more sophisticated form of social organization than is closed society. In a closed society, there is only one concept of how society should be organized: That's the authorized version, which is imposed by force. Within open society, citizens are not only allowed but required to think for themselves, and there are institutional arrangements that allow people with differing interests, backgrounds, and opinions to coexist in peace.

The Soviet system was probably the most comprehensive form of closed society in human history. It penetrated practically all aspects of existence: political and military as well as economic and intellectual. At its most aggressive it even tried to invade natural science—as the case of Trofim Lysenko showed.* To make a transition to open society required a revolutionary change in regime that could not be accomplished without outside help. This insight prompted me to rush in and establish Open Society Foundations in one country after another throughout the former Soviet empire.

But the open societies of the West lacked this insight. In 1947, following the devastation of World War II, the United States launched the historic Marshall Plan to rebuild Europe; after the collapse of the Soviet system, such an initiative was unthinkable. I proposed something like it at a conference in the spring of 1989 in Potsdam, which was then still part of East Germany, and I was literally laughed at. William Waldegrave, a minister in Margaret Thatcher's foreign office, led the jeers. Thatcher was a staunch defender of freedom—whenever she visited communist countries she insisted on meeting with dissidents—but the idea that open society needs to be constructed and that the construction may require—and deserve—outside help was apparently beyond her understanding. As a market fundamentalist, she did not believe in government intervention. In fact, the communist countries were left largely to fend for themselves; some made the grade, but others did not.

There is much soul-searching and finger-pointing going on with regard to Russia. Articles are being written asking Who lost Russia? I am convinced that we—the Western democracies—are largely responsible and that the sins of omission were committed by the Bush and Thatcher administrations. The record of Chancellor Helmut Kohl's Germany is more mixed. Both in extending credits and in making grants, Germany was the largest financial contributor to the Soviet Union and, later, to Russia, but Kohl was motivated

*Trofim Lysenko was an agronomist who tried to prove, in support of Marxism, that acquired traits can be inherited.

more by the desire to buy Russian acquiescence in German reunification than to help transform Russia.

I contend that if Western democracies had truly engaged themselves, Russia could have been firmly established on the road toward a market economy and an open society. I realize that such a contention runs counter to prevailing views. It is counterfactual because, in fact, the economic reform efforts were dismal failures. One would have to believe in the efficacy of foreign aid to argue that the outcome could have been different. But foreign aid has a bad record, and the idea that governmental intervention could actually help an economy goes against the prevailing market-fundamentalist bias. So attention is concentrated on who did what that went wrong. But it is that same market-fundamentalist bias that must be held responsible for the outcome. It militated against a genuine engagement to assist the Soviet Union and later Russia.

People felt sympathy, but of an inchoate sort. Open societies in the West did not believe in open society as a universal idea, the realization of which would justify considerable effort. This was my greatest disappointment and misjudgment. I was misled by the rhetoric of the Cold War. The West was willing to support the transition with words but not with money, and whatever aid and advice was given was misguided by a market fundamentalist bias. The Soviets and then Russians were receptive, even eager, for outside advice. They realized that their system was rotten and tended to idolize the West. Alas, they made the same mistake as I: They assumed the West would be genuinely concerned.

I had set up a foundation in the Soviet Union as early as 1987. When Mikhail Gorbachev phoned Andrei Sakharov in his exile in Gorki and asked him to "resume his patriotic activities in Moscow," I realized that a revolutionary change was in the making. I have described my experiences elsewhere.* What is relevant here is that

---

*George Soros, *Underwriting Democracy* (New York: Free Press, Macmillan, 1991).

in 1988 I proposed setting up an international task force to study the creation of an "open sector" in the Soviet economy, and somewhat to my surprise—I was then an obscure fund manager—my proposal was accepted by Soviet officials.

The idea was to create a market sector within the command economy, selecting an industry like food-processing, which would sell its products to consumers at market rather than command prices (with an appropriate system for transfer from command prices to market prices). This open sector could then be gradually enlarged. It soon became evident that the idea was impractical because the command economy was too diseased to nurture the embryo of a market economy. That is, the problem of transfer pricing could not be solved. But even such a harebrained idea from an insignificant source was supported at the highest level. Prime Minister Nikolai Ryzhkov ordered the heads of the major Soviet institutions—Gosplan, Gosnab, and so on—to participate. It is true that I was able to attract Western economists like Wassily Leontief and Romano Prodi to participate from the Western side.

Later on I put together a group of Western experts who provided advice to different groups of Russian economists preparing competing economic reform programs. Then I arranged for the authors of the principal Russian proposal for economic reform—the so-called Shatalin Plan—led by Grigory Yavlinsky, to be invited to the 1990 IMF/World Bank meeting in Washington. Gorbachev wavered over the plan and finally decided against it. He balked at two issues: the privatization of land, and the simultaneous dissolution of the Soviet Union along with the formation of an economic union. I still think the Shatalin Plan would have provided for a more orderly transition than did the actual course of events.

Soon thereafter Gorbachev fell from power, the Soviet Union disintegrated, and Boris Yeltsin became the president of Russia. He entrusted the economy to Yegor Gaidar, head of an economic research institute, who had studied macroeconomic theory from the standard textbook of Rudi Dornbusch and Stan Fischer. Gaidar tried to apply monetary policy to an economy that did not obey monetary signals. State-owned enterprises were continuing to produce according to plan, even if they were not getting paid for it. I remember calling Gaidar in April 1992 to point out that debt between companies was rising at a rate that was equal to one-third of the GNP; he acknowledged the problem but carried on regardless.

When Gaidar failed an uneasy balancing act followed, and eventually Anatoly Chubais, from a different research institute, emerged as deputy prime minister in charge of the economy. He gave priority to the transfer of property from the state to private hands. He believed that once state property was privatized, the owners would start protecting their property and the process of disintegration would be arrested.

That is not how it worked out. A scheme for distributing vouchers, which citizens could then use to purchase state-owned companies, became a free-for-all to grab the assets of the state. Managements took control of companies by cheating workers out of vouchers or buying up shares on the cheap. They continued to siphon off earnings and, often, assets into holding companies based in Cyprus, partly to avoid taxes, partly to pay for the shares they acquired, partly to build up assets abroad owing to a lack of confidence in what was going on at home. Fortunes were made overnight even while there was an extreme shortage of money and credit, both in rubles and in dollars.

Out of these chaotic conditions the rudiments of a new economic order began to emerge. It was a form of capitalism but it was a very peculiar one and it came into existence in a different sequence from what could have been expected under normal conditions. The first privatization was the privatization of public safety, and in some ways it was the most successful. Sundry private armies and mafias were set up, and they took charge where they could. The managements of state-owned enterprises formed private companies, mainly in Cyprus, which entered into contracts with the state enterprises. The factories ran at a loss, did not pay taxes, and fell into arrears in paying wages and settling debts with other companies. The cash flow was siphoned off to Cyprus. New banks were formed, partly by state-owned companies and state-owned banks, partly by newly emerging trading groups. Some banks made fortunes by handling the accounts of various state agencies, including the Russian Treasury.

Then, in connection with the scheme for privatizing state companies by the distribution of vouchers, a market for stocks was born before the mechanisms for registering stocks and efficiently settling transactions were properly in place—and long before the enterprises whose stocks were traded started to behave like companies. A culture of lawbreaking became engrained long before appropriate laws and regulations could be enacted. The proceeds from the voucher scheme did not accrue either to the state or to the companies themselves. At first the managers had to consolidate their control and service the debts they had incurred in the process of acquiring control; only afterward could they begin to generate earnings within the companies. Even then, it was to their advantage to hide rather than report earnings unless they could hope to raise capital by selling shares. But only a few companies reached that stage.

These arrangements could be justly described as "robber capitalism," because the most effective way to accumulate private capital if one had hardly anything to start with was to appropriate the assets of the state. There were, of course, some exceptions. In an economy starved of services, it was possible to make money more or less legitimately by providing them, for example, through repair work or running hotels and restaurants.

Foreign aid was left largely to two international financial institutions—the IMF and World Bank—because Western countries were unwilling to put up money from their own budgets. I was opposed to this arrangement on the grounds that the IMF is institutionally ill-suited for the job. It operates by getting governments to sign a letter of intent to adhere to conditions governing stability of currency and central budget, among other requirements, and it suspends payments if a government fails to meet the conditions. When a country does not have an effective government, this method practically guarantees that the program will fail. That is what happened in Russia. The central government was unable to collect taxes, and the only way it could meet the money-supply targets was by refusing to meet budgetary obligations. Wage arrears and debts between companies built up to unmanageable levels. I argued that a more direct, intrusive approach was needed, and it would have been eagerly accepted at the time. But that would have meant putting up real money, and the Western democracies balked at the prospect.

When the IMF extended a $15 billion loan to Russia, I argued in an article published in the *Wall Street Journal* on November 11, 1992, that the money should be earmarked for the payment of social security benefits and that the disbursement of the funds should be closely monitored. Because of the undervaluation of the ruble, pension payments were only $8 per month, so the money would have been sufficient to pay all the pensions. My proposal was not given serious consideration because it did not fit into the IMF mode of operation. So I set out to show that foreign aid could be made to work.

I set up the International Science Foundation with $100 million (the eventual disbursements reached $140 million). Our first act was to distribute $500 each to some 40,000 of Russia's best scientists in the hope that this would encourage them to stay in Russia and continue their scientific work. This took only $20 million, and it allowed these scientists to survive for a year. The criteria for selecting the recipients were open, transparent, and objective: The scientists must have published three articles in the leading scientific publications. The distribution was accomplished in a few months, with an expense ratio of less than 10 percent, and the scheme assured payments in dollars to each recipient throughout the former Soviet Union. This proved that my proposal for controlling the disbursement of funds was practical.

The rest of the money was spent to support research on the basis of an internationally organized peer-review process in which the most famous scientists of the world participated. (Boris Berezovsky, who later became an infamous oligarch, contributed $1.5 million for travel grants for reasons of his own. This was the only Russian contribution.) All the funds were committed in less than two years.

My reasons for supporting scientists were complex. I wanted to demonstrate that foreign aid could be successful, and I selected science as the field of demonstration because I could count on support from members of the international scientific community, who were willing to donate their time and energy for evaluating the research projects. But the mechanics of the emergency aid distribution could have been made to work for pensioners as well as scientists.

There were other arguments in favor of helping scientists. During the Soviet regime many of the best brains had joined research institutes where independent thinking was more tolerated than in the rest of Soviet society, and they produced science that was at the cutting edge of human accomplishments. It was a somewhat different strain from Western science—more speculative and less advanced technically except in a few priority areas. Scientists were also in the forefront of political reform. Andrei Sakharov was particularly well known and admired, but there were many others. In addition, there was the danger that nuclear scientists would be enticed away by rogue states.

The entire undertaking was a resounding success and gave my foundation an unassailable reputation. There were many attacks against us because we engaged in controversial programs. For instance, we ran a competition for new textbooks free of Marxist-

Leninist ideology and were accused of poisoning the minds of students. On one occasion the Duma conducted hearings on charges that we were acquiring scientific secrets on the cheap, although all research sponsored by the foundation had to be published and belonged to the public domain. The entire scientific community rose in our support, and so the Duma ended up passing a vote of thanks. When I say that history would have taken a different course if the Western democracies had come to the aid of Russia after the collapse of the Soviet system, I can therefore rely on my own experiment. Imagine how differently Russians would feel about the West today if the IMF had paid their pensions when they were on the verge of starvation.

I abstained from personally investing in Russia, partly to avoid any conflict of interest but mainly because I did not like what I saw. I did not interfere, however, with my fund managers who wanted to invest, and I also approved their participation in a Russian-run investment fund on equal terms with other Western investors.

I attended the World Economic Forum in Davos in January 1996 where the communist presidential candidate, Gennadi Zyuganov, was well received by the business community. I met with Boris Berezovsky and said to him that if Zyuganov was elected he, Berezovsky, would hang from a lamppost. I wanted him to support Grigory Yavlinsky, whom I considered the only honest reformer among the candidates, but I was naive. I did not realize to what extent Berezovsky was involved in dirty dealings with Yeltsin's family. According to his own public statements, my warning about his safety concentrated his mind. He got together with the other leading Russian businessmen who were attending the Davos conference, and they formed a syndicate to work for Yeltsin's reelection.

That is how they became the oligarchs. It was a remarkable piece of political engineering: Yeltsin started with an approval rating of lower than 10 percent, and they succeeded in getting him reelected.

The campaign was managed by Anatoly Chubais. I do not know the details, but I can use my imagination. When one of Chubais's aides was caught leaving the Russian White House—the headquarters of the prime minister and his government—with some $200,000 in a suitcase I am sure it was not play money. The oligarchs extorted a heavy price for their support of Yeltsin. They received shares in the most valuable state-owned companies as security against loans they made to the state budget in an infamous "loans for shares" scheme. After Yeltsin won the election, these companies were put up for auction and the oligarchs divided them up among themselves.

I know Chubais well. In my opinion, he is a genuine reformer who sold his soul to the devil in order to fight what he called the "red-brown menace"—a combination of socialism and nationalism—which he believed would come to dominate Russia unless he did something to prevent it. After Yeltsin's reelection, he again took charge of the economy, but he had difficulty controlling the oligarchs. I was greatly encouraged when Yeltsin brought Boris Nemtsov, the reformist governor of Nizhny Novgorod, into the government and treated him as his adopted son. Chubais was tainted by the elections, but Nemtsov was clean: He could stand firm where Chubais could not. I took this as a signal that the Yeltsin regime, under the leadership of Chubais, genuinely wanted to move away from robber capitalism toward legitimate capitalism. The budget deficit and money supply were kept within bounds, and back taxes began to be collected. Inflation and interest rates declined. Shareholder rights were better respected, and the stock market boomed. Foreign money poured into stocks and debt instruments. Russian borrowers could obtain five-year loans at only 250 basis points above the London interbank rate.

It was against this background that I decided in 1997 to participate in the auction of Svyazinvest, the state telephone holding company. I agonized over the decision, being all too aware of the pervasive corruption in Russia. It would have been easier to keep my hands clean by sticking to philanthropy, but I felt that Russia needed foreign investment even more than philanthropy. If Russia could not make the transition from robber capitalism to legitimate capitalism, all my philanthropy was in vain. So I decided to participate in a competing bid for Svyazinvest that turned out to be the winning one. This was the first genuine auction in which the state was not shortchanged. Although we paid a fair price—just under $2 billion, nearly half put up by my funds—I calculated that it would prove to be a very rewarding investment if the transition to legitimate capitalism came to pass.

Unfortunately that is not what happened. The auction precipitated a knockdown, drag-out fight among the oligarchs, a falling-out among thieves. Some of the oligarchs were eager to make the transition to legitimacy while others resisted it because they were incapable of working in a legitimate manner. The main opponent of the auction and its outcome was Boris Berezovsky. After his allies lost the auction, he vowed to destroy Chubais. I had a number of heart-to-heart talks with him, but I did not manage to dissuade him. I told him that he was a rich man, worth billions on paper. His major asset was Sibneft, one of the largest oil companies in the world. All he needed to do was to consolidate his position. If he could not do it himself, he could engage an investment banker. He told me I did not understand: It was not a question of how rich he was but how he measured up against Chubais and against the other oligarchs. They had made a deal, and they must stick to it. He must destroy or be destroyed himself.

I came to witness at close quarters an astonishing historic spectacle in which powerful oligarchs tried to reverse the results not only of the auction but of the entire government effort to control the oligarchs. It seemed as if I were watching people fighting in a boat as it drifted toward a waterfall. As part of a campaign of charges and countercharges, Berezovsky revealed that Chubais had received $90,000 from a phony book contract, which was in fact the other oligarchs' payment for his services as Yeltsin's campaign manager. Chubais was weakened and distracted by the constant need to defend himself. Tax collections required his personal intervention if they were to go forward, and tax revenues fell. There was a dangerous drift downward in the economy in 1998 just as the Asian crisis began to make its effects felt. It culminated in Russia defaulting on its internal debt in August 1998, which shook the international financial markets.

Korean and Brazilian banks that had invested heavily in the Russian market had to liquidate their positions. Some leading Moscow banks were also exposed because they had large speculative bond positions and were also carrying uncovered forward contracts in the ruble. There had been some precarious moments in December 1997, but they had passed. Interest rates were sharply raised and government spending reduced, but the Duma balked at passing the laws necessary for structural reform. On March 24, 1998, Yeltsin dismissed Viktor Chernomyrdin as prime minister and on April 24 forced the Duma to accept Sergei Kiriyenko, a young technocrat recommended by Gaidar and Chubais, as replacement. For a brief moment, Russia had a reformist government, the best it has seen since the breakup of the Soviet Union, and in July 1998 the IMF came through with a loan of SDR 8.5 billion (about U.S. $11.2 billion), of which SDR 3.6 billion (about U.S. $4.8 billion) was disbursed. But it was not enough.

At this point, I shall turn to what I call a real-time experiment. I started it just before the final meltdown. I reproduce faithfully the notes I wrote during a two-week period while the crisis unfolded.

A Real-Time Experiment

Sunday, August 9, 1998

Ruble (spot)	=	6.29
Ruble Forwards*	=	45%
GKO†	=	94.52%
Prins‡	=	21.79%
S&P	=	1,089.45
U.S. 30-year Treasury Bond	=	5.63%

I had not been following developments in Russia closely until the last two or three days—I was too busy writing this book. I was aware that the situation remained desperate even after the IMF agreed to an $18 billion bailout package. Interest rates on Russian government debt remained at astronomical levels—between 70 percent and 90 percent for one-year ruble-denominated treasury bills (GKOs). The syndicate which had bought 25.1 percent of Svyazinvest—the Russian telephone holding company—and of which we were the largest foreign participants, was approached by the Russian government to provide a temporary bridge loan leading to the sale of the next tranche of 24.9 percent in Svyazinvest. It was in our interest to make the sale a success but I did not like the idea of throwing good money after bad—that is why I decided to focus on the situation.

It soon became obvious that the refinancing of the government debt presented a seemingly insurmountable problem. The IMF program had assumed that the domestic holders of the debt would roll over (reinvest) their holdings when they matured; the only question was at what price. If the government was successful in col-

---

*Implicit interest rates on one month nondeliverable forward contracts for rubles traded in dollars.
†Yield on ruble-denominated Russian government treasury bills.
‡Yield on dollar-denominated Russian government bonds.

lecting taxes, interest rates would eventually come down to tolerable levels, say 25 percent, and the crisis would be over. What this line of reasoning left out of account was that much of the debt was held by domestic holders who were not in a position to roll over their maturing GKOs at any price. Corporations were being forced to pay taxes, and what they paid in taxes could not be reinvested in GKOs. More importantly, the banking sector, with the exception of Sberbank, the state-owned savings bank, had bought GKOs with borrowed money. Due to the decline in the Russian stock and bond markets most of these banks were insolvent and even those which were solvent were unable to renew their credit lines. As a result, not only were they not buyers, some of their existing holdings had to be liquidated in order to meet margin calls. Much of the credit had come from foreign banks, some of whom tried to liquidate their own positions as well. Waves of selling depressed the dollar-denominated Russian debt to record low levels. There was a full-blown banking crisis in progress.

A banking crisis is usually contained by the central bank intervening and providing liquidity, for instance by lending money against collateral at concessionary rates; but in this case the central bank was prevented from doing so by the terms of the IMF agreement. That is what made the situation seemingly insoluble.

On Friday, August 7, I telephoned Anatoly Chubais, who was on vacation, and Yegor Gaidar, who was minding the store. I told them that in my view the situation was terminal: the government would be unable to roll over its debt after September even if the second tranche of the IMF loan was released. To aggravate the situation, the Ukrainian government was on the verge of defaulting on a $450 million loan arranged by Nomura Securities coming due next Tuesday. In these circumstances I could not justify participating in a bridge loan: the risk of default was too great. I saw only one way out: to put together a large enough syndicate to cover the Russian government's needs until the end of the year. It would have to be a public and private partnership. The Svyazinvest group could participate with, say, $500 million, but the private sector on its own could not come up with enough money. I asked how much would be needed. Gaidar told me, $7 billion. This assumed that Sberbank, the only bank that has large deposits from the public, would be able to roll over its holdings. For the time being the public was not withdrawing deposits from the banks on a significant scale. "That means the syndicate would have to be formed with $10 billion," I said, "so as to reestablish public confidence." Half would have to come from foreign government sources, such as the Exchange Stabilization Fund (which is under the control of the U.S. Treasury) and the other half from the private sector. The syndicate would come into operation when the second tranche of the IMF loan is released in September. It would underwrite one-year GKOs starting at, say, 35 percent p.a., gradually dropping to say 25 percent. (The current rate is around 90 percent.) The program would be announced in advance; that would attract some public buying: it would make sense to invest at 35 percent when a credible program is in effect to reduce the rate to 25 percent by the end of the year. If successful, only a small portion of the $10 billion would be actually used. Both the public and private component would be difficult to put together, but I was willing to try. Gaidar was understandably enthusiastic.

I called David Lipton, Undersecretary in charge of International Affairs at the U.S. Treasury. He was fully aware of the problem but they had not even thought of using the Exchange Stabilization Fund. The sentiment in Congress was strongly opposed to any kind of bailout. I said I was aware of it but I saw no alternative. There was a panic and it was in our national interest to support a reform-minded government in Russia. If there was private participation it ought to make a bailout politically more palatable. Still, it would require the Russians to make a strong case on Capitol Hill. It would be also very difficult to line up the private participants because they consisted of investment banks and speculative investors like us and they could not be so easily mobilized by the authorities as the large commercial banks.

Just to explore all alternatives, I called Gaidar again and asked him whether it would be possible to impose a charge on those GKO holders who want to take cash on redemption. He said that would be counterproductive because it would destroy the credit standing of the GKOs. He was right of course.

As of the present moment, I believe that without my scheme the government will default with cataclysmic consequences; even with the scheme, most of the Russian banks will be wiped out but it would be a mistake even to try to salvage them.

Tuesday night, August 11

Ruble (spot)	=	6.30
Ruble Forwards	=	91%
GKO	=	147%
Prins	=	23.92%
S&P	=	1,068.98
U.S. 30-year Treasury Bond	=	5.60%

I talked briefly with Lipton on Monday. The U.S. administration had reached no conclusion yet. He promised to call again. On Tuesday there was a collapse in the Russian financial market. Trading on the stock market was temporarily suspended. Government bonds sank to new lows. Even the international markets were affected. The scheme I have proposed is no longer feasible. Only a larger rescue package of minimum $15 billion could stabilize the market and no private investor could be expected to put up money. Lipton left for Moscow without calling me. I heard through the grapevine that he was exasperated going without anything to offer. I decided to write the following letter to the *Financial Times*:

Sir, The meltdown in Russian financial markets has reached the terminal phase. Bankers and brokers who had borrowed against securities could not meet margin calls and forced selling swamped both the stock and the bond markets. The stock market had to be temporarily closed because trades could not be settled; prices of government bonds and Treasury bills fell precipitously. Although the selling was temporarily absorbed, there is a danger that the population will start again to withdraw funds from savings accounts. Immediate action is required.

The trouble is that the action that is necessary to deal with a banking crisis is diametrically opposed to the action that has been agreed with the International Monetary Fund to deal with the budget crisis. The IMF programme imposes tight monetary and fiscal policy; the banking crisis requires the injection of liquidity. The two requirements cannot be reconciled without further international assistance. The IMF programme had assumed that there would be buyers for government bonds at a price: as the government proceeded to collect taxes and slash expenditures interest rates would come down and the crisis would abate. The assumption was false because much of the outstanding debt was held on margin and credit lines could not be renewed. There is a financing gap that needs to be closed. The gap will become bigger if the general public starts withdrawing deposits.

The best solution would be to introduce a currency board after a modest devaluation of 15 to 25 per cent. The devaluation is necessary to correct for the decline in oil prices and to reduce the amount of reserves needed for the currency board. It would also penalize the holders of ruble-denominated government debt, rebutting charges of a bail-out.

About $50bn of reserves would be required: $23bn to cover MI [narrow money supply] and $27bn to cover the shortfall on domestic debt refunding for the next year. Russia has reserves of $18bn; the IMF has promised $17bn. The Group of Seven [G7] needs to put up another $15bn to make a currency board feasible. There would be no bail-out of the banking system. With the exception of a few institutions that hold public deposits, banks can be allowed to fend for themselves. Government bond prices would immediately recover and the sounder financial institutions would survive. Some $40bn is held by Russians in foreign currencies. With a currency board they may be tempted to buy ruble-denominated government bonds at attractive yields. If they do, the G7 standby credit would not need to be used. The reduction in interest rates would help the government to meet its fiscal targets.

If the G7 were willing to put up $15bn right away, the situation could be stabilised even without a currency board, although it might take longer and the damage would be greater. It would also be difficult to accomplish a limited currency adjustment without a currency board because the pressure for further devaluation would become irresistible, as it did in Mexico in December 1994.

If action is delayed, the cost of a rescue will continue to mount. The cost would have been only $7bn a week ago. Unfortunately, international financial authorities do not appreciate the urgency of the situation. The alternatives are default or hyper-inflation. Either would have devastating financial and political consequences.

Thursday, August 13

Ruble (spot)	=	6.35
Ruble Forwards	=	162%
GKO	=	149%
Prins	=	23.76%
S&P	=	1,074.91
U.S. 30-year Treasury Bond	=	5.65%

After I had written my letter to the *Financial Times*, the Deputy Governor of the Russian central bank imposed some restrictions on the convertibility of the ruble. It had a devastating effect on the Russian market: Stocks opened 15 percent lower and did not rally very much. My letter received a lot of attention but the emphasis was on my advocating devaluation, not on my proposal for a currency board. It became one of the factors in what has come to be called Black Thursday. I was accused of speculating against the ruble. That is not at all what I intended. I felt obliged to put out another statement as follows:

> The turmoil in Russian financial markets is not due to anything I said or did. We have no short position in the ruble and have no intention of shorting the currency. In fact, our portfolio would be hurt by any devaluation.
>
> The purpose of my letter to the *Financial Times* was to issue a wake-up call to the G7 governments. While the Russian government is doing everything in its power to cope with the situation, it cannot succeed without further assistance from abroad.

Friday, August 14

Ruble (spot)	=	6.35
Ruble Forwards	=	162.7%
GKO	=	172%
Prins	=	23.01%
S&P	=	1,062.75
U.S. 30-year Treasury Bond	=	5.54%

I talked to Treasury Secretary Rubin and stressed the urgency of the situation. He was fully aware but his concern was not shared by the other G7 governments, which were largely beyond reach on holidays. I was contacted by Senator Mitch McConnell and I urged him to call Rubin to assure him of Republican support in what would be a very risky operation. Late in the day I was approached on behalf of Kiriyenko. He is still looking for a $500 million bridge loan but that is no longer realistic. I offered to fly to Moscow to discuss the larger issues if it would help.

Sunday night, August 16

Ruble (spot)	=	6.35
Ruble Forwards	=	162.7%
GKO	=	172%
Prins	=	23.01%
S&P	=	1,062.75
U.S. 30-year Treasury Bond	=	5.54%

I spent most of the weekend on Russia. I gave an interview on Echo Moskva radio station explaining my position, and my statement was read on Russian TV. I hope that I managed to correct the false impression that I was advocating devaluation when I was pleading for a currency board or that I could benefit from devaluation in some way. Spoke to Gaidar several times. Prepared an article advocating the currency board solution and sent it to him for approval. Just now (6:30 a.m. Monday, Moscow time) he told me that he had spoken to Larry Summers [deputy secretary of the Treasury] and there was no help available; they will have to act unilaterally. I said my article was no longer relevant but he urged me to publish it anyhow. I won't.

Tuesday, August 18

Ruble (spot)	=	6.80
Ruble Forwards	=	305%
GKO*	=	
Prins	=	29.41%
S&P	=	1,101.20
U.S. 30-year Treasury Bond	=	5.56%

On Monday, all hell broke loose. Russia imposed a moratorium

*Trading in GKOs was suspended as of August 17, so no figures are available in this category for the remainder of the tables.

and widened the trading band on the ruble, effectively devaluing it by up to 35 percent. What is worse, Russian banks are not allowed to honor their foreign obligations. This created havoc among their foreign counterparties, who dumped Russian securities at any price. David Lipton called me for a technical explanation and suggested I write them a memo.

On re-reading it I find it rather garbled. The point I was trying to make is that it is still not too late to look for a constructive resolution of the crisis in Russia. The G7 should offer to put up the hard currency which is needed to set up a currency board *provided* the Duma passes the laws which are needed to meet the IMF conditions. There are two possibilities: the Duma could agree to it or it could reject the offer. In the first case, the value of the ruble would be reestablished, the ruble debt could be restructured in an orderly fashion, and the structural reforms (putting companies that don't pay taxes into bankruptcy, etc.) could be implemented. Most Russian banks would go broke and the international banks and funds that had contracts with those banks would suffer losses; but Russian government obligations would regain some value, the better banks would survive, and the meltdown would be arrested. In the second case, the meltdown would continue but the onus would fall on the Duma. Yeltsin could dissolve the Duma, call elections, and implement the reforms. If they are successful, they would be endorsed by the electorate. Even if Yeltsin failed to rise to the occasion or the reforms were less than successful, we would have done what we could and we would have kept the flame of reform alive in Russia. It is a high risk strategy but doing nothing poses an even bigger risk.

Saturday, August 22

Ruble (spot)	=	7.15
Ruble Forwards	=	443%
GKO	=	defaulted
Prins	=	36.05%

S&P	=	1,081.18
U.S. 30-year Treasury Bond	=	5.43%

International markets were badly affected by the Russian crisis in the last two days. For instance, the German stock market dropped 6 percent on Friday. I find it surprising that it took so long for the penny to drop. My partner assures me that the U.S. stock market made a very good temporary bottom on Friday and we were buyers of stocks and sellers of put options. By the way, we did not trade any Russian securities during the entire period of this real-time experiment.

I tried to push my idea with everyone who would listen during the week but to no avail. It could have helped the political situation in Russia. As it is, the Duma will not pass the laws and the IMF will not disburse the second tranche of the package. With no more money coming from abroad in the foreseeable future, Yeltsin will have to scuttle the present government and find a new source of support at home. But where? The oligarchs are fatally weakened. Gazprom and some of the oil companies remain. Is it back to Chernomyrdin? He is certainly aspiring. But no regime can succeed, because the political will to remedy the structural defects is lacking. The downside is open ended.

Sunday, August 23

Yeltsin dismissed the government and reappointed Chernomyrdin. Now I can't predict it anymore.

Wednesday, August 26

Ruble (spot)	=	10.00
Ruble Forwards	=	458%
GKO	=	defaulted
Prins	=	42.83%

S&P = 1,084.19
U.S. 30-year Treasury Bond = 5.42%

There is no limit to how far a meltdown can go. The disintegration of the Russian banking system is occurring in a disorderly fashion. Banks have suspended payments and the public has panicked. The terms of the GKO conversion offer were announced and at first they were quite well received but the ruble has gone into a free fall, making the offer practically worthless. The international financial system is experiencing a few disruptions. There may be $75–100 billion of currency contracts outstanding and it is unclear which of them will be honored. A credit agency has downgraded Germany's largest commercial bank. A faint element of credit risk has been introduced into international inter-bank swap transactions. It is likely to be temporary but it may reveal other weaknesses because of the high degree of leverage employed. European and U.S. stock markets have shuddered but are likely to regain their composure. The meltdown in Russia is terminal with incalculable political and social consequences.

That is the end of the diary.

The effect of the Russian default on the international financial markets has already been discussed. The effect on the Russian economy was less devastating than expected. The default on treasury bills brought relief to the budget; the recovery in oil prices helped both the fiscal and the trade balance; and the devaluation announced by Yeltsin in the summer of 1998 led to increased demand for domestic products. After an initial shock caused by the collapse of the banking system, the economy hit bottom and began to recover. The banks and the oligarchs suffered serious losses, but within a year Russian GNP was higher than before the financial crisis. Even the foreign creditors were offered settlements that they found advantageous to accept.

Russia's political and social evolution has been far less satisfactory. Yeltsin's family, under the guidance of Boris Berezovsky, had been looking for a successor who would protect them against prosecution after the presidential election. They finally found one in Vladimir Putin, director of the Federal Security Service. In the summer of 1999, he was made prime minister and selected as Yeltsin's candidate for the presidency. There was a flare-up in Chechen terrorist activity. When Shamil Basayev, a Chechen guerrilla leader, invaded neighboring Dagestan, Putin reacted vigorously. Russian security forces attacked the Chechens and Putin issued an ultimatum, announcing that Dagestan would be cleansed of terrorists by August 25. The target date was met. The Russian population responded to Putin's handling of the situation enthusiastically, and his popularity skyrocketed.

Then a series of mysterious explosions in Moscow destroyed entire apartment houses, killing some three hundred people as they slept. In the panic that ensued, fear and anger were directed against the Chechens, assisted by a carefully orchestrated campaign among the print and TV media. Putin invaded Chechnya, and the Duma elections were held in an atmosphere of war hysteria. Very few candidates dared to oppose the invasion.

Grigory Yavlinsky was among the few. He supported the antiterrorist campaign in Dagestan but drew the line at invading Chechnya proper. The popularity of his party (Yabloko) dropped precipitously and barely met the threshold 5 percent vote required for representation in the Duma. A hastily concocted government party, Unity, without any coherent program, came in second to the Communists, with 23 percent. The Union of Rightist Forces, led by Chubais, Sergei Kiriyenko, and other reformers, embraced Putin and scored quite well with 8.6 percent. Yevgeni Primakov, who with the backing of Moscow Mayor Yuri Luzhkov had been considered the favorite candidate for the presidency, was decisively defeated; their party got only 13 percent. Using the momentum generated by the victory in the Duma elections, Yeltsin announced his resignation on

New Year's Eve, virtually assuring Putin's election as his successor. Primakov withdrew his candidacy.

Putin's phenomenal, out-of-nowhere rise had an eerie resemblance to the political machinations that secured Yeltsin's reelection in 1996. From long experience with Berezovsky, I see his hand in both operations. I first met him in connection with his $1.5 million contribution to the International Science Foundation when the executive director of the foundation, Alex Goldfarb, introduced us. I already described our well-known conversation at Davos; subsequently Berezovsky claimed that it was this conversation that induced him to form a syndicate for the reelection of Yeltsin. During 1996 we had a number of very frank discussions about the election campaign; I got to know how he operates.

Then we became adversaries in the Svyazinvest auction, but we continued to talk. I tried to convert him from robber capitalist to legitimate capitalist; he tried to use me in his campaign for the chairmanship of Gazprom—by far the most powerful commercial entity in Russia. In June 1997 he invited me to Sochi to visit Viktor Chernomyrdin, who had been chairman of Gazprom before he became prime minister, and subsequently flew me back to Moscow in his private plane. Berezovsky told me that both Chubais and Nemtsov supported his candidacy. I did not believe him, so I asked Nemtsov. That was the first he had heard about it. "Over my dead body" was his reaction.

Afterward I had lunch with Berezovsky at his "club," which was decorated, deliberately or not, much like a Hollywood depiction of a mafia hangout. I was the only guest. I did not tell him what Nemtsov said, but I did tell him that I had asked Nemtsov and that he denied any knowledge about Berezovsky's quest for the chairmanship of Gazprom. This made Berezovsky very angry, and his anger gave me the chills. I literally felt that he could kill me. And though he did not say so directly, he made me feel that I had betrayed him by talking to Nemtsov. It was a turning point in our relationship. We continued to talk to each other—on one occasion

Berezovsky flew to New York to see me—but from then on I tried to keep my distance.

As I have said, the falling-out among the oligarchs, and the conflict between Berezovsky and Chubais in particular, was a bizarre episode, although not as bizarre as the promotion of Putin as Yeltsin's successor. Berezovsky saw the world through the prism of his personal interests. He had no difficulty in subordinating the fate of Russia to his own. He genuinely believed that he and the oligarchs had bought the government by paying for Yeltsin's reelection and that the government had reneged on the bargain by allowing a genuine auction for Svyazinvest. He was determined to bring down Chubais for betraying him. When I warned him that he was pulling down the tent around him, he answered that he had no choice; if he showed any weakness he could not survive.

I could not understand this at the time, but in retrospect it makes perfect sense. Berezovsky could not make the transition to legitimacy; his only chance for survival was to keep people entangled in the web of illegitimate relationships that he had woven. He had a hold on Yeltsin because of the illegitimate favors he had arranged for Yeltsin's family. For instance, he had made Yeltsin's son-in-law a manager of Aeroflot; the airline's hard-currency revenues were diverted to a Swiss company called Forus, which, it was explained to me, meant just that: "For us." This gave him power over Yeltsin that none of the other oligarchs enjoyed. Berezovsky also had a hold on Chubais, and when the chips were down he did not hesitate to use it. The $90,000 Chubais received in the form of a phony book contract caused his temporary downfall.

This is the perspective I bring to bear on subsequent events. Berezovsky and Yeltsin's family were looking for a way to perpetuate the immunity they enjoyed under the Yeltsin administration. They tried a variety of ways, some quite farcical. At one point Yeltsin, at Berezovsky's instigation, informed the president of the Duma that he was going to nominate Nikolai Aksyonenko as prime minister, but Chubais intervened; the official document sent to the Duma nominated Sergei Stepashin. Subsequently Stepashin was pushed out of office. Berezovsky's situation turned desperate when the scandal over the laundering of Russian illegal money in U.S. banks broke in 1999, for he realized that he could no longer find refuge in the West. One way or another he had to find a successor to Yeltsin who would protect him. That is when the plan to promote Putin's candidacy was hatched.

During the flight from Sochi to Moscow in 1997 Berezovsky had told me stories about how he had paid off the anti-Russian military commanders in Chechnya and Abkhazia. So when Chechen leader Shamil Basayev invaded Dagestan, I smelled a rat. I set up a test: Would Basayev withdraw by the deadline set by Putin? He did. Even so, I could not quite believe that the explosions in the Moscow apartment buildings could be part of a plan to justify war. It was all too diabolical. It would not be unique—Russian history is replete with crimes committed by agents provocateurs, from Azev the spy during the tsarist period to Kirov's murder, which was used to justify Stalin's purges—but it would nevertheless be in a class by itself.

Still, I could not rule out the possibility. From Berezovsky's point of view the bombing made perfect sense. These terrorist attacks would not only help elect a president who would provide immunity to Yeltsin and his family; they would also give Berezovsky a hold over Putin. So far, no evidence has surfaced that would contradict this theory.

While we may never find out the truth about the Moscow explosions, there can be no doubt that the war in Chechnya propelled Putin to victory. I find this distressing, to say the least. Between 1994 and 1996, during the previous Chechen war, the Russian population was upset when it viewed on TV the devastation and suffering caused by the invasion of Chechnya. The protests by mothers of enlisted soldiers and human rights activists like Sergei Kovalev helped bring about a negotiated settlement. This time the reaction of the Russian population strongly contrasted with its previous attitude. Admittedly the Chechen terrorists must bear a large share of the blame; they captured aid workers and journalists, held them for ransom, and often killed them. Fred Cuny, the hero of Sarajevo, perished in this way. There is hardly anybody left who dares to get involved with helping Chechens or with publicizing the atrocities they have suffered. There has also been a masterful manipulation of public sentiment against them. The fact remains that the attitude of the Russian population is very different from what it was a few years ago.

At the beginning of the post-Gorbachev era, Russians had a positive aversion to violence. In fact, very little blood was spilled in the early days, and on the rare occasions when people were killed—in Tblisi, Georgia, in Vilnius, Lithuania, and in the October 1993 siege of the Duma—public opinion turned against those who used force. Not anymore. By electing Putin in March 2000, the Russian people have become implicated in the bloodshed in Chechnya.

There is a theory that a victim who has been sufficiently brutalized can become drawn to violence. The pattern seems to fit the case of many violent criminals and it also seems to apply to ethnic violence.* The Serbs have long considered themselves victims, and Slobodan Milosevic could exploit this sentiment in pursuing a policy of ethnic cleansing. Something similar seems to have happened in Russia.

Putin will try to reestablish a strong state, and he may well succeed. In many ways, that would be a desirable development. As the Russian experience taught us, a weak state can be a threat to liberty. An authority that can enforce the rules is indispensable for the functioning of a market economy. By accomplishing the transition from robber capitalism to legitimate capitalism, Putin may well preside over Russian economic recovery; my investments in Russia—including Svyazinvest—might finally pay off.

But Putin's state is unlikely to be built upon the principles of

*See Richard Rhodes, *Why They Kill: The Discoveries of a Maverick Criminologist* (New York: Knopf, 1999).

open society; it is more likely to be based on the demoralization, humiliation, and frustration that the Russian people experienced after the collapse of the Soviet system. Putin will seek to reestablish the authority of the state at home and the glory of Russia abroad. Russia is not lost; on the contrary, it may revive under Putin. But the West has lost Russia as a friend and ally and as an adherent to the principles of open society. One thing is crystal-clear: The prospect we face in Russia could have been avoided if the open societies of the West had been more firmly committed to the principle of open society themselves.

In his farewell speech, Yeltsin asked for the forgiveness of the Russian people:

> For the fact that many of our hopes did not materialize. For things which to us seemed simple but turned out arduous. I want to ask forgiveness for the fact that I was not able to justify the hopes of some people who believed that we would be able to move forward in one swoop from a gray totalitarian and stagnant past to a bright, rich and civilized future. I believed it myself. But it did not work out like that. In some way, I was too naive.

What Yeltsin did not say is that he and many others had put their faith in the West, but the West did not live up to their admittedly exaggerated expectations. I can speak only for myself. At first I thought that Western statesmen simply did not understand what was happening. That Gorbachev was willing to change the system was too good to be true, so they wanted to test him. They set hurdles, and when Gorbachev jumped over them, they set higher hurdles. Eventually they had to admit that the change was for real, but in the meantime they lost all respect for Russia as a superpower. They started treating Russians like beggars. They found money in the Nunn-Lugar Act to help them with nuclear disarmament, but not much for anything else. I remember a Russian economist,

Nikolai Schmelyov, telling me that in 1990 he passed a five-hour flight with then U.S. Secretary of State James Baker begging for assistance—to no avail.

I also remember Alexander Yakovlev, the driving force behind Gorbachev, telling me, much later, how humiliated he felt in his dealings with the Americans. With regret I had to conclude that the West did not care very much for open society as a universal concept. Had it done so, the transition would still have been painful, with dislocations and disappointments, but at least Russia would have moved in the right direction. Russia could have become a true democracy and a true friend of the United States, just as Germany did after World War II and the Marshall Plan. That is not the prospect facing us today.

My foundation remains active in Russia and is receiving strong support from Russian society. We established thirty-two computer centers in provincial universities. This has helped to develop an Internet infrastructure in Russia, and online information is emerging there as an alternative to the increasingly intimidated press. In most of our recent programs, we insist on matching funds from local authorities. For instance, we are supplying books to five thousand local libraries, and we are asking for 25 percent of the cost in the first year, 50 percent in the second, and 75 percent in the third—and we're actually receiving it. When we wanted to introduce an educational reform program in six oblasts, fifteen offered to put up matching funds. I remain committed to supporting the work of the foundation as long as it receives support from Russian society and is allowed to function freely. The quest for an open society is a flame that could not be extinguished even by Stalin's terror. I'm certain that it will stay alive in Russia, whatever its future.

CHAPTER 10

A New Global
Financial Architecture

T he global financial crisis of 1997–1999 is now history. Even if financial markets were to collapse tomorrow, it would have to be considered a new crisis, not an extension of the recent one. The duration of the crisis was much shorter and the decline in economic activity shallower than could have been expected at the time. This is taken as evidence that financial markets have a way of correcting themselves and that the global capitalist system as currently constituted is basically sound. According to conventional wisdom, the deficiencies were in the countries that were hit by the crisis, not in the system itself. The defects are in the process of being fixed. The system will emerge stronger than ever. These observations are reinforced by the fact that the world economy is once again growing.

I do not share this optimistic assessment. I believe that the global capitalist system is far from stable. It is true that some of the disparities that prevailed before the crisis erupted are being corrected, but new disparities have taken their place. Going into the crisis, IMF intervention served to bail out international creditors, creating what is now recognized as a moral hazard. Now the tables are turned: The emphasis is on "bailing in" the private sector—that is, getting creditors to share the burden of rescue operations. This will solve the moral-hazard problem and prevent excessive lending, but no arrangements have been made to make up for the looming *inadequacy* of capital flows to periphery countries. On balance, the global financial system has become less robust because the IMF has lost much of its authority and reputation.

At the height of the crisis there was much talk about the global financial architecture and the need for a new Bretton Woods. The urge for radical reform has now subsided, and any reform that has not already been put into motion is unlikely to be considered. The only radical reform proposal has come from an advisory commission appointed by the U.S. Congress, the so-called Meltzer Commission.* It advocates a drastic downsizing of international financial institutions. While it is unlikely to be implemented—international institutions are not so easy to change—it is likely to exert a constraining, negative effect on their operations. That is a pity. We need stronger, better functioning international institutions, not weaker, beleaguered ones.

Historically, financial crises have always led to the strengthening of regulations. That is how central banking evolved to its present, highly sophisticated stage. Financial markets have become global, and we must strengthen international regulation. But the crisis of 1997–1999 promises to be an exception: The tendency now is to reduce regulation. That is perhaps because the crisis hurt only the periphery, not the center.

*The International Financial Institution Advisory Commission (The Meltzer Commission), Allan H. Meltzer, Chairman, submitted its final report to the United States Congress and Department of Treasury on March 8, 2000.

The reforms currently under way are rather narrow in scope. By and large, they are directed at correcting the structural deficiencies in the borrowing countries and seek to discourage unsound lending. The idea that there may be something structurally wrong with global financial markets has been rejected. The prevailing doctrines of financial economics have not changed. It is assumed that markets, with better information, can take care of themselves or, more exactly, if they cannot take care of themselves then nobody else can; therefore—the argument goes—the main task is to make the necessary information available and to avoid any interference with the market mechanism. Imposing market discipline remains the guiding principle. Transparency and information are the keywords. To use a fashionable metaphor, the goal is to fix the plumbing rather than redesign the entire building.

In no way am I opposed to fixing the plumbing. No doubt, the deficiencies in domestic banking systems were a major factor in determining the extent of the damage. Like a hurricane, the crisis hurt those countries most whose defenses were weakest, and so there is much to be gained by strengthening local banking systems. But that begs the question whether international defenses also need to be strengthened. We should not forget about the larger architecture because the recent crisis has revealed some serious structural weaknesses, and it is important to repair the cracks in the wall before we paper them over.

In fact, some important changes have already occurred in the global financial architecture without people being fully aware of them. By and large, the changes serve to discourage unsound international lending. Undoubtedly that will help to prevent a repetition of the last crisis, which was brought on by unsound lending. In my opinion, however, this may serve to bring on the next crisis, which is likely to be caused by an inadequate flow of funds to the periphery. The situation reminds me of the Maginot Line in France; built to protect the country against the repetition of World War I, it proved useless during World War II.

Deficiencies of the Previous Architecture

In speaking about the global financial architecture, we are basically discussing the role of international financial institutions, especially the International Monetary Fund. Looking at the way the IMF operated before and during the crisis of 1997–1999, we can identify two major deficiencies or, more exactly, asymmetries. One is a disparity between crisis prevention and crisis intervention; the other is a disparity in the treatment of lenders and borrowers. The two are interconnected, and they are part of the system; thus the management of the IMF cannot really be blamed for either. Admittedly, the IMF made several policy mistakes. It insisted on cutting *public* expenditures when the cause of the trouble was located in the *private* sector; it underestimated the severity of the contagion; and in the case of Indonesia it precipitated a run on the banks by closing some banks without first installing a deposit-insurance scheme. But specific mistakes are not our concern here. Our aim is to identify the structural deficiencies, because they are the ones that require structural changes.

Under the prevailing rules, the IMF does not have much say in the internal affairs of member countries except in a crisis when a member country turns to the IMF for assistance. It may visit and consult, but in normal times it has neither the mandate nor the tools to interfere. The primary mission of the IMF is to preserve the system. When it intervenes it has the stability of the system foremost in its mind. It cannot provide any debt relief to the debtor countries during a crisis because that could have a devastating effect on the financial markets. The loans it provides and the conditions it imposes serve to enable debtor countries to meet their obligations. Any debt relief has to wait until the situation calms down.

The IMF does not have enough resources to act as a lender of last resort. It needs the cooperation of the financial markets to make its programs successful, and banks and investment banks know how to exploit their position. In addition, the IMF is controlled by the countries at the center of the capitalist system; it would go against the national interests of the controlling shareholders if the IMF penalized the lenders.

Conditions imposed by the IMF usually include the slashing of budget deficits and the raising of interest rates. The effect is to plunge the borrowing country into a recession, which reduces imports and encourages exports. The resulting trade surplus enables the debtor country to service and pay down its debts. In an emergency, the financial authorities may also put pressure on the lenders to roll over their loans, but they have been careful to maintain the pretense that the lending is voluntary so that the balance sheets of the banks are not unduly weakened while the crisis is in full swing. Later on, when the situation is calmer, there can be a more permanent reorganization of the debt. That is what happened in the great international lending crisis of 1982. Several years after the crisis, outstanding debts were reorganized and so-called Brady bonds were issued.

The net effect of this approach was to place the burden of adjustment mainly on the borrowing countries. They were required to service their debts to the limits of their capacity. The lenders did not get off scot-free, but their losses were much smaller than they would have been absent IMF intervention. For instance, U.S. banks suffered much greater losses in their exposure to the savings-and-loan industry than in their international lending activities in the 1980s. Even so, banks did not like to have their arms twisted. After the experience of the 1980s, they became reluctant to engage in long-term lending; they preferred to sell bond issues to the public rather than put the loans on their own balance sheets. Bondholders are much less susceptible to pressure from the banking authorities than commercial banks, so the switch from direct lending to bond issues strengthened the hand of the lenders and reinforced their preferential position.

This became obvious during the Mexican crisis of 1994. In that crisis, the foreign holders of *tesobonos* (Mexican dollar–denominated treasury bills) came out whole, although the yield on *tesobonos* at the time they were purchased implied a high degree of risk. When Mexico could not pay, the U.S. Treasury and the IMF stepped in, taking investors off the hook. Mexico's taxpayers were left to foot the bill.

This experience played an important role in shaping investor expectations in Russia. Banks, brokers, and hedge funds kept buying Russian treasury bills (GKOs) even when everyone could see the situation deteriorating. Russia was considered too important to fail; the international authorities could be counted on to come to the rescue. Even if GKO holders would have to take a hit, the risk-reward ratio was considered attractive. So people continued buying GKOs at ever-increasing yields until the music eventually stopped. Ironically, the expectation held by GKO holders that they would be bailed out made it difficult for the international financial authorities to do so. The moral hazard inherent in the IMF's method of operation became recognized, and the political pressure against bailing out investors who were speculating on getting bailed out became overwhelming. It left authorities practically powerless to prevent Russia's default.

Herein lies the most important change that has occurred in the global financial architecture in the course of the 1997–1999 crisis: It occurred gradually and almost imperceptibly. Most people are still not fully aware of it.

The Emerging New Architecture

At the beginning of the crisis the two asymmetries we have identified—one between the treatment of lenders and borrowers and one between crisis prevention and intervention—were fully in effect. They largely explain why the Asian IMF programs were so unsuccessful. Take a look at the three Asian countries that turned to the IMF: Thailand, Indonesia, and Korea. All three suffered from a structural imbalance: The private sector had borrowed too much money in hard currency without hedging, and companies did not have enough equity in relation to their indebtedness. Devaluation, when it came, increased the ratio of foreign debt to equity. The high interest rates and the sudden collapse in domestic demand imposed by the IMF programs increased the burden of debt, bringing the solvency of the debtors into question. Lending them more money did not help. What these countries needed was a way to convert debt into equity. But to impose a moratorium and allow a debt-to-equity conversion scheme would have damaged the international banks and bondholders, and the IMF could not even contemplate such a move. Therefore the IMF applied the usual prescriptions, with the usual side effects of plunging the countries into recession.

But the decline in economic activity did not arrest the decline in the currencies because the burden of debt was weighing ever more heavily. Debtors were hustling to cover their hard currency obligations, and international creditors were trying to withdraw whatever assets they could. The currencies overshot—in the case of Indonesia it went into a free fall—causing creditors to suffer severe losses. This was a nasty antidote to the moral hazard. Then came Russia, where the recognition of the moral hazard stood in the way of a bailout. Creditors suffered even greater losses.

By the time the Brazilian crisis came to a climax, moral hazard had become a paramount consideration. The IMF and the treasuries of the various participating countries were reluctant to advance any monies to Brazil without a commitment from the commercial banks to maintain their credit lines. The Brazilian government resisted the pressure because it felt that its credit standing would be adversely affected. Negotiations dragged on, giving banks a chance to run down their credit lines or to establish short positions against them. The climax, when it came, was all the more severe.

By then, the posture of the IMF had changed 180 degrees: Instead of bailing out, "bailing in" became the official policy. Bailing in is, in my opinion, pernicious nonsense. It is nonsense because it means ladling water into a sinking boat; it is pernicious because it makes the boat sink.

The IMF is now unwilling to lend to countries that had paid excessive rates on their bonds unless bondholders are willing to take a hit. The IMF has been looking for a country where it could demonstrate its new approach ever since. It tried with Romania, but Romania did not want to default; it paid off the maturing loans with even more expensive new borrowings before it received the IMF loan that would have enabled it to borrow more cheaply—not a very satisfactory outcome. Eventually the new policy was applied to Ecuadorian Brady bonds, sending a clear message to financial markets that international bonds are not without risk.

One of the reforms currently proposed but not yet implemented is to introduce so-called collective-action clauses into international bonds. This would make it easier to put through debt-reorganization schemes. Not surprisingly the proposal is encountering fierce resistance from bondholders and investment banks.

At the same time, the importance of crisis prevention has been recognized. The various endeavors to establish standards and best practices, particularly in banking, aim at prevention; so do the Contingency Credit Lines recently introduced by the IMF.

So it can be seen that the various reform proposals address one or the other of the disparities we have identified. The recently introduced Contingency Credit Lines have even begun to link the two disparities together. Making the facility available to those countries that follow sound policies provides an incentive for them to do so. I have been advocating such a policy, and I consider it to be the most positive change in the global financial architecture to date. Unfortunately few countries have indicated an interest to avail themselves of the facility. This is not surprising in view of the fact that the availability of the credit line is constrained by the lack of funds. Certain funds—the General Arrangements to Borrow and the New Arrangements to Borrow—are available only for countries that pose a systemic risk; this leaves out smaller countries that are also exposed to contagion. I think the Contingency Credit Lines, to be meaningful, need to be backed by an issue of Special Drawing Rights (SDRs), but that is not in the cards.

The tendency is to reduce rather than increase the powers and resources of the IMF. This is a dangerous trend (as I stated at the outset). All the efforts are directed at discouraging unsound lending. So far so good. But there is now a danger that the flow of funds to the periphery will be inadequate, both in terms of cost and volume. This danger is receiving no attention because the prevailing predilection is to rely on the market mechanism. It is generally acknowledged that the risks of international lending were inadequately priced, and the distortion is attributed to the moral hazard introduced by the IMF. All that is needed, according to this interpretation, is to cure the moral hazard. Actually the moral hazard has now been cured, and that has increased the risks of international lending. In these conditions, it is not sufficient to ensure that the risks are adequately priced; steps must also be taken to reduce the risks. But this proposition does not fit into the prevailing way of thinking.

"Moral hazard" has become the new catchphrase for the market fundamentalists—and a rather effective one at that. It offers moral backing for an institution—namely, the market—that is inherently amoral, and it provides a perfect excuse for resisting any kind of tampering with markets. But the fact remains that it is impossible to maintain lender of last resort or insurance function without incurring the possibility of moral hazard. The Meltzer Commission recommends that the IMF should serve as a quasi-lender of last resort to emerging economies, but in its zeal to eliminate the moral hazard it imposes onerous conditions that would render the IMF ineffective in that role. The Meltzer Commission states that "liquidity loans would have short maturity, be made at a penalty rate (above the borrower's recent market rate) and be secured by a clear priority claim on the borrower's assets." To qualify, countries must open their financial system to foreign competition, ensure that their banks are adequately capitalized, and follow proper fiscal policies as defined by the IMF. It is doubtful whether many countries would qualify and if they did whether it would do them much good. Not much moral hazard there—but not much help to emerging economies, either.

Here I would like to introduce another catchphrase to counterbalance the moral hazard: a level playing field. In global finance, the field was anything but level prior to the recent crisis. The switch from bailing out to bailing in will further tilt the playing field against the periphery. The idea of bailing in involves some kind of sacrifice from the private sector—extending the duration of loans or promising to maintain credit lines. But the private sector is not in the habit of making sacrifices without charging for it. The expectation of being bailed in will make credit more expensive.

The cost of capital is one of the most important variables in competitiveness. So the gap between center and periphery gets even wider. This has already happened. The spreads charged to periphery countries are much higher than they were before the crisis of 1997–1999.

It is widely argued that this is all for the better, as spreads were far too low and periphery countries borrowed far too much. It would be much healthier if borrowings were replaced by direct investments. This argument is valid as far as it goes. Spreads were indeed far too low, and direct investments are more stable and less likely to cause a crash than either portfolio investment or short-term lending. But the problem of an uneven playing field remains; indeed, it is exacerbated by the increased spreads in the cost of borrowing. Multinational corporations, which have greater resources and better access to capital, can outbid, outlast, and outgrow local competition. Take the case of Argentina: All the major banks with one exception are in foreign hands. In the privatization of the state-owned Argentine oil company YPF, the Spanish company Repsol could easily outbid Argentine buyers because it could borrow much cheaper, and eventually it could take over the entire company. The Buenos Aires stock exchange has shrunk to insignificance because many of the leading counters have become subsidiaries of foreign companies.

This may not be so bad. Indeed, the internationalization of the financial system and the spread of multinational corporations could provide the answer to many of the ills of the less-developed world. It could prevent corrupt and dictatorial governments from subordinating the economy to their venal interests, and it could bring the benefits of up-to-date management and technology. But there is a price to pay. Countries already at the periphery would feel and become even more marginalized. This would be politically unacceptable unless it brought visible improvements in living conditions. That is not the case in many parts of the world today.

Corporations are in business to make profits, not to spread benefits. Given the additional risks, they need higher profit margins to operate in the less developed parts of the world. Some arrangements would be needed to compensate for this disparity. As it is, the presence of foreign corporations does not necessarily improve economic and political conditions. On the contrary, foreign corporations often operate in cahoots with corrupt and dictatorial governments. Foreign exploitation is even more objectionable than domestic exploitation, and it may easily provoke a political backlash. History is full of examples: the Boxer Rebellion in China, Perónism in Argentina, the expropriation of oil companies all over the world. The threat of political unrest would have the effect of reducing the value of property in emerging economies and widen the gap between center and periphery. It could cause a contagion spreading from country to country, similar to the financial crisis of 1997–1999.

I do not want to build my case for a more level playing field on the threat of expropriation. As I pointed out in Chapter 7, foreign investment brings much-needed entrepreneurship and technology. Periphery countries might put up with many inequities, because opting out of the system would be even more disadvantageous. But there is something morally wrong about perpetuating inequities, especially if they are avoidable. Morality does not usually enter into hardheaded business calculations, but it should enter into political calculations. People seizing upon a perceived injustice can cause a lot of damage. It is in the interest of the countries at the center of the global capitalist system to foster the economic and political development of periphery countries.

A Modest Proposal

How can we create a more level playing field? I have been concerned about facilitating the flow of funds from the center to the periphery ever since the crisis erupted. I wrote an article in the *Financial Times* (London) on December 31, 1997,* advocating an international credit guaranty scheme. I enlarged on the idea in the original version of this book, arguing that the institution providing the guarantee would have to function as a kind of international central bank. On January 4, 1999, I wrote another article in the *Financial Times*,† arguing the case for an international central bank. I must acknowledge that since the crisis has subsided, these ideas are far

*"Avoiding a Breakdown: Asia's Crisis Demands a Rethink of International Regulation," *Financial Times* (London), December 31, 1997.
†"To Avert the Next Crisis," *Financial Times* (London), January 4, 1999.

too radical. Therefore I propose a more modest reform that does not introduce any radically new ideas yet would make the global financial architecture more balanced and therefore sustainable. My proposal uses the reform elements that have already been introduced and links them together in a way that will make them more coherent and mutually supportive. That is what architecture is supposed to do.

Several measures are addressing the two major disparities we have identified. Those directed at the first disparity are essentially punitive in nature: collective-action clauses for bonds and various arrangements for bailing commercial banks into IMF rescue packages. They are designed to eliminate the moral hazard by making lenders pay for the consequences of unsound lending. Those directed at the second disparity are essentially preventive in nature: better banking supervision, better IMF supervision of macroeconomic and structural policies, greater transparency, and the like. But there is no linkage between the two sets of measures, with one exception: the Contingency Credit Lines, which, however, lack sufficient resources. I contend that the linkage needs to be strengthened by complementing the punitive measures with positive incentives. Specifically I propose mitigating the punitive effect of collective-action clauses by exempting countries following sound policies.

This is how it would work. Under the recently proposed reforms, the IMF is already committed to issue Public Information Notices subsequent to consultations under IMF Charter Article 4, giving its assessment of a country's macroeconomic health and its degree of conformity to established standards and codes of conduct. I propose that the IMF should go one step farther and classify countries according to their performance. In those countries that meet the highest standards, IMF programs would not allow debt restructuring, so that bondholders need not fear that collective-action clauses would be invoked except in the case of individual companies failing. This would enable the countries concerned to borrow in the markets at cheaper rates. In countries with somewhat lower standards, the IMF would not require debt restructuring before entering into a program, while in the case of the lowest standards the IMF would insist on it.

This would give the IMF a powerful preventive tool without encroaching on the sovereignty of member countries. The IMF could prevent excessive borrowing, for instance, by warning a country that it would be downgraded. (There would be no danger of excessive borrowing by countries that are already in the lowest category.)

The IMF assurance would be confined to publicly issued bonds and would exclude bank lines. Providing banks with implicit guarantees was at the core of the trouble in the recent crisis, and it should not be perpetuated. In the case of banks, the leverage that the IMF needs could be provided by varying the capital requirements under the Basle Accord according to the grade awarded by the IMF. The Basle Accord is under review; this could be incorporated in the revised regulations.

I further advocate that the Contingency Credit Line should be strengthened by backing it with a special issue of Special Drawing Rights. A regular issue of SDRs could have inflationary implications; but SDRs earmarked for Contingency Credit Lines could only serve to counteract deflationary pressures.

These three changes taken together would provide both the sticks and the carrots the IMF needs in order to become an effective institution for crisis prevention. Moreover, the carrots would encourage long-term lending, and the sticks would discourage short-term lending. This would be a healthy development.

I believe this proposal makes eminent sense, yet it has run into heavy opposition. For instance, the Council on Foreign Relations's

"Independent Task Force Report on the Future International Financial Architecture" rejected my proposal, and I had to put in a dissenting opinion. One of the objections was that the IMF would not dare to downgrade a country because doing so may precipitate the crisis it was supposed to prevent. But the IMF has an institutional interest in preserving the system, and downgrading a country sooner rather than later would reduce the severity of a crisis. Another objection was that a distinction between those countries that do and do not qualify would create too much of a discontinuity. But the discontinuity would be moderated by distinguishing among countries where debt reorganization would be required, countries where it would be tolerated but not required, and countries where it would not be tolerated. Capital requirements for banks could also be graduated. But the main objection centered on the issue of moral hazard. Wouldn't an IMF guarantee encourage unsound lending? The answer is no. If unsound lending caused a crisis, then the IMF would have to accept the consequences and provide assistance without invoking collective-action clauses. The IMF would be taking a real risk, but there would be no moral hazard involved. It goes to show how the concept of moral hazard is being abused.

The measures I propose—linking the performance of individual countries to the kind of assistance they can expect from the IMF—is hardly revolutionary. It is a scaled-down version of my original loan-guarantee scheme. Alas, even such a modest proposal is simply a nonstarter in today's political environment. The prevailing mood is hostile to any interference with the market mechanism.

Yet the need remains. The success of the Federal Reserve in preserving prosperity in the United States stands in stark contrast to the failure of the IMF to do the same for periphery countries. In the recent crisis, the IMF imposed punitive interest rates, and the countries concerned were plunged into deep recession. But when the crisis threatened the United States the Federal Reserve *lowered* interest rates, and the U.S. economy escaped unscathed.

Admittedly, the situation of the two institutions is far from analogous. The Federal Reserve is in charge of a financial system over which it, and other federal authorities, can exercise control; the IMF has to deal with sovereign states over which it has no authority. One cannot expect the IMF to have provided liquidity to Russian banks in August 1998 the way the Federal Reserve provided liquidity to Wall Street in October 1987. An international financial authority in charge of maintaining the stability of the global financial system has to operate along lines radically different from a national central bank. This does not obviate the need for such an authority.

The most potent objection to strengthening the IMF is that it lacks the methodology for distinguishing between sound and unsound economic policies.* I accept the validity of this objection, especially in light of recent developments. Both the IMF and the United States Treasury, which calls the tune at the IMF, have gone out of their way to appease the market-fundamentalist tendencies of Congress. This bodes ill for the IMF's capacity to set correct policy guidelines for individual countries. After a flawed performance in the 1997–1999 crisis and now under attack, the IMF seems to have lost its way.

I am not in a position to design the methodology the IMF ought to use if it were to act as a kind of international central bank, but I believe the IMF itself would be able to do so if it were given the resources and responsibility. Let's keep in mind that national central banks also lacked the appropriate methodology when they were first entrusted with preventing financial crises and keeping their economies on an even keel, but they developed it and became very successful at their job; the same would happen with the IMF.

*The same objection applies to the Meltzer Commission's recommendations that the IMF should "establish a proper fiscal requirement" for countries eligible for IMF loans.

e IMF some clout for
far in creating a more
ing very little benefit
tries, which as a rule
. For these countries,
nd support from an
to the U.S. Congress

laims against heavily
onomic development
hould be written off
eral creditors. More
s should be prepared
for such countries.
citizen ($1.5 billion
vided the results jus-

here has been wide-
ion with the Jubilee
ed by the refusal of
cost to the World
nate conservatism.
under the current
t as they can service
ynamic. I would go
n some version of a
ital to these coun-

r Commission rec-
business altogether

and be converted int...
should be the respons...
specialize in technica...
Commission is to d...
income countries suc...
ineligible for World F...
required to release th...
the loans are paid d...
amount to a major r...
rich and it would crea...
theless, the Meltzer...
reexamination of the...
today's world.

The World Bank...
countries at a time w...
was contributed mai...
ized countries, again...
markets with an A...
requires that its loan...
rowing countries. T...
lending activities: It...
The guarantees bec...
recipient governmer...
open societies.

The government...
more nefarious infl...
Bank: They push l...
loans that may creat...

Originally the V...
ture projects, but ...
radically reoriented...
human and social...
be carried out muc...

with other elements of society besides the central government—the private sector, local government, and NGOs. The World Bank has a large and competent staff—too large, according to the Meltzer Report—drawn mainly from the Third World, familiar with local conditions and concerned with social issues. It is hamstrung, however, by having to deal with and through governments. In my opinion, the main benefit of the lending operations is that they throw off some discretionary funds. Under the Wolfensohn regime, the World Bank has embarked on some much needed social initiatives, from microlending to distance learning, but in relation to its discretionary spending it is indeed severely overstaffed. It could become much more effective if it had at its disposal more discretionary funds (i.e., funds not tied to a guarantee from the central government of the recipient country). The funds could be used for lending or outright grants or for a combination of both (as, for instance, in microlending).

The Meltzer Commission recommends changing the name of the World Bank to the World Development Agency. I am very much in favor of such an agency, but I do not dare to advocate that the World Bank should get out of its bread-and-butter lending business because I am afraid that in the current political atmosphere it would lead to a reduction in the World Bank's resources, not to an increase in its discretionary funds. That is, in effect, what the Meltzer Commission is proposing. It has a highly restrictive definition of eligibility: Countries with a per capita income in excess of $4,000 would be excluded, and starting at $2,500 official assistance would be limited. Callable capital would be reduced in line with the declining loan portfolio; the International Finance Corporation would be merged into the World Development Agency and its $5.3 billion capital returned to shareholders; and the Multilateral Investment Guarantee Agency would be dissolved. It all amounts to a massive resource transfer from the World Bank to the rich countries.

I agree that the World Bank's lending business is inefficient, no longer appropriate, and, in some ways, counterproductive because it reinforces the role of the central government in the recipient countries. But I cannot agree that the role of the proposed World Development Agency should be as restricted as the Meltzer Commission would have it. There is too much poverty remaining in countries like Russia, Brazil, and Indonesia. Less-developed countries also suffer a disparity in the cost of capital. Local enterprises, particularly the small and medium-sized ones, are penalized vis-à-vis multinationals. Therefore there is no justification for returning capital to the rich countries or canceling the callable capital of the World Bank. On the contrary, the callable capital ought to be used more actively by offering credit enhancements to small and medium enterprises.

Converting the World Bank into an aid and development agency is not without pitfalls. These kinds of agencies are notoriously inefficient and the discipline to assure cost effectiveness is yet to be invented. But the challenge is well worth accepting. Just as the central banks managed to develop a discipline for keeping the economy on an even keel, a World Development Agency could do the same for dispensing aid. The management of the agency ought to be made more independent of the donor governments. The bane of international aid is that the interests of the donors take precedence over the needs of the recipients. At the same time, steps must be taken to prevent the interests of the staff from dominating the agency. This would be best accomplished by putting a time limit on employment. At present the World Bank is staffed by highly qualified people, mainly from Third World countries, whose primary goal is not to have to go home. The best way to hold the agency accountable would be to insist that it should spend its available resources within a limited period. This would oblige it to come back to the donor countries for replenishments. Having to fight for survival is likely to stimulate the institution more than any of the conventional methods of control.

This is not what the Meltzer Commission had in mind. Nevertheless, I am pleasantly surprised to find some common ground with its report. I consider most of its members to be market fundamentalists. Undoubtedly they had to make some concessions on the poverty front to gain the approval of one of the members, Jeffrey Sachs; even so, I am delighted by their support of a World Development Agency. It goes to show that market fundamentalism and open society are not diametrically opposed; the differences are more nuanced.

I take exception to the implication in the Meltzer Report that the frequency and severity of financial crises are due more to the moral hazard introduced by the IMF than to the inherent instability of financial markets. That instability is never acknowledged in the report; neither are the existence of an uneven playing field and the need for preventive action by the IMF. Still, the Meltzer Commission does recognize poverty as a problem that requires the active intervention of richer countries. It seems to agree that economic development requires institutional as well as, by implication, political reform. I welcome the incisive tone of the report. I do not agree with all its arguments, but at least it gives me something to argue with. As a general rule, I find market fundamentalists more creative and radical in their thinking than old-fashioned liberals. They have the benefit of having the wind behind their backs. I would not dare to advocate converting the World Bank into a World Development Agency, for fear that it would be shrunk into insignificance; but they are not afraid because that is exactly what they want to accomplish.

I do agree with the Meltzer Commission that the mission and operating methods of international financial institutions need to be reexamined. Now that the immediate crisis has passed, complacency has set in. Still, the best time to introduce reforms is when there is no immediate emergency. The reforms I have in mind are somewhat different from the Meltzer Report. I shall elaborate them further in Chapter 11, where I discuss the global political architecture. In this chapter, I want to round out my discussion of financial markets.

Currency Regimes

The great unresolved problem of the international financial system is the currency regime. We do not have a clearly defined exchange-rate system at present. The major currencies are free to fluctuate against each other, but we do not have a free float, because it is often felt that the authorities ought to intervene (occasionally they do). The minor currencies range from a totally free float to a totally fixed exchange rate backed by a currency board, with most currencies situated somewhere between.

Experience shows that whatever currency regime prevails it is bound to be flawed. Freely floating currencies are inherently unstable because of trend-following speculation; moreover, the instability is cumulative, because trend-following speculation tends to grow in importance over time. Yet fixed exchange-rate regimes are dangerous because they are too rigid, and breakdowns, when they occur, can be catastrophic. The in-between arrangements are particularly troublesome. Currency pegs were the immediate cause of the Asian crisis. I often compare currency arrangements with matrimonial arrangements: Whatever regime prevails, its opposite looks more attractive.

The effect of the 1997–1999 crisis has been to discredit the in-between arrangements. Currency boards have held, but any less rigorously fixed exchange-rate system failed to withstand attack. Most of the currency pegs have broken, and countries that tried to protect their currencies have fared less well than those that allowed them to depreciate. As a result, we are left with two extremes: currency boards and floating exchange rates, with a preponderance of the latter. Many experts try to justify this polarization, but they have a difficult task because experience has shown that neither extreme is tenable: The instability of the interwar currency arrangements had led to Bretton Woods, and Bretton Woods has, in turn, broken down. I believe the current situation is unstable and will not last.

In certain situations, a currency board is justified. That is the case for countries that are applying for membership in the European Union and for the Balkan countries that hope to benefit from the Stability Pact for Southeastern Europe (see Chapter 11). But the disadvantages of a currency board are amply demonstrated in the case of Argentina. When Brazil devalued, Argentina was left with an overvalued currency, and the obvious escape route was blocked by the currency board. Argentina finds itself in the worst of all possible worlds: high unemployment coupled with high interest rates. It must adopt painful policies to reduce both the budget and trade deficits. The situation is analogous to that of Britain in 1925 when it reestablished the gold standard at an unsustainable exchange rate, as analyzed by J. M. Keynes in *The Economic Consequences of Mr. Churchill*. No way has yet been found to adjust the exchange rate under a currency board when the currency has become overvalued.

Freely floating exchange rates also have grave disadvantages: They make it risky to borrow in foreign currencies and expose the local currency to speculative attack. In the absence of other alternatives, countries may be driven to impose capital controls. This could render the countries that seek to keep their capital markets open more vulnerable, eventually causing a systemic breakdown. The need to develop an alternative is pressing, even if the urgency is not felt. Small countries such as Thailand are particularly exposed.

The exchange-rate system is one of those problems that does not have a permanent solution. The only hope is to alleviate the problem through a process of trial and error. A promising start would be to reduce the range of fluctuations among the major currencies. Swings in excess of 50 percent are beyond tolerable bounds. Paul

Volcker, former chairman of the Federal Reserve, advocates introducing target zones for major currencies. While the intention is admirable, the method proposed is not. Formal target zones provide exactly what the name implies: targets for speculators to shoot at.

Exchange-rate stability is desirable, but it is impossible to determine what the equilibrium or central rate ought to be. Take the current circumstances. The United States has a trade deficit in excess of 3 percent of GNP and rising, suggesting that the dollar should fall; yet the economy is in danger of overheating, suggesting the need for a strong dollar. Conversely, Euroland (the eleven members of the euro zone) and Japan both have trade surpluses, adding strength to the currencies, but weak economies, indicating currency weakness. Correction of the economic imbalance and the trade imbalance would therefore require currency moves in opposite directions. The likelihood is that the currencies will in fact move, first in one direction and then in the other. The trick is to figure out when the changes in direction will occur—and in what order—because they will be intimately interconnected with the fortunes of the various financial markets and economies. The actions of the authorities will have great influence on the outcome without actually determining it because of the unintended consequences. One thing is certain: The situation cannot be understood in terms of equilibrium.

To impose a target zone on the authorities would be counterproductive because it would reduce their room to maneuver. Stability needs to be pursued by more subtle means, and an important part of the balancing act is to adjust the methods to prevailing conditions. Authorities and markets are engaged in a never-ending cat-and-mouse game: Both sides need to adjust to each other's behavior. The authorities need to keep markets and economies on an even keel. But that is not their only goal. They want to assure growth, control inflation, and, depending on the political complexion of the government, promote their vision of social justice. They also want to pull the blanket to their side: to benefit at the expense of others. Target zones cannot be reconciled with this multiplicity of objectives.

Still, the stability of the global system ought to rank higher than it does at present. The belief that the system will always right itself is a self-defeating prophecy. The system *did* right itself, and I was wrong when I predicted its imminent demise, but it was saved by the actions of financial authorities in response to imminent danger. Market fundamentalism could undermine the resolve of the authorities to intervene in case of need.

At present the power and responsibility for the global financial system lies mainly with the United States. U.S. financial authorities are aware of that and try to live up to it, but their primary responsibility is for the economy of the United States. If domestic and international considerations come into conflict, there can be no doubt which will prevail. The position of the Federal Reserve is analogous to the position of the Bundesbank within the ERM in 1992, and we all know that the ERM broke down. The conflict between domestic and international considerations was less clear-cut during the 1997–1999 crisis; nevertheless it is obvious that the United States fared better than the rest of the world.

I have no solution for this problem. All I can do is draw attention to it. It would be helpful if the American electorate and Congress became more aware of the precariousness of the current arrangements, but the resilience of markets militates against any structural reforms. I have proposed three small steps, but even they are unacceptable. I believe that the instability of the international financial system has no architectural solution at present; it is more a challenge for day-to-day management. This management can be successful only if public officials reject the fundamentalist assumption that free markets left to themselves will automatically move toward equilibrium and produce socially acceptable results.

In the longer term, there could be a permanent solution: abolishing national currencies. The creation of the euro is showing the way. It is increasingly realized that having a national currency is a handicap for a small economy. In their distress, some Latin American countries are moving toward adapting the dollar as their national currency; but that will make their dependence on policy decisions made in the United States even more apparent. National currencies cannot be abolished without creating an international central bank, and that is a long way away. Right now the trend is in the opposite direction.

Derivatives, Swaps, and Spreads

Could volatility in currency markets be reduced by making it less profitable to the professionals? Nobel Prize–winning economist James Tobin believes so, and I am inclined to agree with him, but I also believe that the invention of derivatives has made the Tobin tax proposal difficult to apply. The following section, devoted to the role of derivatives, is meant to stimulate discussion, not to provide a prescription.

Derivatives are constructed on the basis of the theory of efficient markets. The fact that they have become so widely used would seem to imply that the theory of efficient markets is valid. I disagree, but I have to be careful how I state my disagreement; as I mentioned before, I have not studied the theory of efficient markets in sufficient detail, nor have I spent much time on how derivatives are constructed. Beta, gamma, and delta are, for the most part, Greek letters to me. This may come as a surprise from a "financial wizard" like me, but it is a fact. It is also an expression of my lack of confidence in the theory of efficient markets.

As I understand it, volatility can be measured, and it is possible to buy insurance against volatility by paying a premium for options.

Those who assume the risk by selling options can either offset the risk against their existing positions or reinsure themselves by engaging in so-called delta hedging. This is a complex strategy, but it boils down to a rather crude method of limiting risk. It involves the seller of the option buying back a certain portion of the underlying security as the price moves against her. Delta hedgers are usually professional market makers who derive their profits from the spread between bid and asked prices and limit their risks by delta hedging.

Properly executed, this strategy should yield profits over the long run, but delta hedging creates automatic trend-following behavior. As the market moves in a certain direction, the delta hedger automatically moves in the same direction, buying when the price goes up, selling when it is going down. In this way, the market makers transfer their risk to the market. If the efficient-market theory were valid, this would mean that the risk disappears. I contend that the theory is false. In my view, volatility cannot be measured with any degree of certainty because the act of measurement can affect that which is measured in a reflexive fashion. Specifically the practice of delta hedging can create a risk of instability that was not present before. It all depends on whether the positions of the market makers add up or cancel each other out. As a general rule, they cancel out because different market participants move in different directions. Once in a blue moon, the risks pile up on one side of the market and delta hedging can touch off a discontinuity in price movements. On these occasions, efficient market theory breaks down. The occasions are rare enough not to discourage an otherwise profitable business, but when they occur they can have a devastating impact. The 1987 stock market crash was a case in point.

Risk management, as it is practiced in the proprietary trading departments of commercial and investment banks, sets limits to the amount of loss a trader can incur. It works the same way as delta hedging. It forces the trader to reduce trading positions when they move against her. This is, in effect, a self-imposed stop-loss order, which reinforces the trend that caused the loss in the first place. The dangers of risk management as it is currently practiced became evident when Long Term Capital Management got into its difficulties.

Trend-following behavior in general and delta hedging in particular tend to increase the volatility of markets, but the market makers benefit from volatility because they can charge a higher premium on options; the buyers of the options cannot complain because the higher premium is justified by the higher volatility. There may be hidden costs to the public, but they are well hidden. As former Fed Chairman Paul Volcker has said, everybody complains about volatility but nobody will do anything about it because the public cannot complain and the market makers in derivatives make a profit coming and going—by creating volatility and by selling insurance against it.

Derivatives have become increasingly sophisticated, and some carry a higher risk of causing a discontinuity than others. The 1987 stock market crash was precipitated by the widespread use of a delta-hedging technique marketed under the name of portfolio insurance. Those who bought the insurance became more heavily invested in the market than they would have been otherwise. When a market decline activated the insurance, the sudden volume of selling created a discontinuity, and the market crashed. To prevent a recurrence, regulators introduced so-called circuit breakers—temporary trading suspensions that destroy the assumption of continuity upon which delta-hedging programs are based.

Similarly dangerous derivative instruments are in widespread use in currency markets, but nothing has been done to discourage their use. For instance, "knockout" options expire when a certain price limit is reached, leaving the buyer of the option without insurance. Knockout options used to be rather popular among Japanese exporters because they are much cheaper than regular options. When they were all knocked out at the same time, in February 1995, a stampede ensued that drove the yen from about 100 yen to the dollar to below 80 yen within a few weeks. Unbalanced option positions have caused other large and seemingly unjustified currency movements at times. The situation cries out for regulation—or at least supervision—but again, as Volcker explained, there has been no constituency clamoring for it.

Generally speaking there are no margin requirements or size limits for derivatives, swaps, and forward transactions, except when they are executed on registered exchanges. Banks and investment banks acting as market makers can carry these commitments as off–balance sheet items. These instruments have developed in an age when people believe in the self-correcting capacity of financial markets. By contrast, margin requirements on stock purchases are left over from a bygone age. If my contention is correct, and some of the recently invented financial instruments and trading techniques are based on a fundamentally flawed theory of financial markets, the absence of margin requirements may pose a serious systemic risk.

On a more fundamental level, we ought to reconsider our attitude toward financial innovations. Innovation is regarded as one of the main benefits of free markets, but in the case of financial markets innovations can create instability. We ought to view financial innovations differently from the way we view better mousetraps, breakthroughs in communication technology, and other inventions. This will require quite an adjustment, because the best brains in the world have been attracted to the financial markets, and the combination of computer capacity and efficient market theory has produced an explosive growth in new financial instruments and new types of arbitrage. The dangers that they carry have been ignored because markets are supposed to be self-correcting, but that is an illusion. The innovative instruments and techniques are not properly understood either by the regulators or the practitioners; therefore they pose a threat to stability.

As I understand it, efficient market theory works with the idea that as long as the price clears the market it is in permanent equilibrium. I work with the opposite idea: In my view, markets are in permanent disequilibrium because of the radical uncertainty that participants must cope with. I think the very idea of measuring risk is flawed because it disregards reflexivity. Long Term Capital Management believed in the idea that risks can be measured, and that belief changed the magnitude of the risk that LTCM encountered in its operations.

Perhaps derivatives and other synthetic financial instruments ought to be licensed in the way new issues of securities must be registered with the Securities and Exchange Commission. It goes against the grain that the creative energies of innovators should be subjected to constraints administered by plodding bureaucrats, but that is precisely what I suggest. Innovations bring intellectual excitement and profit to the innovators, but maintaining stability or, more exactly, preventing excesses ought to take precedence.

When I say this I speak against my own personal interests and predilections. I am a man of the markets, and I abhor bureaucratic restrictions. I try to find my way around them. For instance, I limit the number of funds I advise so I do not have to register with the Securities and Exchange Commission. But I do believe that financial markets are inherently unstable; I also recognize that regulations are inherently flawed: Therefore stability ultimately depends on a cat-and-mouse game between markets and regulators. Given the ineptitude of regulators, there is some merit in narrowing the scope and slowing down the rate of financial innovations.

The Russian meltdown in August 1998 revealed some of the systemic risks. The failure of LTCM, a hedge fund that pioneered the use of risk management techniques based on efficient market theory, demonstrates the failure of the theory. The fact that a rescue effort had to be orchestrated by the Federal Reserve indicates that a systemic risk was involved. As I mentioned before, LTCM carried a balance sheet of over $100 billion on an equity base of less than $5 billion. In addition, it had off–balance sheet liabilities in excess of $1 trillion. The dislocations caused by the Russian meltdown eroded the equity base until it was down to $600 million at the time of the rescue. If LTCM had been allowed to fail, the counterparties would have sustained losses running into the billions, especially as they carried similar positions for their own account. As it is, the counterparties banded together under the prodding of the Federal Reserve and put additional capital into the failing company to permit a more gradual unwinding. The Federal Reserve did what it is supposed to do: prevent systemic failure. Once the emergency has passed, the system ought to be reexamined, and a recurrence prevented. Reform could be superficial, as it was after the 1987 stock market crash with the introduction of so-called circuit breakers, or it could be more fundamental. I hardly need to repeat that I favor a more fundamental rethinking because I believe that our current views about financial markets are based on false premises.

Still, I am not sure whether the introduction of margin requirements on swaps and derivatives or other regulations would reduce volatility, because this would also reduce the amount of capital market makers are willing to devote to their businesses. The net effect of regulation could be to reduce the "depth" of the market rather than reduce volatility.

In the case of currency markets, this could be a good thing. At present the authorities find it difficult to intervene because the volume of transactions—the depth of the market—is too great. If markets were shallower, the authorities could regain their influence. By reducing volatility, they could reduce the demand for hedges and diminish the influence of trend-following behavior. Trade- and investment-related transactions would become more influential, and exchange rates would become more closely correlated with the economic "fundamentals" than they are at present.

Hedge Funds and Banking Regulations

Following the bailout of LTCM there has been much talk about regulating hedge funds. I believe the discussion is misdirected. Hedge funds are not the only ones to use leverage; the proprietary trading desks of commercial and investment banks are the main players in derivatives and swaps. Most hedge funds are not even engaged in those markets. Soros Fund Management, for instance, is not in that line of business. We use derivatives sparingly and operate with much less leverage. LTCM was in some ways exceptional: It was, in effect, the proprietary trading desk of an investment bank (Salomon Brothers) transplanted into an independent entity. Having proved successful, it was beginning to spawn imitators. Even so, hedge funds as a group did not equal in size the proprietary trading desks of banks and brokers, and it was the threat that LTCM posed to those institutions that prompted the Federal Reserve to intervene.

I am not defending hedge funds, and I believe that hedge funds should be regulated like any other market participant. They are difficult to regulate because many operate offshore, but if the regulatory authorities cooperate this should not present insurmountable difficulties. Hedge funds should be neither exempted from regulation nor singled out for special treatment.

In my opinion, regulation and supervision ought to be applied at the point where credit is extended, namely, commercial and investment banks. The regulatory authorities have the power to intervene at that point, and they can bring entities operating offshore under their jurisdiction. The trouble is that they may lack the expertise. Financial transactions have become extremely complex, and it has become practically impossible for a supervisor to assess leverage and risk by looking at the books from the outside. Regulators used to impose margin requirements, so-called haircuts, and the like.

This approach has become impractical because rules of thumb are difficult to apply to the sophisticated instruments that have recently been introduced. Market participants can use those instruments to write circles around the regulators. Many derivatives have been specially designed to evade regulations. The most blatant cases occurred in Japan, where international investment banks made an industry out of so-called wash transactions. I used to be surprised by some anomalous market movements that could be explained only by maneuvers designed to meet Ministry of Finance requirements. Credit Suisse recently had its license revoked in Japan for trying to cover up past activities in this field.

U.S. regulators have recognized that they cannot measure the risks from the outside and are better off relying on the risk-management techniques developed by the banks themselves. The trouble with this approach is that banks only guard against risk as it affects them individually and disregard the risks that their behavior may pose for them collectively. As I said earlier, their risk management is just a sophisticated stop-loss order. When many stop-loss orders are triggered concurrently, they can cause a cascade. That is what happened during the LTCM crisis. Financial institutions are likely to be more cautious while the LTCM crisis remains vivid in their memory, but that may bring only a temporary reprieve.

The Basle Accord of 1988 introduced certain capital requirements for commercial banks operating internationally. The yardsticks they applied were crude and, as it turned out, aggravated the global financial crisis of 1997–1999, particularly in Korea. International banks doing business with Korea were exempted from setting up special reserves once Korea became a member of the Organization for Economic Cooperation and Development, and this encouraged the banks to lend to Korea. To top it off, the Korean central bank required only loans over one year of maturity to be registered, so that most borrowing was done for less than one year and the central bank had no idea of the amounts involved. These factors made the crisis, when it erupted, more intractable. The Basle Accord is now under revision, and these anomalies are likely to be removed.

Capital Controls

It used to be an article of faith that capital controls should be abolished and the financial markets of individual countries, including the banking system, opened up to international competition. Prior to the recent crisis, the IMF had even proposed amending its charter to make these goals more explicit. The experience of the Asian crisis has given us pause. The countries that kept their financial markets closed weathered the storm better than those that were open. India was less affected than the Southeast Asian countries; China was better insulated than Hong Kong. Opinion is now more divided.

It is widely recognized that short-term capital flows can be destabilizing,* and there is much praise for the so-called Chilean model. Chile imposed deposit requirements on capital inflows that penalized short-term capital movements. Chile also reformed its social security system, which provided a domestic source of long-term capital. As a result, it was relatively unscathed by the Mexican crisis of 1994–1995 and the global crisis of 1997–1999.

On their own, short-term capital movements probably do more harm than good. As the Asian crisis demonstrated, it is risky for a recipient country to allow short-term capital inflows to be used for long-term purposes. The proper policy is to sterilize the inflow. That is usually done by accumulating reserves, which is costly and tends to attract further inflows. The main justification for keeping capital markets open, then, is to facilitate international trade and the free flow of long-term financial instruments such as stocks and bonds.

*No surprise. As a student I read studies detailing the destabilizing effect of "hot money" movements during the interwar period.

It is also recognized that the premature opening of capital markets among the newly industrialized countries in Asia was a major contributing factor to the crisis of 1997–1999. In the Asian model, the banking system was used for political ends. The managements of banks became accustomed to taking their instructions from their political masters, and they were ill-prepared to compete in open markets. This was true even for Japan, which has a democratic government; it applied with much greater force to countries with autocratic and corrupt regimes.

Experience has shown how difficult it is to correct this defect. Japan, the world's second largest economy, has been struggling with it for years and is not yet out of the woods. The problem extends beyond the management of commercial banks to the supervisory authorities. The central banks of Indonesia, Korea, and Thailand, not to mention Malaysia, acquitted themselves poorly during the crisis.

Economist Paul Krugman has shown that individual countries may benefit from imposing capital controls, and Mahathir of Malaysia has demonstrated it in practice. But keeping capital markets closed is undesirable on political grounds. Capital controls are an invitation for corruption and the abuse of power. A closed economy is a threat to liberty. Mahathir followed up the closing of capital markets with a witch-hunt against his political rival, Anwar Ibrahim.

But open capital markets also impose a political price. In global markets, multinational corporations and financial institutions enjoy considerable advantages over local ones. They have better access to capital, a broader base to finance research and development, and a broader distribution of risks. Without protective measures for local enterprises, multinationals are liable to swallow them whole. The Asian model of development was so successful exactly because it protected the accumulation of local capital.

More important, open capital markets tend to deprive a country of control over its destiny. Policy decisions are made at the center of the global system, with domestic considerations in mind. This can have unfortunate consequences even where there is no difference in wealth between center and periphery. That was the case in the European Monetary System, where the actions of Bundesbank caused a breakdown of the ERM in 1992. In the global capitalist system most periphery countries are dependent on the center for the supply of capital. That limits their freedom of action. They need to maintain the confidence of foreign investors—or else all hell will break loose. It could be argued that this is a good thing because it subjects governments to market discipline. But market discipline, as it applies to a periphery country, is somewhat perverse: It requires raising interest rates at a time of recession. It reinforces disequilibrium rather than counterbalancing it. That is not what Keynes prescribed.

There is no doubt that open capital markets would be a highly desirable, if not indispensable, feature of a global open society. But capital markets may not stay open unless we find ways to preserve stability and create a more level playing field. In the absence of collective measures, each country has to look out for its own interests, which in turn may lead to the imposition of capital controls. Based on the lessons learned during the crisis of 1997–1999, countries under duress are more likely to resort to capital controls than before. This may give them some temporary relief, but in shaking investor confidence it would also hurt other countries that seek to keep their markets open. Capital controls qualify as beggar-thy-neighbor policies that could disrupt the global capitalist system. Unfortunately our ammunition for combating such an eventuality is being depleted. Right now we are in the process of weakening international financial institutions in the name of eliminating the moral hazard.

CHAPTER 11

The Global Political Architecture

In the wake of the global financial crisis, there has been much talk about the global financial architecture. Practically no discussion has taken place on the global political architecture. This is a strange omission, given that international politics is full of conflicts, and arrangements designed to address them are much weaker compared to the financial arena.

We have not had a political upheaval comparable to the global financial crisis, but we have had a plethora of local conflicts, and in the absence of an effective peacemaking mechanism some of them proved rather devastating. If we look at a single continent—Africa—the conflicts have been too countless to enumerate. Admittedly they do not endanger the global capitalist system, but the same cannot be said of the nuclear-arms race between India and Pakistan or the tensions in the Middle East and the Balkans, not to mention Taiwan. The previous incarnation of global capitalism came to an end with World War I. I do not wish to raise the specter of another world war, but I do believe that the system could be disrupted by political developments just as easily as by financial instability; more likely the two will feed off of one another to create upheaval.

It seems that local conflicts have become increasingly difficult to overcome. During the Cold War they were contained by a larger conflict that pitted the two superpowers against each other. Each side tried to keep its own house in order and exploit the weaknesses of the other. The arrangement was far from ideal, and some local conflicts festered for years, but few were neglected and none were allowed to escalate into a full-scale war between superpowers. Today they must become full-blown crises before they receive attention, and even then the political will to deal with them is difficult to muster.

Most local conflicts arise from relations within a sovereign state: ethnic tensions, corruption, repression, breakdown of central authority. Eventually they can spill across national borders, but until then they can fester under the protective umbrella of national sovereignty. That is why so many grow into full-blown crises.

International relations used to be concerned with relations among states; nowadays what goes on within states has become more important, and there are no effective arrangements to deal with internal conflicts. The rules that govern international relations apply to relations among states. Within states, sovereignty is supposed to prevail except to the extent that a state has abdicated or delegated its sovereignty by international treaty. The arrangements governing relations among states are far from adequate, but there is a much greater deficiency with regard to conditions within states. There is no effective mechanism to prevent crises from developing. Any external intervention constitutes interference with sovereignty. Because crisis prevention requires some degree of external interference, the current arrangements are crisis-prone.

This is nothing new. The principle that sovereign states should be allowed to decide how they treat their subjects was established in the Treaty of Westphalia in 1648 after thirty years of religious warfare. Since then international relations have been based on the principle of national sovereignty.

Sovereign nations are guided by national interests. The interests of the states do not necessarily coincide with the interests of their own citizens, and states are even less likely to be concerned with the citizens of other states. There are few safeguards built into these arrangements to protect the interests of the people. The United Nations has adopted the Universal Declaration of Human Rights, but there is no enforcement mechanism. There are some international treaties and institutions, but their influence is confined to the narrow sphere that the sovereign nations have assigned to them. Events within the borders of states are thus largely exempt from international supervision.

Still, people living under repressive regimes need outside protection. States are more likely to abuse their power in relation to their own citizens than in relation to other states because they are subject to fewer constraints. For people living under repressive regimes, assistance from the outside is often the only lifeline. But people living elsewhere have little interest in coming to their aid. By and large, people living in democracies are ready to defend their own freedom when it is endangered. But there is not enough support for open society as a universal principle. How severe is this deficiency? Could it be corrected? We shall examine the prevailing attitude toward international relations first and the actual state of affairs afterward.

Geopolitical Realism

International relations are not well understood. They do not have a scientific discipline to rely on, although there is a doctrine called "geopolitical realism" that claims scientific status. Just like the theory of perfect competition, geopolitics has its roots in the nineteenth century, when science was expected to provide deterministic explanations and predictions. According to geopolitics, the behavior of states is largely determined by their geographical, political, and economic endowments. Henry Kissinger, the apostle of geopolitics, contends that the roots of geopolitical realism go back even farther, to Cardinal Richelieu, who proclaimed that "states have no principles, only interests."* This doctrine has some similarity to the doctrine of laissez-faire: Both treat self-interest as the only realistic basis for explaining or predicting the behavior of a subject. For laissez-faire, the subject is the individual market participant; for geopolitics, it is the state. Closely allied to both is a vulgar version of Darwinism, according to which the survival of the fittest is the rule of nature. The common denominator of the three doctrines is that they are based on the principle of self-interest and exclude all moral or ethical considerations. In the case of geopolitics, this means the national interest, which does not necessarily coincide with the interests of the people. The idea that the state ought to represent the interests of citizens is beyond its frame of reference. There are, of course, other views about international relations that take into account moral considerations, but they are considered soft and idealistic. The authorities of the state often feel that they cannot afford to stray too far from geopolitical realism in dealing with other states.

This perspective yields some strange results. Geopolitical realism could not cope, for instance, with popular opposition to the war in Vietnam. More recently it could not deal with the disintegration of states such as the Soviet Union and Yugoslavia. According to geopolitics, a state is a state is a state. We are taught to think of them as pawns on a chessboard. What goes on inside the pawns is not the business of geopolitics.

*Henry Kissinger, *Diplomacy* (New York: Simon and Schuster, 1995).

Interestingly, economic theory suffers from a similar weakness. Geopolitics is based on the state; economics is based on the isolated individual, *homo economicus*. Neither construct is strong enough to sustain the weight of the theory that is built upon it. The economic beings are supposed to possess perfect knowledge, both of their own needs and of the opportunities open to them, and to be able to make rational choices based on that information. We have seen that these assumptions are unrealistic; we have also seen how economic theory has wiggled out of the difficulty by taking both preferences and opportunities as given. But we are left with the impression that people are guided by their self-interest as isolated individuals. In reality, people are social animals: The survival of the fittest must involve cooperation as well as competition. There is a common flaw in market fundamentalism, geopolitical realism, and vulgar social Darwinism: the disregard of any motivation other than narrow self-interest.

No World Order

Turning from ideology to reality, let us look at the actual state of affairs in international relations. The distinguishing feature of the current situation is that it cannot be described as a "regime." There is no political system to correspond to the global financial system; moreover, there is no consensus that a global political system is either feasible or desirable.

This is a relatively recent state of affairs. Until the collapse of the Soviet empire, one could point to a regime in international relations—the Cold War—and it was remarkably stable: Two superpowers representing two different forms of social organization were locked in deadly conflict. Each wanted to destroy the other, and both prepared for it by engaging in a nuclear-arms race. As a consequence, each became strong enough to wreak havoc on the other if attacked. This prevented the outbreak of outright war, although it did not prevent skirmishes at the margin and jockeying for position.

A balance of powers, such as that represented by the Cold War, is generally recognized as one way to preserve peace and stability in the world; the hegemony of an imperial power is another; an international organization capable of effective peacemaking could be a third. At present we have none of the above.

The United States remains the sole surviving superpower, but it has no clear view of its role in the world. During the Cold War, the United States was both a superpower and the leader of the free world, and the two roles reinforced each other. With the disintegration of the Soviet empire, this cozy identity also disintegrated, but people failed to realize it. The United States could have remained the leader of the free world, but to do so it ought to have cooperated with other democratic-minded countries, first to help lay the foundation for democracy in former communist countries, then to strengthen the international institutions necessary to maintain a global open society. On two previous occasions when the United States emerged as the leader of the free world—at the end of World Wars I and II—it did exactly that: It sponsored the League of Nations, then the United Nations. However, both efforts proved futile. In the first case, Congress refused to ratify the League of Nations; in the second, the Cold War rendered the United Nations largely ineffectual.

The opportunity to reinvigorate the United Nations presented itself when Mikhail Gorbachev became the head of the Soviet Union. Gorbachev was hoping to make the United Nations function the way its founders had intended by forging an alliance with the United States. It was the most coherent part of his program, called *novoye myshlenie* (new thinking), elaborated by the only segment of the Soviet bureaucracy that supported his reforms—the Foreign Ministry. His ideas for economic reform were far less coherent; he was expecting his prospective ally, the United States, to ride to his rescue.

One of Gorbachev's first acts was to make good on the Soviet arrears to the United Nations. Then he came before the UN General Assembly to make an impassioned plea for international cooperation. It received short shrift. The United States suspected a ruse and wanted to test his sincerity. When he met the test, new tests were designed. By the time he made all the concessions demanded of him, conditions in the Soviet Union had deteriorated so much that the Western leadership could conclude that it was too late to extend the assistance that Gorbachev had hoped for. Still, neither Gorbachev nor his successor, Boris Yeltsin, posed any serious difficulties to the proper functioning of the UN Security Council for about five or six years.

The opportunity to make the Security Council function the way it was originally intended was dissipated, first by an unfortunate incident in Somalia and then by the conflict in Bosnia. The Somalia experience established the principle that U.S. soldiers would not serve under UN command—although they were not under UN command when the incident occurred. It also taught the U.S. government that the public has a very low tolerance for body bags. Nevertheless the Bosnia crisis could have been better contained if the Western permanent members of the Security Council had agreed among themselves. The task could have been assigned to NATO—as it was in the end—and the tragedy could have been avoided. In 1992 Russia would have posed no objections. But, cowed by the Somalia experience, President Bill Clinton exerted no leadership, and the United Kingdom, which was president of the European Community at the time, preferred to send peacekeepers where there was no peace to keep. The fighting and atrocities dragged on until finally the United States took a firmer line.

In the aftermath of the Bosnia conflict, the United States has come to believe that nothing will get done unless it takes the lead. Europe cannot get its act together, and the independence of the United Nations is seen as an affront to U.S. leadership. Under congressional pressure, the United States did not even pay its dues to the United Nations. After the debacle in Rwanda, it is no exaggeration to say that the United Nations is less effective today than it was during the Cold War. At the same time, the United States has been reluctant to take the lead on most international issues, lacking domestic support. As a result, problems fester until they reach a crisis point where they can no longer be ignored. This state of affairs is clearly unsatisfactory. There is an urgent need for the profound rethinking and reorganization of international relations.

Toward a Global Open Society

I have argued that we cannot have a global economy without a global society. But how can the idea of a global society be reconciled with the sovereignty of states? States have interests but no principles. How can the global common interest be left in their care? Only if the citizens of democratic states exert influence on governments and make them responsive to the needs of a global society.

I propose that the democratic states of the world should form an alliance with the purpose of creating a global open society. This would involve two distinct but related tasks: fostering the development of open societies throughout the world, and establishing certain rules and institutions that would govern the behavior of states toward their citizens and one another. This is a rather grandiose project, and it could be dismissed as an utopian idea; but open society recognizes the limitations imposed by reality. Perfect solutions are not attainable. We must therefore content ourselves with the second-best: imperfect arrangements that can be improved by a process of trial and error. The arrangements must vary according to time and place. Above all we must remember that well-intended actions often have adverse unintended consequences. This is particularly true of external interventions. When people try to impose their version of the ultimate truth on others it is liable to lead to religious, ideological, or communal warfare and there will be no end to the fighting. That is what happened in the Thirty Years' War. By basing the international political architecture on the principles of open society, this danger could be avoided. Open society rests on the recognition that the ultimate truth is beyond our reach. We must accept that people have different views and interests and we must find ways to allow them to live together in peace.

The creation of a global open society would inevitably involve some external meddling in internal affairs. It follows both from the principle of fallibility and the principle of sovereignty (which is today's reality) that to the greatest extent possible the intervention should be consensual and constructive rather than coercive. The emphasis should be on crisis prevention rather than punitive intervention. Prevention cannot start early enough, but at an early stage it is impossible to identify potential trouble spots. The best way to prevent crises is to foster the development of open societies throughout the world. The development has to be economic as well as political. The point is well made by Amartya Sen when he defines development as political freedom.*

I believe the concept of open society could provide some guiding principles to govern international relations, but to serve in that capacity the abstract concept must be transformed into an operational one. To prepare a blueprint for a global open society would run counter to the principles of open society; it would also be an exercise in futility. Open society cannot be designed from first principles: It must be created by the people who live in it.

Open society as an operational concept needs to be developed by every society and every age for itself. A global open society has to be created by the open societies of the world working together. That is exactly what I propose.

The process that Karl Popper recommends is piecemeal social

---

*Amartya Sen, *Development as Freedom* (New York: Alfred A. Knopf, 1999).

engineering. I am not entirely happy with the term, because in times of revolutionary regime change, the tempo is too fast to allow us the luxury of piecemeal action; that is why events spin out of control. The collapse of the Soviet system was such a moment in history. But that moment has passed, and, as I argued earlier, we missed a historic opportunity. The international political scene is now much calmer, with specific problems slowly coming to the boil. Therefore a piecemeal approach is appropriate. Accordingly I shall focus on a particular case—the disintegration of Yugoslavia—that raises the issues confronting us in a particularly poignant way. I shall try to build the case for a global open society by proceeding from the particular to the general.

The Disintegration of Yugoslavia

Since the original publication of this book, the crisis in Kosovo came to a head. NATO intervention constituted an important precedent, in which an alliance of democratic states intervened in an internal conflict within a sovereign state in the name of universal principles, even if those principles were not properly defined.

The intervention was successful, but it was a close run, and raised many troubling issues. The spectacle of NATO planes dropping bombs from high altitudes was profoundly disturbing, and in many ways it was directly counterproductive. It accelerated the ethnic cleansing it was supposed to interdict; it temporarily silenced the domestic opposition to Slobodan Milosevic; and it divided the world rather than uniting it behind the universal principles it invoked. The eventual outcome mitigated some of these ill effects, and it is only too tempting to forget about the troubling issues and proclaim victory. But that would not be justified by the current state of affairs. The fall of Slobodan Milosevic has not resolved the problems that he has helped to create. The process of disintegration can be reversed only by integrating the region into the economic and political community of Europe. The need is recognized by the political leaders of Europe; it is now a question of execution. The fate of the former Yugoslavia and its neighbors constitutes a test case for open society.

Let's take a closer look at the disintegration of Yugoslavia. I have some direct knowledge about the subject. I have Open Society Foundations operating in every Balkan country with the exception of Greece and Turkey. Prior to the Kosovo crisis we had branches of the Yugoslav foundation in Kosovo and Montenegro; these have now been converted into independent foundations.

I was in Belgrade in April 1990 and met with Prime Minister Ante Markovic on the day he announced the formation of a federal party that would contest the elections in each of the republics. We were negotiating about setting up an Open Society Foundation to which the federal government would provide matching funds. At that time Yugoslavia was economically much better situated than Poland. It had been more open and prosperous than Poland during communist times. Both countries had suffered a bout of hyperinflation, and both countries introduced an IMF-sponsored stabilization program—better known as the "big bang"—on January 1, 1990. Yugoslavia had the advantage of experts trained by the international financial institutions in Washington, and the program was much more advanced than in Poland. Prices were actually falling in April—that was why Ante Markovic chose to launch his party then. Subsequently Milosevic ran up a big budget deficit in Serbia, wrecking the stabilization program and winning the Serbian elections.

I was also in Belgrade in June 1991 just before the outbreak of hostilities in Slovenia and Croatia. I had breakfast with U.S. Ambassador Warren Zimmerman, who told me that Secretary of

State James Baker had just visited Belgrade and told the leaders of the Yugoslav army that the United States would have no objections if they declared a state of emergency, secured the frontiers, and held internationally supervised federal elections within six months. I also met with Foreign Minister Leko Loncar, who told me that the European Community had offered a loan of 3 billion ecu, no small amount, if only Yugoslavia would stay together, but he was not hopeful. More than half the federal budget went to support the army, which was largely under Serbian domination; more than half the federal budget came from customs revenues collected in Slovenia. No wonder that the army was anxious to secure its main source of revenue and Slovenia was reluctant to provide it. When it came to armed conflict, the first move of the Yugoslav army was to try to take possession of the border posts in Slovenia, but the Slovenians were more determined and prevailed.

As the Yugoslav federation broke up, I set up foundations in each of the successor republics. It was to my lasting regret that I had delayed the process in the hopes of securing matching funds from the federal government. There was a group of intellectuals committed to transforming Yugoslavia into a democracy who had sought my support; I made them responsible for running the foundations. They were opposed to the nationalist emotions that became increasingly dominant as the breakup of Yugoslavia proceeded and the atrocities multiplied. They remained eager to cooperate with each other; they saw the conflict not in terms of Serbs, Croats, Bosnians, and Albanians but in terms of open versus closed society. This put them at loggerheads not only with the ruling regimes but also, in the case of Croatia, with society at large. The Croatian foundation was in danger of being confined to a ghetto of its own creation, and reluctantly I changed the leadership to make the foundation more acceptable to a broader segment of society.

When the Bosnia crisis erupted and Sarajevo came under siege, I committed $50 million to the UN High Commission for Refugees

(UNHCR). That was in December 1992. My thought was that by sponsoring voluntary organizations to go into the country I would also draw in UN peacekeepers to protect them, which would help prevent atrocities. This turned out to be a false track. Still, I retained some degree of control over my gift, and the money was exceptionally well spent. Under the leadership of a particularly gifted relief organizer, Fred Cuny, who was subsequently killed in Chechnya, an alternative water supply was established, electricity was brought in through a tunnel, a plasma manufacturing unit was installed in the hospital, people were given seeds to grow vegetables on small plots and balconies, and so on. Nevertheless, I considered my gift an admission of defeat: It would have been much better if the crisis could have been prevented and the money would have been spent in countries that were not being destroyed.

I visited Sarajevo in November 1993, flying in an Ilyushin, one of the world's largest aircraft, carrying gas pipes that Fred Cuny was going to use to extend the natural gas supply system. It was a scary trip, with the Ukrainian crew tightening and loosening the straps that held the pipes together as the plane banked to one side or the other; we were sitting on a bench alongside the pipes that could have crushed us if the straps had slipped. In Sarajevo, I was supposed to attend the inauguration of the water supply. Cuny had built a modular water purification plant in Texas and had it transported in segments. They barely fit inside the Ilyushin and could be removed from the hold within eight minutes—the permitted turnaround time in Sarajevo. They were then installed inside a road tunnel alongside the river; the water was drawn from the river and purified. Cuny even found a disused reservoir on a nearby hill left over from the Austro-Hungarian monarchy where water could be stored and distributed by gravity. Unfortunately the local authorities did not give permission for the water to be turned on. We never found out why—either because it would have interfered with a water-distribution racket or because the government needed gory pictures on CNN showing people being killed while they waited for water. I had to threaten going public with my protest before permission was granted.

The Open Society Foundation in Bosnia and Herzegovina had a separate identity from the humanitarian relief operation. Its goal was to support civil society, and it kept a distance from the authorities. It sustained the spirit of resistance that appealed to the conscience of the world. It certainly appealed to my conscience. My visit merely confirmed what I already knew from a distance: their heroic commitment to the values of open society.

On my return I stopped off in Zagreb and had my one and only meeting with President Franjo Tudjman. He accused me of supporting traitors in his country and spreading a dangerous new ideology called open society. The foundation continued to incur the enmity of the government for its support of independent media. Government control over the media was more complete in Croatia than in Yugoslavia, and there was less opprobrium from Europe because of religious and historical links. It left the foundation somewhat isolated and exposed.

I also became deeply involved in Macedonia. Greece had imposed an embargo on Macedonia, in a dispute over its name, that severely disrupted the Macedonian economy. Macedonia is landlocked and gets its oil supplies from Greece. At the beginning of 1993, I gave Macedonia a loan of $25 million to enable it to buy sufficient oil to see it through the winter. Macedonia was a multiethnic society with a large Albanian minority. It could survive as an independent country only if it treated all its citizens equally, and the government seemed to recognize the force of this argument. That was why I felt it so important to rush to their aid. The government repaid the loan, but otherwise it did not quite live up to its promises. Perhaps it tried but ran into too much opposition from the Macedonian intelligentsia. In particular, no Albanian-language instruction was allowed at the university. When an illegal Albanian university was set up in Tetovo, I begged President Kiro Gligorov not to rise to the provocation but to no avail: Blood was shed. When I publicly expressed my disappointment I became persona non grata with the government. The feeling was mutual. I was distressed to observe the gradual deterioration in public morals. In the early days of independence and during the Greek embargo, I sensed a lot of public spirit, even idealism, in the government. When Yugoslavia came under embargo the situation changed. Smuggling and other illicit activities spread corruption. There was a murder attempt against President Gligorov that narrowly missed its target. I found that previously honest government officials gave up the struggle and became cynical about corruption.

Our foundation in Yugoslavia proper was always at loggerheads with the regime, but it managed to establish strong roots within civil society. In addition to its support of independent media and other grants that incurred the wrath of the government, the foundation engaged in many activities—particularly in public health, education, culture, and support for refugees—of which the government could not openly disapprove. At one point the registration of the foundation was withdrawn, but it continued operating, and eventually the registration was restored. Subsequently when I visited the foundation in June 1997, I was received by Milan Milutinovic, then foreign minister. We had, to use the diplomatic vernacular, a frank discussion.

The Yugoslav foundation had branches in Vojvodina, Montenegro, and Kosovo. The Kosovo branch supported the parallel system of education that the Albanian population established when it was excluded from the official system. Although most of the foundation's support went to Albanian causes—including Albanian-language media—it did not operate along ethnic lines, and when I visited Kosovo in 1997 I met at the foundation people drawn from all elements of civil society. The Albanian member of the foundation board, Veton Surroi, was—and remains—an important voice for reason and moderation. He played a crucial role in saving the Rambouillet Conference (February 6 to 23, 1999), which preceded the military intervention in Kosovo, from total failure.

I should also mention my involvement in Albania and Bulgaria. In Albania, I became engaged in the physical reconstruction of schools. This was a deviation from our usual approach, which is confined to what goes on inside schools, but it was rendered necessary by the fact that many schools had been destroyed when the communist regime was overturned. We managed to establish an efficient construction operation that was free of corruption and engaged the communities in the rebuilding effort. I knew we had succeeded when a contractor donated money to rebuild the school in his home village. Subsequently, when the Berisha regime was violently overthrown in 1997, many buildings were again destroyed, but not one of our buildings was touched. Our computers were looted from the warehouse, but not from the schools. Those events taught me that the Albanians have strong ethical standards and that the rejection of government should not be equated with a lack of public morality. On the whole, I had a very positive experience in Albania, and the foundation enjoys widespread support and respect. The same is true in Bulgaria.

I offer these details partly to establish my credentials and partly to state my perspective (or bias). My foundations were fighting for an open society but to no avail. Still, I believe that losing battles are worth fighting; I also believe that if the Western powers had been guided by the principles of open society the battle might have been won. It is not appropriate to detail my contacts with Western policymakers; suffice it to say that I was often critical of Western policies both publicly and privately, and my public statements helped me to get a private hearing. For instance, I had several discussions with the then secretary-general of the United Nations, Boutros Boutros-Ghali, and I argued that he should have resigned rather than accept a peacekeeping mission that could not be carried out—but resignation was farthest from his mind. I was advocating a firm line against both Milosevic and Tudjman, and I felt a strong sense of personal responsibility when we finally took a firm line in Kosovo—not because I was consulted (I was not) but because I was in favor of it.

I do not want to give a blow-by-blow account of events in Yugoslavia, only some general observations. First, the Western democracies—Europe and the United States—were intimately involved. I have already mentioned Secretary of State Baker's visit and the European offer of a 3 billion ecu loan. I would argue that the involvement should have started even earlier, when Milosevic abolished the autonomy of Kosovo and Vojvodina or when he wrecked the economic reform program, and it should have been more firmly based on the principles of open society. International involvement cannot start early enough, but even then success cannot be assured.

Second, no Western democracy had its national interests at stake, but Europe and the United States had a collective interest in what happened in Yugoslavia. Perhaps because of that, Western policy lacked unity and clarity of purpose. Most of the time, the aim was to preserve the status quo and to avoid armed conflict. This was true in June 1991 when Secretary of State James Baker agreed to the declaration of a state emergency; it was true in Bosnia, where the Western powers chose humanitarian intervention in lieu of armed intervention—Article 6 peacekeeping instead of Article 7 peacemaking under the UN Charter. This was also true in the Kosovo crisis, in which the United States explored every avenue to Milosevic. When in the fall of 1998 Milosevic engaged in a large-scale anti-insurgency campaign against the Kosovo Liberation Army (KLA), displacing some 400,000 Kosovo Albanian villagers, U.S. envoy Richard Holbrooke reached an agreement with Milosevic that introduced into Kosovo unarmed observers from the Organization for Security and Cooperation in Europe (OSCE). The observers were withdrawn and the Rambouillet Conference arranged only after Milosevic broke the agreement and allowed the atrocities to continue in the presence of the observers. Close study of the events leads me to the conclusion that Milosevic wanted to be bombed in order to carry out a well-prepared, large-scale ethnic cleansing that would prepare the ground for de facto partitioning of Kosovo.

Generally speaking, Western democracies were relatively insensitive to the internal political conditions prevailing in the various republics; they were much more influenced by religious, historical, and national considerations. For instance, Germany insisted on the recognition of Croatia and Slovenia as independent countries without making adequate provisions for the protection of Serbian minorities. France, Greece, and to a lesser extent the United Kingdom sympathized with the Serbs. Prejudice against Muslims was widespread in Europe. The United States concluded the Dayton Accords without dealing with the festering problem of Kosovo. The leader of the Kosovo Albanians, Ibrahim Rugova, believed in nonviolent resistance, putting his faith in the Western democracies; after Dayton he started losing influence, and the KLA gained ground. It is no exaggeration to say that the Kosovo crisis in 1999 was a direct consequence of the Dayton Accords in 1995.

Western policymakers should have recognized that the conflict in Yugoslavia was not only between Serbs, Croats, Bosnians, and Albanians but also between open and closed society. This recognition would have made policymakers more sensitive to issues like the lack of independent media and rigged elections. It would have discouraged them from building on repressive regimes like those of Slobodan Milosevic, Franjo Tudjman, and to a lesser extent Alija Izetbegovic in Bosnia; they wouldn't have ignored the problems in Kosovo for a decade.

Third, external intervention was clearly unsuccessful. It took many forms, but none worked. In Bosnia, the international community intervened within the framework of the United Nations, and the results were disastrous. Learning from that experience, in Kosovo the Western powers relied on NATO, but the results were not much better; in the end UN authority had to be invoked to forge a settlement. Earlier the United Nations had imposed an economic embargo with unintended adverse consequences. Shady businessmen could break the sanctions with the help of the authorities. This led to unholy alliances between the ruling regimes and mafia interests in Yugoslavia and some neighboring countries. The European Community even tried preventive action by promising a loan if Yugoslavia stayed together, but to no avail. In short, nothing worked. The military intervention in Kosovo did achieve its immediate military objective, but it did not bring peace.

Eventually, Milosevic was swept from power by the Serbs themselves. International pressure undoubtedly contributed to Milosevic's fall but it cannot be said to have been engineered by the Western powers. On the contrary, their policies often hindered the emergence of a strong and united opposition. The U.S. in particular insisted on treating Vuc Drascovic as part of the opposition, instead of recognizing that he was a disruptive influence. The Western powers were slow in allowing the towns controlled by the opposition to receive relief from the oil embargo; they were even slower in extending aid to Djukanovic in Montenegro, who was opposed to Milosevic.

If the Djukanovic regime in Montenegro could have provided economic stability while the Yugoslav dinar lost its value, the Milosevic regime could have been destabilized much more surely than by all the bombing. As it turned out, Milosevic could exert sufficient pressure on Montenegro to be able to steal the elections there.

The way events unfolded in Kosovo also played into Milosevic's hands. There were a proliferation of organisations. Authority was divided between the NATO-led military (KFOR) and a civil authority established by the United Nations (UNMIK). The civilian authority has in turn four pillars: UNHCR for humanitarian affairs; the United Nations for interim civil administration; OSCE for political institution-building; and the European Union for economic reconstruction. To make matters worse, UN headquarters in New York want to exercise detailed control over UNMIK.

The lack of funding and the confusion of authorities has confounded the UN administration at every step. It could not pay teachers and other civil servants, restore essential public services, establish the rudiments of a judicial system, or even provide civilian registration documents.

Six months after the settlement of the Kosovo crisis, order was not restored and people could not feel safe. KFOR troops succeeded in protecting themselves, but not in protecting the civilian population. The United Nations was unable to field an adequate police force. The situation has improved since then, but the damage could not be undone. The Serbian population has taken refuge in enclaves, Roma peoples have been chased away, and the Albanian population lives in fear. This has enabled Milosevic to claim the Serbian votes in Kosovo as well.

These circumstances emboldened Milosevic to call elections, but, as usual with successful despots, he overreached himself. The strength of the opposition surprised everyone, including themselves, and the size of the turnout trumped the number of votes Milosevic could steal. In the end, victory went to those who were willing to fight losing battles.

The Lessons of Yugoslavia

Events in Yugoslavia support my general argument not only with regard to fighting losing battles but also with regard to external intervention. Punitive intervention tends to be ineffective and is often counterproductive. This is true of economic sanctions, peacekeeping, and military action. Crisis prevention cannot start early enough, and it must be based on the principles of open society. Even so, there can be no assurance that preventive action will be successful; therefore we cannot do without punitive sanctions. These sanctions would be morally and politically better justified if all the constructive options had been fully exhausted.

In the early stages, crisis prevention is relatively painless and inexpensive; later, the damage and costs escalate exponentially. The trouble is that crisis prevention, however early it starts, will not necessarily succeed. It is part of the concept of open society that not every problem has a solution. For instance, with the best will in the world, nothing could have preserved the status quo in Yugoslavia.

If Western democracies had objected in 1989 when Slobodan Milosevic abolished the autonomy of Kosovo, it is possible that Milosevic might not have been able to consolidate his power in Serbia, and there could have been a more peaceful transition to a new regime. But if prevention fails, then military action might become unavoidable. Even then, early action can be the least costly. The damage would have been much less if NATO had intervened when the Yugoslav navy bombarded Dubrovnik in December 1991.

One of the main obstacles to early crisis intervention is an adverse risk-reward ratio. Nobody earns laurels for solving crises that have not yet erupted; if the prevention is successful, no crisis arises. Only the failures register. What government or institution is willing to accept such odds?

I believe the obstacle could be overcome with the help of the moral argument I proposed earlier: When it comes to doing the right thing, people must be prepared to fight the losing battles. I should like to bring this point home by looking at a crisis area that has not yet emerged into public consciousness: the Ferghana Valley.

The Ferghana Valley

Few people have even heard of the Ferghana Valley, which connects Uzbekistan, Tajikistan, and Kyrgyzstan. Even fewer are aware that serious trouble is brewing there. I would not know it either if I did not have foundations in those countries. Uzbekistan is the largest and strongest state in the region, endowed with oil and minerals and subject to a repressive regime. The repression is directed primarily against Islamic fundamentalism, and by treating all manifestations of Islamic religion as a manifestation of fundamentalism the regime has plenty to repress. Kyrgyzstan, a neighbor, is smaller and much poorer. It has a democratically inclined but ineffectual president. Tajikistan has been devastated by several years of civil war, which was only recently settled. Borders within the Ferghana Valley are difficult to police, and the valley itself is easily accessible from Afghanistan. The valley is in economic decay, with drug trafficking and terrorism taking hold. Armed incidents are more frequent in Kyrgyzstan than Uzbekistan exactly because Uzbekistan is more authoritarian. Presidential elections were scheduled in Kyrgyzstan for October 2000, with significant opposition expected. Under pressure from all sides, the administration has increasingly resorted to repressive measures, intimidating the media and arresting potential presidential candidates. There is no reason to believe that those candidates would be any more democratic than the incumbent. The outlook is bleak.

Repression and terrorism are mutually reinforcing. We are in the early stages of escalating conflict. In this respect, the situation is reminiscent of Yugoslavia in 1990. What to do? I do not see a strategy to reverse the prevailing trend, which leaves me two options: continue doing what our foundations do best—support education, civil society, and the rule of law—or abandon the entire effort. The effort seems futile, and in some respects it may even prove to be counterproductive. For instance, if we succeed in enforcing the rule of law in Kyrgyzstan because the president is relatively well intentioned, he is liable to lose the election to a tougher character. But I am convinced that it would be a mistake to pull out.

The Ferghana Valley represents a case where it is worthwhile to continue irrespective of near-term results. We are sowing the seeds of open society, and some of those seeds will take root. The prospective loss ratio is daunting, but the seeds that survive may become extremely valuable exactly because so few will have survived. I recall that in Hungary, when I wanted to establish a business school, the best candidates to head it up had studied abroad on a Ford Foundation scholarship twenty-five years previously.

The conclusion I have reached is not entirely satisfactory, because it does not offer a way out of the current crisis. That in itself seems to undermine the case for crisis prevention. We have identified a crisis at a relatively early stage, we want to prevent it, yet we cannot find a way to do that. But that is the human condition: Not every problem has a solution. The likelihood that a crisis in the Ferghana Valley is unavoidable actually strengthens the case for the kind of work my foundations are undertaking. I have argued that crisis prevention cannot start early enough and that it is best pursued by laying the groundwork for open societies. If we knew how to prevent crises, my prescription might be too wasteful; as it is, it may be the best available option. And even if it is wasteful, it certainly is not useless. There are times when it is possible to find a promising strategy. In the early stages of the collapse of the Soviet system, I could almost always envision some promising strategies, and I tried to advocate them, although without success. There are other times when no strategy seems to work, for the trend is already set. The dissolution of Yugoslavia was a case in point; the Ferghana Valley may be another. In these cases, we have to fall back on Sergei Kovalev's prescription and keep fighting the losing battles. Paradoxically, it will ensure ultimate victory because people who are willing to fight losing battles keep the flame of freedom alive. Society comes closer to the ideal of open society than it would be if people merely pursued their self-interest. That is the justification for doing the right thing irrespective of what others do.

Foreign Aid

When I advocate constructive intervention for the sake of building open societies, I am advocating foreign aid. In a sense, that is what my foundations do, and that is what I advocate for the alliance of open societies.

Foreign aid has acquired a poor reputation, and rightly so. It is an entrepreneurial activity, more difficult in many ways than running an enterprise for profit, yet it has been reduced to a bureaucratic exercise. Bureaucracies tend to be more concerned with self-preservation than with carrying out their mission. Accountability is an essential feature of democracy, but it encourages defensive behavior, second-guessing, and recrimination. We hold public servants to higher standards than businessmen. We tolerate losses in business but not in foreign aid. No wonder that those in charge avoid risks even at the cost of avoiding success.

In arguing for foreign aid, I am going against the grain. Market fundamentalism seeks to liberate economic activities from any kind of official interference, and it must be acknowledged that it has produced some wonderful results by unleashing the creative energies of the human intellect. And here I go, trying to impose the dead hand of bureaucracy.

That is not what I stand for. I recognize the merits of a market economy. I believe they lie exactly in unleashing creative energies, not in producing equilibrium. But the profit motive is not sufficient to sustain society. The market economy is only one part of open society. There must be some effort to foster the development of open societies, and it must have a constructive component because punitive sanctions on their own cannot do the job; neither can they be morally justified. That means that we must engage in foreign aid in full awareness of its imperfections.

I believe that it is not beyond the capacity of the human intellect to be as creative in the pursuit of social goals as it is in the pursuit of profit.

I have tried to demonstrate this in my own philanthropic activities. I have created what I call a "fractal version" of open society, establishing a network of foundations governed by boards composed of nationals of the countries they serve. I rely on them to decide what the foundation ought to do, and they take responsibility for their actions. I am often surprised by what they do. Some of the best programs are those that I never envisioned. Admittedly it is a hit-and-miss affair. We have had some great successes, some indifferent results, and occasional failures that require a change of personnel.

I wish this approach could be replicated on a larger scale, but I realize it cannot be done. Indeed, my own foundation network has reached a scale where it has lost some of its erstwhile flexibility and begun to take on the character of a bureaucracy. Still, I am an independent agent. I can afford to admit and correct my mistakes; that is why my efforts have been for the most part successful. Politicians and public servants do not enjoy such luxury, for they must justify their actions in the eyes of a hostile public. This makes them risk-averse in situations where it is difficult to produce positive results without taking risks.

Official foreign aid cannot possibly be as effective as my philanthropic endeavors (although it can make up in quantity what it lacks in quality). Still, we cannot do without it if we want to build a global open society. The same argument applies to other forms of official intervention: The fact that it is ineffective does not mean that it is unnecessary; it means that we should try to make it more effective. Rule-based incentives are preferable to government-administered programs. That is why the global political and financial architecture becomes so important. But even in administered programs it should be possible to unleash the creative energies of people who care—there is no reason why entrepreneurship should be confined to the pursuit of profit.

The Stability Pact for Southeastern Europe

This brings us back to the Balkans. I spoke of the disintegration of Yugoslavia as a hopeless situation where nothing worked. After the fall of Milosevic, the situation has changed. An opportunity has arisen to engineer a positive outcome, and it is imperative that we seize it. The opportunity was recognized even before the revolution in Serbia. I was not the only one who was profoundly shaken by the moral issues raised by the NATO bombing. It was widely felt that European involvement in the Balkans has been far too timid and reactive and the European Union needed to develop a positive, proactive policy toward the region that would prevent crises rather than react to them. The point was first made to me by Javier Solana, NATO secretary-general at the time, *before* NATO's intervention. My foundation network started working on a comprehensive program for the region, but we were preempted by the Centre for European Policy Studies (CEPS), a think-tank in Brussels, whose plan had the endorsement of Romano Prodi, president-elect of the European Commission. Rather than reinventing the wheel, we adopted that plan as the basis for our thinking. We organized a workshop of twenty-five policy institutes from the region in Ljubljana for July 18–20, 1999, and issued a declaration that was an elaboration of the CEPS proposal.

The key idea is to bring the countries of the region closer together by bringing them closer to Europe. The European Union can act as the magnet because the people in the region are attracted to it. Breaking down the customs barriers separating countries from one another and from the European Union would eliminate a prime source of corruption and political interference. The countries of Southeastern Europe would receive budgetary support that would enable them to use the euro as their currency. The budgetary support would have political conditions that would lay the groundwork for open society. Aid would be dispensed on a regional rather than bilateral basis. Participating countries would be obliged to compete for investment finance and technical aid instead of being able to control the flow of funds and exploit it for personal and political gain.

This is a comprehensive plan that would avoid a repeat of the mistakes made in Bosnia. The reconstruction of Bosnia failed for two main reasons: The territory is too small, and the political authorities have their dirty fingers in every pie. The regional approach would eliminate both shortcomings. A common market and a common currency, buttressed by the infrastructure of a market economy, would allow economic development. There is a lot more to be done on the social and political side and in coming to terms with the sins and traumas of the past, but the way to a better future is clearly mapped out.

It is not difficult to generate local support for this plan, because Europe holds tremendous appeal for the region. My network of foundations has been mobilizing civil society behind it. The various governments are eager to cooperate. There is also a lot of support within the European Union. In addition to Romano Prodi, government figures in Germany, Italy, Britain, and other countries have spoken along these same lines. The U.S. government is also supportive, especially as the costs would be borne primarily by the European Union.

The difficulty is to get the European Union to exercise leadership. Only the EU can set the terms on which the countries in the region can gain access to the European common market. But the EU is institutionally ill-suited to carry out an initiative akin to the Marshall Plan. The costs would be quite modest because the region is tiny in economic terms, smaller than the Netherlands. Nevertheless, money is a problem. Member countries are strongly opposed to increasing the budget of the European Union; they want to retain control over their funds by going through donor conferences. This would undermine one of the key ideas behind the plan: Countries in the region should compete for support, rather than donors competing with each other and allowing gatekeepers to divert the funds to their own purposes.

The other problem is organization. In translating the concept into reality, the foreign ministries of the European Union countries devised the Stability Pact, which is nothing but an empty framework waiting to be filled with content; the finance ministries don't like the framework and refuse to provide funds. The bureaucrats of the European Union don't like it either. They are used to bilateral, government-to-government dealings; their preferred route is to conclude so-called Stability and Association Agreements with individual governments. As a result, the regional, nongovernmental approach would be lost.

There are certain moments when history is more open-ended than at other times. We failed to take advantage of such a moment in the Soviet Union in 1989; we are at such a moment in the Balkans at the beginning of the new century. There is not much we can do about Chechnya: The more we protest, the more we feed the bitterly nationalistic mood in Russia. But it is well within our powers to change the course of events for the better in the Balkans. The Balkans are not the only problem area in the world – there are almost too many to list: Indonesia (which could be Yugoslavia writ large), Chechnya, the Ferghana Valley, Congo, Angola, Kashmir, Taiwan, and on and on. Still, the fate of the Balkans poses a direct challenge to NATO. If we are not willing to engage constructively, then we have no right to interfere punitively; and if we are not willing to intervene in the internal affairs of a sovereign but repressive state, then we cannot hope for an open society.

I am hopeful that the idea of an open society will pass the test on this occasion. Much hangs in the balance – not just the fate of the former Yugoslavia but also the future of the European Union and the validity of the concept of open society.

CHAPTER 12

The Open Society Alliance

P roceeding from the specific to the general, I should now like to build the case for a global open society. I have proposed an alliance of democratic countries with a dual objective: fostering the development of open societies throughout the world, and establishing some ground rules to govern the behavior of states toward their citizens and each other. The Open Society Alliance would have to be led by the developed democracies; therefore I shall start by examining the current conditions in the United States and the European Union—to discuss the problems of Japan would take us too far afield. The Alliance would have to have a military as well as a developmental component; therefore I shall examine NATO before discussing the Alliance itself. The Alliance would be able to operate within or outside the United Nations; therefore I shall examine the prospects for reforming the United Nations before I make the final case for creating the Alliance.

The United States

The United States is the sole remaining superpower, and its military superiority is greater than ever. It would be in a position to create a global open society if it had a clear vision what it should look like. Unfortunately the United States does not have a clear view of its role in the world, or, more exactly, its views are internally inconsistent. The United States is suffering from a crisis of identity without even realizing it.

There have always been two main themes in U.S. foreign policy: geopolitical realism, and what may be called "open society idealism." The United States is exceptional among history's Great Powers in its commitment to certain universal principles, brilliantly expressed in the Declaration of Independence and reaffirmed in the Atlantic Charter (which was in turn reflected in the Preamble of the UN Charter). Even Henry Kissinger acknowledges what he calls "American exceptionalism."*

The two tendencies are often at loggerheads. Theodore Roosevelt can be said to embody the geopolitical approach, Woodrow Wilson the open society vision. On balance, idealism tends to lose out to national, institutional, and other vested interests, but policies must be couched in moralistic terms in order to satisfy public opinion. The net result is an element of hypocrisy in U.S. foreign policy.

During the Cold War the United States enjoyed the best of all possible worlds: It could be both superpower and leader of the free world. U.S. foreign policy also had the benefit of bipartisan support. This harmony was disrupted by the Vietnam War when foreign policy and domestic politics came into direct conflict. Domestic opposition eventually made it impossible to pursue the Vietnam War. The experience left deep scars and bitter memories.

The Cold War ended with the internal collapse of the Soviet sys-

*Henry Kissinger, *Diplomacy* (New York: Simon and Schuster, 1995).

tem and the implosion of the Soviet empire. This was seen as a great victory for the United States. But the nature of the victory was never properly understood because the two roles—superpower and leader of the free world—were fused. Neither was it clear what the free world stood for: capitalism or open society. Was the collapse brought about by aggressive U.S. pursuit of the Strategic Defense Initiative (the so-called Star Wars scheme), the superiority of capitalism, or the yearning for freedom within the Soviet empire? The response to the collapse was equally confused.

U.S. foreign policy has remained confused ever since. There can be no doubt that we like being the sole remaining superpower. But we also wish to be the leader of the free world, as during the Cold War, and that is where confusion creeps into the picture. During the Cold War the free world was threatened in its very existence and sought the protection of a superpower. Western democracies banded together in NATO, which was under United States domination. But the Cold War is over, and the threat has been removed. Other countries no longer have the same reasons to submit to the will of a superpower. Therefore to remain the leader of the free world we ought to change our behavior. We ought to lead by building a genuine partnership and abide by the rules that we seek to apply to others.

We have chosen a different way. We feel that our superpower status ought to confer special privileges and we are entitled to dominate the international institutions to which we belong. We were eager to expand NATO; we belong to the World Trade Organization, the International Monetary Fund, and the World Bank, but only because we can dominate them.* We have gone out of our way to bash the United Nations. And under the influence of hard-line conservative leaders like Senator Jesse Helms we are absolutely

---

*Compared to the IMF, the World Bank is more independent of U.S. influence; even so, its outspoken senior vice president and chief economist, Joe Stiglitz, found it appropriate to resign when his views annoyed the United States.

opposed to any infringement of our sovereignty. Still, we are willing to infringe on the sovereignty of others in the name of human rights and democracy. We have no tolerance for body bags, yet we impose trade sanctions and drop bombs from high altitudes in defense of our principles. Our principles are supposed to have universal validity, yet we insist on judging how and when they should be applied. There is a double standard at work that is liable to offend the rest of humanity, and Americans are not even aware of it.

Our posture could be justified on the grounds of military superiority: The United States is the only superpower and therefore can call the shots. But this cannot be reconciled with our claim to be the leader of the free world. That is where our position becomes internally inconsistent. And while we see ourselves with the right on our side, others see mainly the arrogance of power.

The United States enjoys military superiority , but it is not willing to act as the sole policeman of the world. It is better so, because the United States does not derive sufficient benefits from the global capitalist system to justify the sacrifices that preserving peace single-handedly would entail. Neither is world domination easy to reconcile with open society.

But the world does need rules and standards of behavior and the means to enforce them. In their absence, the strong would lord it over the weak, both internationally and internally. The rules of behavior can be established only through international consent. If they were imposed unilaterally by a superpower it would be an instance of the strong lording it over the weak. That is where being a superpower and claiming to be leaders of the free world come into conflict.

It may be a shocking thing to say, but the United States has become the greatest obstacle to establishing the rule of law in international affairs. There are repressive regimes that maintain an iron grip over their subjects, but in projecting their power abroad they are acutely aware that they might awaken a slumbering giant. The United States is anything but repressive at home, yet it flaunts its power internationally more than any other country. It does act occasionally as an aggressor when it sees no danger of body bags— bombing a pharmaceutical factory in Sudan, for example. Even more to the point, it is aggressive in refusing to cooperate. It refuses to make good on its dues to the United Nations; it hesitated to replenish the IMF during the global financial crisis; and it imposes sanctions unilaterally at the drop of a hat or, more exactly, at the instigation of domestic constituencies. The United States was one of only seven countries that voted against establishing the International Criminal Court (ICC). The other recalcitrants were China, Iraq, Israel, Libya, Qatar, and Yemen. The Pentagon, which objected to U.S. military personnel coming under international jurisdiction, went so far as to instruct U.S. military attachés based in U.S. embassies around the world to enlist the military leaders of their host governments to lobby against the International Criminal Court. This was a particularly questionable tactic in countries where civilian authority over the armed forces is not firmly established.

The United States has at least a plausible argument against the ICC, namely that the ICC might not provide the same guarantees to American citizens as the United States Constitution.* But there is no justification for Congress' failure to ratify uncontroversial international agreements such as the Law of the Sea Convention and the Convention on Biological Diversity. The United States is one of only nine nations who have not ratified the latter Convention—along with Afghanistan, Kuwait, Liberia, Libya, Malta, Thailand, Tuvalu, and Yugoslavia—not very distinguished company."

It does *not* go without saying that the United States should cooperate with others. Those who are guided by geopolitical realism or

---

*I disagree with this argument because the issue does not arise as long as a U.S. court is willing to try the case as for instance in the My Lai massacre.

market fundamentalism or the crude Darwinism that equates the survival of the fittest with economic and military power may not see any reason why the United States should accept any limits to its sovereignty. Only if we want to live in an open society does it follow that we must subordinate our sovereignty to universally valid rules and standards of behavior. As I have been at pains to point out, a genuine choice is involved: Without fully realizing the implications, the United States has opted to exercise its power to the detriment of international cooperation.

The United States could regain its position as leader of the free world by forming an alliance of like-minded states devoted to promoting the principles of open society internationally and internally within individual countries. But this would require a radical change of attitude—from high-handed unilateralism to a more cooperative approach. Is such a change possible?

I believe it is. The United States has long maintained a commitment to the ideals of open society, starting with the Declaration of Independence. According to public-opinion surveys, the United Nations, despite its current paralysis, is still more popular with the public than Congress or the president. All that needs to be done is to recapture this latent support for international cooperation.

Prior to the 2000 U.S. elections a conservative majority in Congress has stood firm against international cooperation. Its stance is not necessarily representative of public opinion. An uneasy alliance prevails between market fundamentalists and various adherents to the idea of national sovereignty ranging from the isolationism of religious fundamentalists, to the America-first approach of trade unions, and to the unilateralism of Jesse Helms. And though they are united in their opposition to multilateral institutions, they have rather different objectives in mind. Market fundamentalists object to government intervention in the economy; religious fundamentalists oppose liberal standards, such as abortion rights, imposed by the state. Market fundamentalists are against international cooperation for the same reason that they dislike big government: They want to give business a free hand. Isolationists, trade unionists, and religious fundamentalists are against it for the opposite reason: They resent the threat that global markets pose to their values and interests. It is amazing how these disparate groups have been able to reconcile their differences by focusing on a common enemy, namely, governmental and international authority. I expect that they will find this unity increasingly difficult to maintain as they move closer to achieving their objectives.

The crucial choice confronting the United States is between a unilateral and a multilateral approach. The former leads to the reestablishment of a balance of powers and the prospect of armed confrontation between opposing blocks; the latter to a global open society. It is unlikely that the choice will be presented to the American electorate in such stark terms in the November 2000 elections—multilateralism is too long a word to serve as an election slogan. Albert Gore is clearly more sympathetic to the idea than George W. Bush but he is likely to find it too risky to make it an election issue. Nevertheless, foreign policy is likely to loom larger in the 2000 elections than in 1992 when Bill Clinton deliberately deemphasized the subject, and the prevailing sense of economic well-being may well translate into greater sympathy towards international cooperation.

After the elections there could be a reconfiguration of the domestic political scene, with internationalists of various stripes coming together to support a global open society. It could happen on a bipartisan basis, because there are some traditions within both parties that could be reactivated. In the Democratic Party, it is the liberal, New Deal tradition; in the Republican Party, it is the internationalist, free-market tradition. All that is needed is for Republican supporters of globalization to recognize open society as a desirable goal. As the Meltzer Report's endorsement of a World Development Agency indicates, that is not as far-fetched as it sounds.

Usually it takes a crisis to prompt a meaningful change in direction. One would have hoped that the crises in Kosovo and East Timor and Africa were shocking enough to focus the mind. If we must wait for a crisis that adversely affects the U.S. position in the world, then the opportunity for America to lead humanity toward a global open society may be lost. Therefore it is imperative to establish open society as an objective of U.S. policy while the United States maintains its status as the undisputed superpower.

The European Union

In the creation of the European Union, we have witnessed a gigantic experiment in what Karl Popper called "piecemeal social engineering." It is worthwhile to explore this development more closely because it raises the crucial issue of our time: how to overcome the obstacles posed by national sovereignty to the pursuit of the common interest. In the creation of the European Union, the issue was not confronted directly; if it had been, the process could not have gone as far as it has. Rather it was approached indirectly, by identifying a concrete objective and gathering sufficient support behind it. It started with the Coal and Steel Community, and it has reached as far as the common currency. Each step forward produced some kind of imbalance that could be corrected only by taking another step forward.

Nothing could be more appropriate to an open society. Still, the process is fraught with uncertainty, and it is hard to say just how much further it will progress. Each step is resisted, mainly because of the expectation that it will lead to additional steps in the same direction. These fears are well founded. The creation of a common currency, for instance, is liable to prove unsound without a common fiscal policy. Whether it will be possible to gather sufficient political support for introducing a common fiscal policy remains an open question.

The entire process is running into difficulties. It has been driven by a political elite and is losing the support of the masses. The idea of a united Europe was immensely enticing, especially while the memory of World War II was fresh and Europe lay exposed to the Soviet menace. The reality of the European Union, however, is much less alluring. Politically it is still an association of states that have delegated some sovereignty to the larger Union. In the economic sphere, where the delegation has occurred, the single market works remarkably well; but in the political sphere there has been practically no delegation, and the results are disappointing. Every such association of states suffers from what has been called a "democratic deficit."* The interests of the state do not necessarily coincide with the interests of the people who belong to it, but in a democratic state the people can exercise control over the behavior of the government through their elected representatives; in an association of states, that control is lacking because the decisionmaking power is vested in governments, not the people.

The administration of the European Union is in the midst of an acute crisis. The central administrative body, the European Commission, is subject to the authority of the European Council, which is made up of the governments of the member states. The Council is guided more by national interests than by the common interest. Therefore even pedestrian decisions take on the character of international treaties—difficult to reach, even more difficult to alter. The members of the Commission are appointed on the basis of national quotas, and the Commission's work suffers from all the faults of a bureaucracy that serves not one master but fifteen. Bureaucrats tend to protect themselves against their political masters by avoiding decisions for which they could be blamed. When

*William Maynes, "America's Fading Commitments," *World Policy Journal* (Summer 1999).

they are responsible not to one master but fifteen, the effect is para-lyzing; the democratic deficit is reinforced by a deficit in decision-making capacity. It is hardly believable, but each Directorate is an island unto itself, and one Commissioner cannot give orders to another. The member states go out of their way to block expenditures in order to keep down their contributions to the EU budget; at the same time, their Ambassadors in Brussels work full-time to appropriate as much of the EU budget to their national benefit as possible. All expenditures, whether for agriculture, scientific research, or foreign aid, have to go through the same cumbersome procedures. What the people see from the outside is a top-heavy bureaucracy that works in convoluted ways shrouded in secrecy. It does not seem to be responsible to any public constituency even though the European Parliament has recently been given some additional powers of oversight and the previous Commission fell as a result of a parliamentary investigation of corruption. The bureau-cracy is demoralized and the public is disenchanted. The European Parliament continues to be held in low esteem, as demonstrated by low turnouts in recent elections.

A growing minority rejects the idea of Europe and espouses nationalistic and xenophobic tendencies. It is to be hoped that the political elite will be able to galvanize public opinion in favor of another step forward, and this time that step must be directed against the political elite itself. The people must assert direct politi-cal control over the EU government. Such a move would have to confront the issue of national sovereignty more directly than before, and its success would be far from assured. In fact, failure may lead to the disintegration of the European Union, for integra-tion is a dynamic process: If it does not move forward it is liable to move backward. It is against this background that the problems of membership enlargement will have to be resolved. The outlook is truly precarious.

To make matters worse, the European Union has been singularly unsuccessful in the area of foreign policy. The second pillar of the Maastricht Treaty was devoted to a common foreign policy, but it did not impinge on the sovereignty of member countries. The result was predictable: No common policy emerged. Foreign policy remained subordinated to the internal politics of member countries. The common policy was discredited in the very act of negotiating the Maastricht Treaty: As part of the horse-trading leading up to the treaty, the former foreign minister of Germany, Hans-Dietrich Genscher, obtained European recognition for an independent Croatia and Slovenia, thereby precipitating the war in Bosnia. The European Union has rarely been able to speak with a single voice on foreign policy matters, and even then it was the voice of a small power. This was evident in the way the European Union handled the disintegration of Yugoslavia—very, very cautiously. This profile may change now that the European Union has appointed a foreign policy czar, Javier Solana, the former secretary-general of NATO, but even so there is no consensus that the European Union should become a great power. The current situation is unsatisfactory to say the least, and the European Union, like the United States, needs a good dose of soul-searching when it comes to international relations. The Stability Pact for Southeastern Europe serves as the test case.

There are many foreign policy matters where member countries have definite national interests that differ from those of other members, particularly in the area of trade and investment. It would be difficult to justify a delegation of powers to the European Union in such matters. Take a simple example: diplomatic representation in international organizations. Britain, France, and Germany have different financial and industrial interests that could not be adequately represented by the European Union.

Still, there are issues where the common interest ought to take precedence over the interests of the individual member states. In these cases the common interest usually extends beyond the European Union. What happens in the Balkans, the Middle East, North

Africa, and the former Soviet Union is of concern not only to Europe but to the United States and the rest of the world. Having open societies is a common interest for all open societies. To pursue that goal requires cooperation that extends beyond the European Union to the United States and other democratic countries.

It can be seen that most foreign policy issues ought to be handled either at a higher or a lower level than the European Union. The European Union is in need of forging an alliance of democratic states—even more so than the United States.

NATO

It so happens that there already is an alliance with an appropriate membership: NATO. But NATO is a military alliance, and the task of fostering open societies is anything but military. NATO does have a political dimension, and its political objectives are stated explicitly in terms of fostering democracy. That is not surprising, because NATO is a creature of the Cold War. But the political dimension was never activated and remained an unused appendage of the military alliance.

After the end of the Cold War, NATO became an institution without a mission. Its objectives had to be rethought. An intense discussion ensued, but it was framed by the military nature of the alliance. There were voices that argued for a new kind of alliance that would also include Russia, but there were others that were dominated by geopolitical considerations. In the end, a compromise was reached: NATO would expand eastward, incorporating some former members of the Warsaw Pact, establish a Partnership for Peace with other former communist countries, and keep the possibility of additional future members open-ended. Eventually three new members were added: Poland, Hungary, and the Czech Republic. Romania and Slovenia campaigned hard for inclusion but failed;

Slovakia was excluded on political grounds; other countries were not seriously considered.

I attempted to participate meaningfully in that debate by organizing a conference at the Central European University in Budapest. It was attended by many, including Manfred Wörner, the then secretary-general of NATO and a man of great integrity fully committed to the principles of open society; he was terminally ill at that time. I published a pamphlet in which I argued many of the same points I argue today, namely, that the postcommunist world needs a different kind of alliance and the Partnership for Peace needs to be coupled with a Partnership for Prosperity. But the proposal was too radical. In order to ratify NATO expansion, all the forces in its favor had to be accommodated: the geopoliticians and cold warriors as well as those who were more concerned with fostering open societies. NATO expansion was an uneasy compromise between preserving and reinforcing the division of Europe and promoting the principles of open society, with the balance tilted in favor of the former. The results show it. Take the case of Belarus: Alexander Lukashenko established a presidential dictatorship that destroyed democracy in Belarus and also posed a threat to democratic forces in Russia; but Russia embraced Lukashenko because the threat posed by NATO expansion was considered more important. In this case, NATO expansion worked directly against the interests of open society.

In the case of Kosovo, NATO intervened in defense of open society principles. No NATO country had a vital national interest at stake, but there was a common interest in resisting yet another instance of ethnic cleansing. The Western democracies had a history of failure in dealing with the disintegration of Yugoslavia, but on this occasion they were ready to take a firm stand. There was an internal division within the U.S. administration, with the State Department in favor of a NATO ultimatum and the Defense Department opposed to it. Eventually it was the commander of NATO forces, General Wesley Clark, who tipped the scales in favor of intervention. The Pentagon never forgave him for it: It waged war against General Clark as much as against Milosevic. For instance, it sabotaged the use of Apache helicopters. And he was given early retirement.

The Kosovo crisis was a traumatic event for me personally. I had been an advocate of a firm line against Milosevic, so I felt a personal sense of responsibility for what happened even though I had no part in the decisionmaking process. I was in favor of military action, but I was deeply distressed by the results. In my opinion the bombing could be justified only if it were followed by constructive action that would bring peace and prosperity to the region.

The case against Milosevic was airtight. Not only did he commit documented atrocities for which he was indicted by the Hague tribunal; he also broke an international agreement he had signed only a few months before. But the manner in which NATO acted was less reassuring. Dropping bombs from high altitudes confirmed the gap between the value of American lives and the lives of those whom they were supposed to help. The intervention did not prevent ethnic cleansing; on the contrary, it accelerated it. Even the motives for intervention were in doubt: Did it serve to punish Milosevic, protect the inhabitants of Kosovo, or demonstrate the military might of NATO? It should be remembered that NATO was approaching its fiftieth anniversary: Would it not be glorious to celebrate it with a military victory?

But instead of uniting the world in condemnation of Milosevic, NATO intervention divided it. The outcome was also in doubt. By ruling out the use of ground troops, President Bill Clinton made it much harder to prevail, and when Milosevic finally yielded control over Kosovo it came as a genuine surprise to everyone concerned. I hate to think what would have happened if he had held out.

In my opinion, two major factors persuaded him to back down. One was the role of the Kosovo Liberation Army; the other was the role of Russia. (The bombing also had an effect when it began to infringe upon the rule against hitting civilian targets.) Although President Clinton had ruled out ground troops, there were KLA troops on the ground, and when they engaged the Yugoslav army it became vulnerable to air attack. Albanian fighters on the ground turned out to be more threatening to the Yugoslav army than NATO troops would have been. Russia played a double role. On the one hand, Viktor Chernomyrdin was immensely helpful by disabusing Milosevic of any hope of Russian support; NATO owes him a debt of gratitude. On the other hand, the Russian army surprised NATO by moving in to the Pristina airport ahead of it; it took some maneuvering to finesse the Russian military presence. This schizophrenia reflected a split between political and military considerations: Politically Russia needed to earn points with the West because of its economic and financial dependency; militarily, NATO was considered a threat.

The Open Society Alliance

The Kosovo conflict has reinforced my conviction that NATO needs to be complemented with a political alliance whose explicit purpose is to promote the values and principles of open society. Military intervention in support of human rights always comes too late, and it is often counterproductive. The emphasis ought to be on crisis prevention.

Crisis prevention cannot start early enough. The earlier it starts, the less coercive it needs to be. Diplomatic or economic pressure may be sufficient, and rewards can be more effective than punishments. For instance, the Baltic states are eager to be associated with Europe. Latvia and Estonia enacted restrictive citizenship laws that sowed the seeds of potential conflict with Russia. The European Union and the Organization for Security and Cooperation in Europe applied persistent pressure and brought about a change in the treatment of minorities. Latvia and Estonia are now candidates for EU membership. If the international community had expressed its displeasure when Milosevic abrogated the autonomy of Kosovo in 1989, he could not have consolidated his power because the federal government was not under his control at that time. If NATO had intervened when the Yugoslav navy bombarded Dubrovnik in December 1991, the Bosnia crisis could have been avoided.

A political alliance could best prevent crises by promoting the values and principles of open society. What would that entail?

There is no single design for open society. Countries have different traditions, with different levels of development. What makes a society open is that its citizens are free to decide how society should be organized. But there are some preconditions for ensuring that citizens will enjoy that freedom. The Open Society Alliance would be concerned with establishing and preserving those preconditions: a democratic constitution, the rule of law, freedom of speech and press, an independent judiciary, and other important aspects of liberty. Again, there are no objective, incontrovertible criteria by which those preconditions can be judged. The Open Society Alliance would have to establish its own criteria in full awareness of its own fallibility. It would give each society the greatest possible latitude in deciding its own character.

What distinguishes the Age of Fallibility from the Age of Reason is that we have come to recognize that reason does not provide unequivocal, incontrovertible solutions. Take law: Roman law and Anglo-Saxon law are quite different in character. It would be inappropriate to promote one over the other, but it would be more than appropriate to insist on the rule of law. Or take the independence of the judiciary: There is no fail-safe method for ensuring it; even the independence of the U.S. judiciary has become endangered in recent years thanks to partisan politics. Still, it would be desirable to improve the independence and competence of the judiciary within every state.

The goal of the Alliance would be to coordinate the activities of member countries in promoting a global open society. There are two distinct but interconnected objectives to be accomplished: One is to help the evolution of open societies within individual countries; the other is to foster the development of international law and international standards of behavior.

The Open Society Alliance would pursue the first goal by a judicious combination of sticks and carrots. Access to trade and investment would loom large in both categories. That is where the global political architecture becomes contiguous with the global financial architecture, because many of the sticks and carrots would be financial. It will be recalled that the emerging new financial architecture is singularly lacking in incentives. I proposed strengthening the capacity of the IMF to reward countries that follow sound policies. I endorsed the Meltzer Commission's recommendation that the World Bank be converted into a World Development Agency on condition that its resources be enhanced rather than reduced and its uncalled capital be used more actively for guaranteeing credits to small and medium enterprises. I supported debt forgiveness for poor countries that implement economic and political reforms. Additional measures may be needed on a case-by-case basis. The Stability Pact for Southeastern Europe is one such case.

The criteria applied by the IMF in deciding what constitutes sound policies would be primarily financial; but there is no hard and fast dividing line between the financial and the political. A transparent, professionally run, well supervised banking system that cannot be misused for political gain would be a great help in the development of open society; financial transparency is but a short step from a free and open press, and in countries where freedom of the press is restricted, the financial papers often offer the best political coverage. A World Development Agency could use more explicitly political criteria in dispensing aid, especially if it adopted Amartya Sen's idea of development as freedom.

There are many areas where democratic countries have competing interests; they would continue to pursue them competitively. But in applying the sticks and carrots they must act cooperatively. That means subordinating themselves to collective decisions. Take the issue of trade sanctions: They could be effective only if collectively applied. The United States is in the habit of imposing sanctions unilaterally; it would have to renounce that habit. Still, all members would have to agree to implement sanctions that had been collectively approved; otherwise they could not remain members of the Alliance.

Punitive interventions in the internal affairs of individual countries would be kept to a minimum because they have unintended adverse consequences. Trade sanctions have proved counterproductive: They tend to strengthen the regime they are supposed to undermine because the smugglers need the support of the regime and they have to support it in return. In the case of Yugoslavia, blacklisting the supporters of the regime has proved much more effective. There is a strong case to be made for substituting blacklisting for trade sanctions whenever possible. It would hit those who deserve it and would weaken, rather than strengthen, the regime it seeks to punish.

Military intervention is even less desirable as a method of exerting pressure than are trade sanctions. Not only does it hurt the country whose people it seeks to help; it is also difficult to sustain. Democracies don't suffer body bags gladly. The goal of the political alliance should be to obviate the need for military action. The availability of incentives and the prospect of blacklisting ought to ensure voluntary compliance in most cases. There will be exceptions, of course, which is why a military alliance is also needed. When it comes to military action, the fact that it was preceded by preventive action should give it greater legitimacy. Even so, the use of force ought to be treated as an admission of defeat.*

The Open Society Alliance would have to be separate from

---

*The Organization of American States has provided a useful precedent. The Santiago Resolution of 1991, requires the secretary general of the OAS to convene a meeting of the hemisphere's foreign ministers within ten days after a coup or other interruption of a legitimate, elected government. Resolution 1080 has been used four times: Following the coup in Haiti in 1991, the "auto-coups" in Peru in 1992 and Guatemala in 1993, and the threat to the government of Paraguay in 1996. In each case, this mechanism helped rally effective political support for the restoration of constitutional democracy.

NATO so that it would not be swamped by the military aspect. In order to enjoy greater legitimacy than NATO, it should have a broader membership: It should be open to any country that subscribes to its objectives irrespective of geography. Given the disparity between periphery and center, however, the Alliance should include as many members from the periphery as possible. Given the paucity of mature democracies at the periphery, aspiring democracies could also be admitted as candidate-members, but special care should be taken that their behavior should reflect their aspirations. It is a common deficiency of international organizations that they rarely expel or suspend members once admitted. The Open Society Alliance ought to be different in this respect.

Membership in the Alliance could never replace foreign policy; promoting open society would always have to compete with other objectives. But the alliance would add an element to international relations that is sorely missing—namely, support and incentives for political and economic development. The Alliance would be most effective in dealing with willing recipients. In countries like Indonesia, it could make the difference between success and failure. Its main instruments for applying pressure to recalcitrant governments would be withholding benefits and ostracizing the leaders of the regime. Every case would require different treatment. Indeed, it may be advisable to form separate coalitions to deal with specific areas: the Balkans, the Ferghana Valley, or Burundi. The Alliance could also address environmental problems such as global warming.

This brings us to the second main goal of the Alliance, which is to foster the development of international law and international standards of behavior. In this context, I shall examine the World Trade Organization, then the United Nations.

The World Trade Organization

The World Trade Organization is a rather opaque institution. Its rules are more complicated than the U.S. Internal Revenue Code and are established by horse-trading behind closed doors. Frankly my eyes used to glaze over when the discussion turned to the WTO; yet it is an important institution that provides the ground rules for free trade worldwide. It has the support of the United States and the European Union, although they are often at logger-heads over particular issues.

Recently the WTO was thrust onto the world stage during its conference in Seattle, Washington. Previously there had been an attempt to establish a charter for international investment, which would have codified the advantages that foreign capital enjoys under the global capitalist system. This was defeated by an international coalition of NGOs. At the Seattle meeting, the United States wanted to introduce the issue of international labor and environmental standards. It gave the NGOs an opportunity to attack the WTO. They formed an impromptu alliance with protectionist forces in the United States, mainly the trade unions, and the Seattle meeting collapsed in pandemonium. That is most unfortunate, because the issues raised at Seattle go to the very heart of a global open society.

Labor and environmental standards are an important common interest that has been neglected by the WTO because it could have been used as an excuse for protectionism. But free trade is also an important common interest. It creates the wealth that allows us to be concerned with labor and environmental issues. Of course, wealth creation also aggravates the very same issues. Which common interest should take precedence is a matter of perspective; both are important. How can they be reconciled? There is no easy solution. If the WTO imposed penalties for the infringement of labor and environmental standards it would penalize less-developed countries because they are the major offenders. It would tilt the playing field even more against them. The less-developed countries would never put up with it, and the WTO would collapse.

This is where a constructive approach ought to come into play. Less-developed countries ought to be compensated for introducing labor and environmental standards. It is the rich countries that want to impose those standards, and poor countries cannot afford them. It stands to reason that the rich countries ought to offer incentives rather than impose penalties. Something similar has already happened in the trading of emission rights. Penalties would destroy free trade; incentives would leave the WTO intact while improving labor and environmental conditions.

NGOs ought to see the larger picture, but all too often they become special-interest advocates. In that sense, they are no better than representatives of business interests, even if they feel more righteous. In a way, then, some NGOs have become like businesses, generating revenues by advocating a cause. While civil society is an important part of open society, the common good cannot be left solely in their care. We need public institutions to protect the public interests. The WTO is such an institution; it would be a pity to destroy it. But it is devoted to the promotion of one common good—free trade—to the exclusion of others. We must find a way to promote the other common goods that we consider important. Could the United Nations help?

The United Nations

It is important to understand what the United Nations can and cannot do. It is a fundamentally flawed institution, for it is an association of states and thus suffers from a democratic deficit. Even if people could control the UN representative of their own country, they have no control over the United Nations organization itself. The democratic deficit is reinforced when some of the member states are not even democratic. Member states exercise patronage in all personnel appointments. The main flaw of the United Nations is that the goals outlined in the Preamble of its Charter are couched in terms of "people" while the organization itself is structured in terms of states; as a result, the United Nations cannot possibly fulfill the promises contained in the Preamble.

This is a regrettable fact, but once we come to recognize it and lower our expectations accordingly, the United Nations could be very useful. As international institutions go, the United Nations has great potential. It has four major components: the Security Council, the General Assembly, the Secretariat, and a number of specialized agencies. Let us look at each in turn.

The Security Council is a well-conceived structure and could be effective in imposing its will on the world if only the permanent members could agree among themselves. The end of the Cold War provided an opportunity for the Security Council to function as it was originally intended, but the opportunity was squandered when the West's three permanent members—the United States, the United Kingdom, and France—failed to agree among themselves how to handle the crisis in Bosnia. They sent peacekeepers where there was no peace to keep. The prestige of UN peacekeeping operations was irreparably damaged. That opportunity is unlikely to reappear in the near future because neither Russia nor China is likely to be as docile as in 1992. The Security Council may be useful in specific instances, but it would be unwise to rely on it as the main instrument for preserving peace.

The General Assembly is a talking shop at present, but it could become more like a legislature making laws for our global society if the Open Society Alliance put its mind to it. An assembly of sovereign states may be ill-suited to carry out executive functions, but it is eminently qualified as an international legislature provided the democratic deficit can be overcome. Unfortunately there is little inclination at present to use the General Assembly for anything more than a talking shop. The Secretariat could also play a more important role than it does now provided the method of selecting the secretary-general were changed. At present, the permanent members of the Security Council have a veto, and the United States, for one, does not want a strong and independent UN secretary-general.

Specialized agencies such as the United Nations Development Program (UNDP), the United Nations Industrial Development Organization (UNIDO), the United Nations Educational, Scientific, and Cultural Organization (UNESCO), and others constitute an element of the United Nations that is open to criticism. Only a few of them function effectively. Appointments are made on the basis of national patronage, not on merit. It is difficult to fire officials and even more difficult to wind up agencies when they no longer have a mission. It is these features that have given the United Nations a bad name.

Bureaucracies are more interested in self-preservation than in carrying out their missions. When a bureaucracy is responsible not to one master but to the entire membership of the United Nations, it is beyond control. An association of states is ill-suited to carry out any executive function. To the extent that there are executive functions to be performed, they ought to be entrusted to specialized institutions with their own executives, budgets, and boards to whom the executives must report. The Bretton Woods institutions, for all their shortcomings, function a lot better than the UN agencies, and even there the boards wield too much power.

Due to the way it has been treated by member states, particularly the United States, the United Nations has lost much of the goodwill and prestige it once enjoyed. In spite of its shortcomings, the United Nations used to possess a certain moral authority and respect. The blue helmet used to give UN soldiers a degree of protection. Much of that is now lost and will be difficult to recapture.

It is widely recognized that the United Nations needs to be reformed. Innumerable studies have been made recommending a variety of reforms, but none could be implemented because member states cannot agree. Therefore the United Nations remains a damaged institution that is difficult to repair.

The Open Society Alliance, more than any other initiative, would have a reasonable chance to make the United Nations live up to its potential if the members of the Alliance could agree among themselves. The Alliance would have the option to work either within or outside the United Nations, giving it leverage that no other reform attempt has had.

How could the Alliance reform the United Nations? It could introduce majority rule and convert the General Assembly into a legislative body. The laws passed by the General Assembly would be valid only in countries that ratify them, but members of the Open Society Alliance would pledge themselves to ratify the laws automatically, provided they have been ratified voluntarily by a qualified majority. Countries that do not abide by the decision of a qualified majority would be excluded from the Alliance. In that way a body of international law could be developed without infringing on the principle of national sovereignty.

What would constitute a qualified majority? I have found the idea of the "binding triad" proposed by Richard Hudson in connection with the United Nations very appealing. It could be adapted to the Alliance. A qualified majority would be constituted by two-thirds of the member countries, two-thirds of their population, and two-thirds of their gross domestic product. But I am not qualified to decide such details; they would have to be decided by the membership of the Alliance.

If the Alliance managed to gain control of the United Nations it would appoint the secretary-general, who would be in charge of the Secretariat, and the Secretariat would guide the legislative work of the General Assembly. The secretary-general's position would be roughly equivalent to the elected leader of the majority party in a democratic state. In view of the greatly enhanced powers of the office, it would be desirable to subject the secretary-general to recall through a no-confidence vote of the Alliance.

The Security Council would retain the same functions, but the permanent members would lose their veto, and the temporary members would be selected by the Alliance rather than rotating on a purely geographic basis. Those permanent members that belong to the Alliance would give up the veto by virtue of belonging to the Alliance, because they would be duty-bound to abide by its qualified-majority decisions. It may be asked why the other two permanent members, Russia and China, should be willing to give up their privilege. The answer is that they may prefer to remain permanent members without veto to seeing the Security Council superceded by another organization to which they do not belong.

It is much more questionable whether the United States would be willing to abide by the rules of the Alliance. It would require a radical change in prevailing attitudes. In reality, the United States has much less to fear from giving up its veto compared to the other permanent members, because it is highly unlikely that the Alliance would go against the wishes of a superpower whose allegiance is indispensable to making it effective.

In the Age of Fallibility we must abandon the assumption of rationality. Still, there are good reasons why a multilateral approach might catch the imagination of the American public. The United States would have much to gain by joining the Alliance because it could share the burden of acting as the world's policeman. The United States could provide logistic and technical support, depending on others to supply the ground troops.

Even without these far-reaching reforms, there is at least one significant step that the United States ought to support now: to establish a permanent capacity within the United Nations to provide civilian police for situations such as Kosovo, Haiti, and East Timor. The UN Secretary General, Kofi Annan, has requested such a capacity, and the Clinton administration has supported it, but Congress has refused to allocate the money.

The Case for the Open Society Alliance

The case for the Open Society Alliance can be built on two arguments. One is prudential, the other idealistic. The prudential argument is that the United States enjoys greater military superiority today than at any other time in its history; the main threat to peace and prosperity comes from internal conditions prevailing in other countries that can be exploited by unscrupulous leaders, and the United States cannot deal with these threats on its own; therefore it needs to form an alliance with like-minded countries.

By spearheading such an alliance, the United States could regain and retain its leadership position in the world because U.S. engagement is indispensable to making the idea a success. By participating in such an alliance, the other democratic countries would gain a greater say in the governance of international relations. They would also have the benefit of a more stable world order.

If the United States continues to act unilaterally, it is only a matter of time before countries resent its dominance so much that they form their own coalition to counterbalance its power; the preeminent position of the United States would be lost. Since a balance-of-power system is far from foolproof in preserving peace, chances for a catastrophic conflagration would be greatly increased.

This argument is valid, but it is difficult to make it convincing because it is all hypothetical. One would have to paint scary scenarios and wait for them to come true to be able to say, "I told you so."

It is an unrewarding exercise, as I have discovered in connection with Russia. I find it more appealing to present the idea on frankly idealistic grounds. A global open society would make the world a better place, and the United States is strong enough and prosperous enough to promote it. This is a simple and inspiring thought. Its weakness is that idealism is considered soft and wooly and tends to lose out to special interests. It has always lost out when it came in conflict with particular interests. The weakness could be overcome by tempering idealism with the recognition of our fallibility. This would moderate our expectations, make us more tolerant of the shortcomings of constructive intervention, and protect us against some of the pitfalls of political activism. Open society is a peculiar ideal that does not aim at perfection. It provides a frame of reference within which idealism can succeed.

It is strange, but the greatest open society in the world—the United States—has never accepted the limitations inherent in the concept of open society. It has set standards for public life that no politician can meet, and it has assumed the right to impose its own standards of human rights and democratic values on other countries. No wonder that our lofty aspirations are doomed to disappointment. We could achieve more by expecting less. Instead of imposing our values, we ought to recognize our fallibility. Instead of acting unilaterally, we ought to participate in forming rules by which we are willing to abide.

The Open Society Alliance would seek voluntary compliance, but even with the best will in the world it cannot always succeed. Therefore the military option cannot be ruled out. Should the Alliance fail to gain control of the Security Council, it could still bypass the Security Council and activate NATO without the authorization of the Security Council, as it did in the Kosovo crisis. The fact that the Alliance has exhausted all constructive options would give its punitive actions greater legitimacy than NATO enjoyed in the case of Kosovo.

Would the Open Society Alliance, whether it operated within or outside the United Nations, be able to avoid the defects that seem to afflict all associations of states, notably the democratic deficit and the decisionmaking deficit? Probably not. But such adverse effects could be mitigated by recognizing them in advance. For instance, it would be possible to institute a sunset clause that would automatically terminate the Alliance after, say, twenty-five years. Whenever a new institution is formed, it is usually permeated by a sense of mission that wears off with the passage of time. This has been true of the United Nations. It generated great enthusiasm when it was formed, but most of its committed supporters are now past the age of retirement. The United Nations would have certainly benefited from a sunset clause. No solution is perfect or permanently valid. Any open society coalition ought to be open to reconsideration and improvement.

The democratic deficit is an inherent problem in all international organizations, but if the Open Society Alliance really succeeded in turning the General Assembly into a legislature, we might just have an overdose of democracy, with every NGO breaking down the doors with legislative proposals. International civil society is capable of great achievements such as the ban on land mines, but with the help of the Internet it could become too much of a good thing. We have all seen what happened at the WTO meeting in Seattle. Fortunately there would be strong safeguards against legislative excesses. The laws would be valid only in the countries that ratify them, and they would have to be ratified by a qualified majority of the Alliance before other members would be obliged to do so. Of course, the laws would also have to survive the scrutiny of judicial review in each country—including by the United States Supreme Court. This would add another set of checks and balances essential to any open society.

While I am rather leery of self-appointed, self-righteous NGOs,

I would have greater confidence in the staff of the Alliance and, if the Alliance captured the United Nations, in the UN staff. It is easy to recruit dedicated staff for international organizations, provided they are selected on merit and not on the basis of national patronage. There are many, many good people serving the United Nations despite all the frustrations. To improve matters, the secretary-general and the heads of the various UN agencies should be given the power to hire and fire and be held accountable for the performance of their organization.

I do not want to go on elaborating the features of an Open Society Alliance because the further I go the more I feel enveloped in an air of unreality. The details would have to be worked out by the participants. The Alliance could take many forms, ranging from a formal alliance to ad hoc coalitions addressing special countries or issues. Viewed in this light, the idea is far from unrealistic; indeed, it is already in the process of being implemented. My foundation network is participating in a number of ad hoc coalitions, ranging from the Landmines Treaty to the Media Development Loan Fund, devoted to fostering independent media in countries where they are needed.

The initiative to create a global open society cannot be expected to come from governments; it must have the support of the electorates. Democratic governments are supposed to be responsive to the wishes of the electorate; unless people genuinely care about the principles of open society, those principles will not prevail.

It may be asked, How can this statement be reconciled with my earlier unkind remarks about the self-appointed and self-righteous guardians of civil society? Very easily. While the impulse for promoting the principles of open society must come from the people, civil society cannot do the job on its own; it must enlist the support of governments. My foundations have found that they can have greater impact if they cooperate with or exert pressure on governments. The impact is twofold: They bring about change in the specific field in which they are engaged, say, prison reform, education, or protection for the mentally disabled; at the same time they also improve the quality of government.

It is important to articulate the grand vision of a global open society; but open society can be approached only one step at a time. That is why I do not want to get lost embellishing on the possible and prefer to focus on the actual. Open society faces a practical test in the Balkans. An informal alliance of democratic states is already engaged there, and it is in their power to succeed. If we acquit ourselves well in the Balkans, it would move us one step closer to the ideal of a global open society.

By the same token, if we fail there, the prospects for a global open society will also be set back. My foundations are committed to making the Stability Pact a success both for its own sake and for the sake of open society. I believe we can create a global open society step by step.

Conclusion

As I release the manuscript of this book to the publisher, I am filled with a mixture of trepidation and great expectations. As I indicated in the introduction, I have been reluctant to part with it. Have I expressed my ideas as well as I could? Are they coherent? Do they mean as much to others as they do to me? These are the questions that worry me. My concerns are reinforced by the fact that I was able to improve the manuscript right up to the last minute. But I have gone about as far as I can on my own. I have learned a lot from other people's criticism, and I can continue to do so after the book is published.

My expectations focus on the Open Society Alliance. I do not know what response my proposal will evoke, but I do know that we need to make progress along these lines if we want to make good use of the possibilities opened up by the development of a global economy. Whether I have convinced others or not, I have managed to convince myself. After a period of frantic activity during which I had a clear idea about what needed to be done, I felt a need to sort out my ideas about open society. I have done so in this book. Once again, I have a clear sense of mission for my foundation network. I shall not spell it out here because it would interfere with my flexibility in carrying it out—there is a parallel here with the problem of making public pronouncements when I was actively engaged in making money—but I can state it in general terms: to foster the civil society component of the Open Society Alliance.

GEORGE SOROS

October 2000

Index

Adaptive behavior, 14, 87, 88, 90
Africa
  conflicts, 301
  foreign aid, xviii
  and political corruption, 150
Age of Fallibility, 345, 354
Age of Reason, 345
Aksyonenko, Nikolai, 260
Albania, foundation in, 316
Alchemy, 46
The Alchemy of Finance (Soros), xxv, xxviii, 48, 64, 66, 69, 77, 84
Allen, Peter, 87
Alliance of democracies, xx, 308
  goals and objectives of, xvi-xvii, 330
  membership of, xviii
  See also Open Society Alliance
America Online, 70
Amorality, of financial markets, 138–141, 160
Annan, Kofi, 355
Antall, Joseph, 192
Argentina, banking and financial system, 275, 287
Asian/Confucian model, demise of, 201–203, 211–215
Asian financial crisis *See* financial crisis of 1997–1999
Association of Asian Nations (ASEAN), 214

Baker, James, 264, 312, 317
Balkans
  open society foundations in, 311
  See also Stability Pact for Southeastern Europe
Bangladesh, microlending programs, 163
Bank for International Settlements, 189
Banking systems
  in Argentina, 275

Chile privatization of, 192
crash of 1929, 188, 195
during financial crisis of 1997–1999, 217–219
hedge fund regulations, 296–298
international central bank, 280
reflexive connection, 65–66
savings-and-loan crisis of 1985–1989, 191, 269
strengthening, 267
transactions vs. relationships in, 113
in the U.S., 99–100
Bank of England, 139
Bank of Japan, 191
Basayev, Shamil, 258, 261
Basle Accord of 1988, 189, 278, 297
Belarus
  foundations banned in, x
  political situation, 342
Berezovksy, Boris, 242, 243, 245, 258, 259, 260
Bergson, Henri, xx, xxi, 115
Berlin, Isaiah, 132–133, 157
Bernoulli, Daniel, 54
Blind spot metaphor, 24
Boom-bust model, 64–69, 83–84, 95–96
  conglomerate boom, 66–69, 80, 148
  construction industry and, 186
  and contraction of credit, 188
  and global capitalist system, 196
  and Internet boom, 69–75, 84
  usefulness of, 233–234
Bosnia crisis
  humanitarian intervention, 317–318
  UN intervention, xv, 307, 312–313, 316–319, 320, 351
Boutros-Ghali, Boutros, 316–317
Brazil
  financial situation, 222, 271, 287

Brazil *(cont.)*
    Russian investments, 246
    and World Bank, 282, 284
Bretton Woods institutions, xiv, 174, 189,
    190, 266, 287, 352
Bulgaria, foundation in, 316
Bundesbank, 289, 300
Burma
    fascism in, xi
    foundations banned in, x
    See also Myanmar (Burma)
Bush, George, 236, 336

Canadian fisheries, 87–88
Capital
    controls on, 175, 298–300
    free movement of, x, 167–168, 174
Capitalist system. *See* global capitalist sys-
    tem
Catholic Church, 31, 156
Centre for European Policy Studies (CEPS),
    326
Chechnya
    political situation, 328
    Russian invasion, 261–262, 313
    terrorist activities, 258–259
Chernomyrdin, Viktor, 246, 256, 259, 344
Chile
    capital controls, 298
    debt crisis of 1982, 191, 192
China
    banking system, 216
    Boxer Rebellion, 204, 275
    controls on information, 181
    economic reform, 202, 203
    economic situation, 223, 224–225, 298
    state-owned enterprises (SOEs), 225
    Tiananmen Square massacre, 224
    and World Bank, 282
Chirac, Jacques, 150
Christianity, 57, 123
Chubais, Anatoly, 239, 244, 245, 246, 248,
    258, 259, 260
Citibank, 99
Citigroup, 226
Clark, Wesley, 342–343
Clinton, Bill, 307, 336, 343
Closed society, vs. open society, 103–109
Cold War, xv, 105, 302, 305–307, 331, 332,
    341

Communications revolution, of the 20th
    century, 173
Communism, 104
    and market fundamentalism, 118
Confucian/Asian model, 201–203
Conglomerate boom, 66–69, 80, 148
Contingency Credit Lines, 272–273, 277, 278
Convention on Biological Diversity, 334
Correspondence theory of truth, 5–7, 15
Council on Foreign Relations, 278–279
Credit, in global capitalist system, 185–190
Cretans, 15
*The Crisis of Global Capitalism: Open Society
    Endangered* (Soros), xxvii, xxviii, xxix,
    66, 227–228
Croatia, resistance to oppression, ix
Cuny, Fred, 262, 313
Currency
    exchange-rate mechanism (ERM), 193,
        289, 300
    exchange-rate system, 286–290
    fluctuations in, 193
    three major currencies, 195
Currency markets
    and boom-bust process, 69
    vicious and virtuous circles, 65
    volatility, 290–295
Currency trading, 56, 216
Cyprus, holding companies in, 139, 240

Darwinism, 94, 304, 305, 334–335
Dayton Accords (1995), 318
Democracy
    capital and the development of, 179–181
    correlation with capitalism, xi
    fostering development of, xvii–xviii
    representative democracy, 146–152
    See also alliance of democracies
Derivatives, 290–295
Descartes, 19, 20
Dialectics, 91–93
Dornbusch, Rudi, 239
Drascovic, Vuc, 319
Druckenmiller, Stan, 233
Dynamic disequilibrium, 79–82, 107–108
    demarcation lines, 109–110

The Economic Consequences of Mr. Churchill
    (Keynes), 287
Economic theory, critique of, 38–57

Einstein's theory of relativity, 16, 82
Encumbered individual, 127–130
Engels, Friedrich, 92, 172
Enlightenment, 51, 52, 121–125
Entrepreneurship, and global capitalist system, 205–206
Epimenides the Cretan, 15
Equilibrium, definition, 63, 76, 111
Equilibrium theory, xiii, xxvi, 19, 45–46, 50–51
   long-term vs. short-term equilibrium, 63
ERM. *See* exchange-rate mechanism (ERM)
European Commission, 326, 338–339
European Community, 307, 312
European Union (EU), xviii, 184, 287, 326–328, 329, 330, 337–340, 344, 349
EU. *See* European Union
Evolutionary biology, 94
Evolutionary systems theory, 14, 16, 17, 87, 89
Exchange-rate mechanism (ERM), 193, 289, 300
Exchange Stabilization Fund, 249

Fallibility, xxii, xxviii, 25, 26–27, 309
   and historical events, 93
   as a universal idea, 121
   See also Age of Fallibility; radical fallibility
Far-from-equilibrium conditions, xxvi, 64, 79, 80, 81, 107–108, 148, 208
Fascism, xi
Federal Reserve
   and interest rates, 71, 191, 206, 223, 280
   monetary policy, 187
   and Russian economic collapse, 294–295
   and U.S. economy, xxvii, 152, 279–280, 289
Ferghana Valley, 322–324, 328, 348
Fertile fallacy, xxvi, 25, 30, 31–32, 58
Feyerabend, Paul, 42
Fidelity, 200
Financial architecture. *See* global financial architecture
Financial crisis of 1997–1999, xiv, xxviii, 65, 69, 74, 77, 142, 152, 170, 208–234
   IMF role in, 219–222
   instability of international finance, 215–219
   reasons for, 194
   recovery from, 194
   unfolding of the crisis, 222–234

Financial hypothesis, 30
Financial markets
   as amoral, 138–141, 160
   as a historical process, xxvi
   reflexivity in, 58–90
   stability of, xiii
Fischer, Stan, 239
Foreign aid, 237, 240–241, 324–326
Frankel, Jeffrey, 87
"Free-rider" problem, 154–155
French Revolution, 123
Freud, Sigmund, 13, 46
Friedman, Milton, 187, 198
Froot, Kenneth, 87
Fundamentals, 75–76
   and participants' bias, 62
   and stock prices, 63–64
   and valuations, 60–61

Gaidar, Yegor, 238, 239, 248, 249, 254
Game theory, 14, 87, 88, 113–114
Gates, Bill, 156
Genscher, Hans-Dietrich, 340
Geopolitical realism, 303–305
German reunification, 65, 193, 237
Germany
   business motivations, 184
   stock market rise, 199
Giddens, Anthony, 14
Glass-Steagal Act, repealed, 188
Gligorov, Kiro, 315
Global capitalist system, 167–207
   as an incomplete regime, 177–181
   asymmetry between lenders and borrowers, 190–194
   boom-bust model and, 196
   center and periphery, relationship between, xxvi, xxvii, 168–169, 172–173
   Confucian/Asian model and, 201–203
   credit, role in, 185–190
   and economic incentives, xix
   empire analogy, 171–173
   entrepreneurship and, 205–206
   expansionism and, 171–173
   future of, 195
   market fundamentalism and, 196–198
   money, role in, 181–185
   triumph of capitalism, 198–204
Global financial architecture, 265–300
   capital controls, 298–300

Global financial architecture *(cont.)*
  derivatives, 290–295
  hedge funds and banking regulations,
    296–298
  a level playing field, 274, 276
  a modest reform proposal, 276–280
  moral hazard, 273, 274
  new architecture (reform proposals),
    270–276
  and the World Bank, 281–286
Global political architecture, 301–329
  geopolitical realism, 303–305
Gödel's numbers, 24–25
Goldfarb, Alex, 259
Gorbachev, Mikhail, 23, 237, 306–307
Gore, Albert, 336
Grameen Bank (Bangladesh), 163
Great Depression (1930s), xiv, 100, 187, 197,
    203
Greenspan, Alan, 187, 223
Group of Seven (G7), 251–252, 255

Hayek, Friedrich, 117–118
Hedge funds, 32, 55, 56, 81–82, 215–216,
    296–298
Hegel, Wilhelm Friedrich, 92
Heisenberg's uncertainty principle, 16, 40,
    44, 45, 83
Helms, Jesse, 332, 335
Historical process, reflexivity in, 10–13,
    91–115
Historic events, 12–13, 91
Holbrooke, Richard, 317
Hong Kong
  banking and financial system, 216, 219
  economic development, 180
  financial crisis, 223, 229, 298
Hudson, Richard, 353
Human behavior
  scientific explanation of, 13
  selfish gene, 93–95
Human condition, 25
Humdrum/everyday events, 12–13, 26, 28,
    91
Hungarian Academy of Science, 104
Hungary
  democratic elections of 1990, 192
  during World War II, 107–108
  foundation in, 104–105

genocide of the Jews, 107
reform communist regime, 192

ICC. *See* International Criminal Court
    (ICC)
IMF. *See* International Monetary Fund
    (IMF)
Imperialism, 172
Indeterminacy, 13, 15, 44
Indonesia
  economic development, 179
  financial crisis, 210, 218–219, 222, 223,
    268, 271, 299
  IMF loans, 271
  political situation, 202–203, 328
  and World Bank, 284
Intel, 199
Interest rates, 71, 191, 206, 223, 280
International Criminal Court (ICC), 334
International debt crisis of 1982, 176,
    190–191, 193, 269
International finance, instability of, 215–219
International Financial Institution Advisory
    Commission. *See* Meltzer Commission
International Monetary Fund (IMF)
  Contingency Credit Lines, 272–273, 277,
    278
  deficiencies of, 268–269
  establishment of, 174
  financial crisis of 1997–1999, role in,
    219–222, 268
  General Arrangements to Borrow, 273
  influence declining, xiv, xix, xxvii, 190,
    266
  international lending policies, 152, 191,
    229, 251, 272
  as lender of last resort, 191, 273–274
  loan to Russia, 241, 249, 251
  New Arrangements to Borrow, 273
  reform proposal, 276–280
  role and mission of, 189, 191, 268
  Special Drawing Rights (SDRs), 273, 278
  strengthening, 346
  U.S. membership in, 332
International Science Foundation, 241–243,
    259
Internet boom, xxvii, 69–75, 77, 84, 206,
    231–232
Izetbegovic, Alija, 319

Japan
  banking and financial system, 212–214,
    297, 299
  business motivations, 184
  during Asian financial crisis, 212–214, 222
  economic development, 179
  interest rates, 191
  recession, 223
  U.S. relations, 203
Jefferson, Thomas, 147
Jesus Christ, 31

Kant, Immanuel, 122, 124, 126, 127
Kay, John, 74
Kennedy, John F., 175
Keynesian economics, 197–198
Keynes, John Maynard, 45, 186, 187, 287,
    300
Khrushchev, Nikita, 12, 97
Kim Dae Jung, 202, 221
Kiriyenko, Sergei, 246, 253, 258
Kissinger, Henry, 304, 331
Kohl, Helmut, 236–237
Korea
  business motivations, 184
  economic development, 179, 223
  economic policy, 202, 223
  financial crisis, 186, 191, 222, 297, 299
  IMF loans, 271
  Russian investments, 246
Kosovo crisis
  Dayton Accords (1995), 318
  NATO intervention, xviii, 310–311, 319,
    320–321, 326–328, 343–345
  UN peacekeeping mission, 317, 327
  See also Yugoslavia
Kosovo Liberation Army (KLA), 317–318,
    343
Kovalev, Sergei, 155, 261, 323
Krugman, Paul, 299
Kuhn, Thomas, 42
Kyrgyzstan, 322–323

Lack of correspondence, 8–9, 20, 26, 93
Lafontaine, Oscar, xiii
"Laissez-faire" doctrine, 196, 197, 304
Land mines ban, 140, 358
Law of the Sea Convention, 334
Laws of mathematics, 24–25

League of Nations, 306
Lee Kwan Yu, 180, 214
Leontief, Wassily, 238
Lipton, David, 249, 255
Lockheed, 139
Logical positivism, 16, 17, 18, 21
Loncar, Leko, 312
London, financial markets, 175
London Club, 190
Long Term Capital Management (LTCM),
    81, 225, 226, 227, 228, 231, 292, 294,
    296–297
Long-term equilibrium, 63
Losonczy, Tamas, xxv
LTCM. *See* Long Term Capital Manage-
    ment (LTCM)
Lukashenko, Alexander, 342
Luzhkov, Luri, 258
Lysenko, Trofim, 236

Maastricht Treaty, 340
McConnell, Mitch, 253
Macedonia, economic and political situa-
    tion, 314–315
Machiavelli, 14
Mahathir, Mohammed, 180–181, 202,
    209–210, 214
Malaysia
  economic development, 179–180
  economic policy, 202, 229
  fascism in, xi
  financial crisis of 1997, 209–210, 216,
    218, 229, 299
  freedom of information restricted,
    180–181
Mandelbrot's fractals, 78
Market fundamentalism, xii, xxiii–xiv, xxvi,
    41, 143–144
  and communism, 118
  and global capitalist system, 196–198
Market mechanism, 169
Market values, xiii, xxvi, 53–54
  vs. social values, 138–142
Markovic, Ante, 311
Marxism, 41, 45, 47, 146, 197
Marx, Karl, 13, 45, 46, 92, 93, 151, 172
Meltzer Commission (International Financial
    Institution Advisory Commission), xix–
    xx, 266, 273–274, 281–285, 336, 346

Merriweather, John, 226
Merton, Robert, 14
Mexico
 financial crisis of 1982, 66, 191
 financial crisis of 1994, 186, 269–270, 298
 tesobonos (treasury bills), 270
 Zapatista Revolution, 204
Michelson-Morley experiment, 82
Microsoft, 199
Military alliances, xvii
Milosevic, Slobodan, 262, 310, 311, 317,
 318, 319–320, 321, 326, 343, 344
Milutinovic, Milan, 315
Money
 major functions of, 181
 role in global capitalist system, 181–185
Morality
 categorical imperatives, 126, 127
 universal principles of, 124–125
Moral philosophy, 125–127
Mortgage Guarantee Insurance Corpora-
 tion ("Magic"), 76
Multilateral Investment Guarantee Agency,
 283
Mutual assured destruction (MAD), xv
Myanmar (Burma), 214

NATO. *See* North Atlantic Treaty Organi-
 zation (NATO)
Natural selection, 94
Nazism, xxi, 107–108
Near-equilibrium conditions, 79, 81, 107
Neier, Aryeh, 133
Nemtsov, Boris, 244, 259
Newton-Smith, William, 25
NGOs. *See* nongovernmental organizations
 (NGOs)
Nongovernmental organizations (NGOs),
 161–162, 282, 283, 349, 357–358
Nonmarket sector, 169
North Atlantic Treaty Organization
 (NATO), xvii, 341–344
 during the Cold War, 332
 expansion, 341–342, 348
 intervention in Kosovo, xviii, 310, 319,
 321, 326, 328, 343–345
Northrop, 139
Novgorod, Nishny, 244
Nunn-Lugar Act, 263

OAS. *See* Organization of American States
 (OAS)
OPEC. *See* Organization of Petroleum
 Exporting Countries (OPEC)
Opening the Soviet System (Soros), 96
Open society
 definition, 130
 origin of term, xx
 specific conditions of, 133
Open Society Alliance, 330–359
Open Society and Its Enemies (Popper), xx, 15,
 103, 136
Open Society Foundations, ix-x, xvii, xxii,
 104–106, 236
 in the Balkans, 311
 in Bosnia and Herzegovina, 314
 and definition of open society, 122
 missions vs. self interest, 34
Open Society Fund, 104
Open Society Initiative for Southern Africa
 (OSISA), 158
Open Society Institute, in the U.S., ix
Organization for Economic Cooperation
 and Development, 297
Organization for Security and Cooperation
 in Europe (OSCE), 317–318, 344
Organization of American States (OAS), 347
Organization of Petroleum Exporting
 Countries (OPEC), 174–176

Paradigm shift, origin of term, 42
Paradox of the liar, 15
Paris Club, 190
Participants, vs. observers, 9–10, 19
Participants' bias, 10–11, 60, 61–64
Partnership for Peace, 342
Partnership for Prosperity, 342
Perfect competition, theory of, xiii, 52, 183,
 196, 304
Performance funds, 32
Peru, fascism in, xi
Philanthropy, 33–34
Philippines, financial crisis of 1997, 210
Playing by the rules, xxvi
Poland, open society foundations, 311
Political architecture, weaknesses in, xiv
Political architecture. *See* global political
 architecture
Polyani, Karl, 172

Popper, Karl, xx, xxi, 15, 103, 107, 117–118, 122, 136
  piecemeal social engineering, 309–310
Popper's scientific method model, 30, 38–41, 47
Prevailing bias, 10–11
  and conglomerate boom, 67–68
  and dynamic disequilibrium, 80
  and prevailing trend, 67–68, 234
Primakov, Yevgeni, 258
Prisoner's dilemma, 87, 89, 113–114
Prodi, Romano, 238, 326, 327
Property rights, 132
Pseudoscientists, 46
Putin, Vladimir, 258, 260, 261, 262, 263

Quantum Endowment Fund, 74
Quantum Fund, 74, 75, 216, 232–233

Radical fallibility, xxv, xxvi, 27–32, 47, 75
Rambouillet Conference (1999), 316, 318
Random-walk hypothesis, 36, 74, 75, 85
Rational expectations theory, 59–60, 61–62, 85, 86, 198
Rawls, 132
Reagan, Ronald, 65, 176, 197, 198
Real estate investment trusts (REITs), 77
Reality, and thinking, 3–37
Reason, rule of, 51, 123–125
Reflexivity, xxii, xxv, xxvi, xxviii, 7–9
  cognitive and participating functions, 7–8, 11, 41
  in context, 14–21
  in financial markets, 58–90
  and the historical process, 10–13, 91–115
  origin of term, 7
  in social phenomena, 38–40
  and social scientists, 41–49
REITs. *See* real estate investment trusts (REITs)
Representative democracy. *See* democracy
Rev, Istvan, 103
Richelieu, Cardinal, xvi, 304
Robbins, Lionel, 52
Rockefeller, John D., 156
Romania, IMF loans, 272
Roma peoples (Gypsies), x
Roosevelt, Theodore, 331
Rubin, Robert, 253

Rulemaking, and playing by the rules, xxvi, 153, 154
Russell, Bertrand, 15, 16
Russia
  and default on internal debt, xxvii, 221, 225–231, 270
  economic reform efforts, 237–239
  excessive lending, 186
  financial collapse, 235–264, 294–295
  financial crisis, 222, 223, 225–231
  foreign aid, 237, 240–241
  investments in, 244–247
  investments in, a real-time experiment, 247–257
  privatization in, 239–240
  Shatalin Plan, 238
  support of scientific research, 241–243
  and World Bank, 282, 284
Rwanda, 308
Ryzhkov, Nikolai, 238

Sachs, Jeffrey, 285
Sakharov, Andrei, 237
Salomon Brothers, 226, 296
Schmelyov, Nikolai, 264
Schutz, Alfred, 14
Scientific hypothesis, 30, 39
Scientific method. *See* Popper's scientific method model
Self-critical attitude, 33
Self-interest, principle of, 304
Selfish gene, 93–95
Self-referent statements, 15, 17, 21
Self-reinforcing behavior, 64–65
Sen, Amartya, xviii, 309, 346
Serbia, foundation in, x
Shoelace theory of history, 92
Short-term equilibrium, 63
Singapore, economic development, 179
Slabbert, Frederik van Zyl, 158
Slovakia, resistance to oppression, ix
Social contract, 123
Social engineering, 309–310
Social justice, 132
Social phenomena, reflexivity in, 38–40
Social responsibility, in business, 161
Social values, xiii, 138–163
  and amorality of financial markets, 138–141, 160

Social values *(cont.)*
  in an open society, 152–163
  and the common interest, 141, 147, 149
  shared social values, 112–113, 114
  in a transactional society, 113–115
  vs. market values, 138–142
  in well-defined communities, 149
Solana, Javier, 326, 340
Solow, Robert, 74, 82
Somalia, UN intervention, 307
Soros Fund Management, 208, 209, 232,
  234, 296
South Africa
  foundation in, 104
  nonprofit enterprises, 162–163
South Korea
  chaebol (conglomerates), 211–212
  financial crisis, 210, 211–212
Sovereign state
  conflicts in, xv, 302
  and national interests, 303, 308, 333
Sovereignty, nation-state, 124, 168
Soviet Union
  collapse of, xxi, xxii, 96–100, 105, 235,
  236, 304, 331–332
  economic reforms, failure of, 97–98
  foreign aid, xviii
  See also Russia
Special Drawing Rights (SDRs), 273, 278
Stability Pact for Southeastern Europe, xviii,
  287, 326–329, 340, 346, 359
Steinberg, Saul, 67
Stepashin, Sergei, 260
Stock market
  crash of 1929, 188
  crash of 1987, 189
  equity leveraging, 65
  in Germany, 199–200
  Japan Nikkei index, 213
  and mutual funds, 200–201
  in Sweden, 100
  technical analysis and, 78–79, 88–89
  thesis about, 77
Suharto, 202, 214, 221, 223
Surroi, Veton, 315–316
Svyazinvest group (Russian telephone holding company), 244–245, 247, 248, 259,
  260
Sweden, stock market, 100

Taiwan
  economic development, 180
  financial crisis, 223
  political situation, 302
  reunification with mainland China, 225
Tajikistan, 322
Technical analysis, 78, 88–89
Thailand
  economic policy, 202, 223
  financial crisis of 1997, 208, 210, 216,
  218, 299
  financial situation, 287
  IMF loans, 271
  political situation, 180
Thatcher, Margaret, 176, 198, 236
Theory of relativity, 16, 82
Thinking, and reality, 3–37
Tractatus Logico-Philosophicus (Wittgenstein),
  16
Transactional society, 113–115
Transportation revolution, of the 19th cen-
  tury, 173
True or false statements, 22
Truth
  correspondence theory of, 5–7, 15
  definition of, 15
  reflexive concept of, 21–23
Tudjman, Franjo, 314, 317, 318
Two Sources of Religion and Morality (Berg-
  son), xx

Ukraine
  financial crisis, 222
  loan defaults, 248
  and political corruption, 150
Uncertainty, element of, 13
Uncertainty principle, 16, 40, 44, 45, 83
United Kingdom, 307
  See also London
United Nations (UN), 350–355
  Bosnia crisis and, xv, 307, 312–313, 351
  establishment of, xiv, 306
  General Assembly, 351–352, 354, 356
  human rights protections, xvi
  reforming, xx, 306–308
  Russian support of, 306–307
  Security Council, 307, 351–352, 354, 356
  Somalia incident, 307
  specialized agencies, 352

United States, foreign policy, 331–337
Universal Declaration of Human Rights,
    303
Universal principles
    relevance of, 120–121
    safeguarding, xii, xvii
UN. *See* United Nations (UN)
Uzbekistan, 322

Value pluralism, 133, 157
Values, 53–57, 110–113
    Asian vs. Western, 214
    exchange vs. intrinsic values, 182–183
    nonmonetary values, 185
    universal values, 134
    See also market values; social values
Value statements, 22
Vietnam War, 304, 331
Vinik, Jeff, 200
Volcker, Paul, 287–288, 292, 293

Wahid, Abdurrahman, 203
Waldegrave, William, 236
Warsaw Pact, 341
Wealth effect, 200
Welfare state, 177, 178
Westphalia, Treaty of (1648), 303
Wilson, Woodrow, 331
Wittgenstein, Ludwig, 16
Wolfensohn, Jim, 282, 283
World Bank
    comparative analysis studies, 90
    establishment of, 174

foreign aid to Russia, 241
    as grant-giving agency, 282
    reform proposals, xix-xx, 281–286
    role of, 189
    U.S. membership in, 332
World Development Agency, 283, 284, 285,
    336, 346
World Economic Forum (Davos, 1996), 243
World Trade Organization (WTO), xv, xx,
    225, 332, 348, 349–350, 357
World War I, 107, 169, 173, 195, 267, 302
World War II, xiv, xxi, 177, 178, 338
    Maginot Line, 267
    Marshall Plan, 236, 264
Wörner, Manfred, 342

Yahoo!, 71
Yakovlev, Alexander, 264
Yavlinsky, Grigory, 238, 243, 258
Yeltsin, Boris, 238, 243–244, 246, 255, 256,
    257, 259, 260, 261, 263, 307
Yugoslavia
    disintegration of, xxix, 304, 310–320, 340,
        342
    ethnic conflict in, xvii, xxi
    foundation in, 315–316
    lessons learned, 320–321
    See also Kosovo crisis

Zimbabwe, fascism in, xi
Zimmerman, Warren, 311
Zyuganov, Gennadi, 243